Swarm Intelligence and Deep Evolution

Evolutionary Approach to Artificial Intelligence

Hitoshi Iba

Department of Information and Communication Engineering
Graduate School of Information Science and Technology
The University of Tokyo, Bunkyo-ku, Tokyo, Japan

CRC Press
Taylor & Francis Group
Boca Raton London New York

CRC Press is an imprint of the
Taylor & Francis Group, an **informa** business

A SCIENCE PUBLISHERS BOOK

First edition published 2022
by CRC Press
6000 Broken Sound Parkway NW, Suite 300, Boca Raton, FL 33487-2742

and by CRC Press
2 Park Square, Milton Park, Abingdon, Oxon, OX14 4RN

© 2022 Taylor & Francis Group, LLC

CRC Press is an imprint of Taylor & Francis Group, LLC

Reasonable efforts have been made to publish reliable data and information, but the author and publisher cannot assume responsibility for the validity of all materials or the consequences of their use. The authors and publishers have attempted to trace the copyright holders of all material reproduced in this publication and apologize to copyright holders if permission to publish in this form has not been obtained. If any copyright material has not been acknowledged please write and let us know so we may rectify in any future reprint.

Except as permitted under U.S. Copyright Law, no part of this book may be reprinted, reproduced, transmitted, or utilized in any form by any electronic, mechanical, or other means, now known or hereafter invented, including photocopying, microfilming, and recording, or in any information storage or retrieval system, without written permission from the publishers.

For permission to photocopy or use material electronically from this work, access www.copyright.com or contact the Copyright Clearance Center, Inc. (CCC), 222 Rosewood Drive, Danvers, MA 01923, 978-750-8400. For works that are not available on CCC please contact mpkbookspermissions@tandf.co.uk

Trademark notice: Product or corporate names may be trademarks or registered trademarks and are used only for identification and explanation without intent to infringe.

Library of Congress Cataloging-in-Publication Data (applied for)

ISBN: 978-1-032-00915-5 (hbk)
ISBN: 978-1-032-00917-9 (pbk)
ISBN: 978-1-003-17636-7 (ebk)

DOI: 10.1201/9781003176367

Typeset in Times New Roman
by Radiant Productions

Preface

Before there can be comprehension, there has to be competence without comprehension. This is nature's way. (...) The process of natural selection itself is famously competent, a generator of designs of outstanding ingenuity and efficacy, without a shred of comprehension.

(Daniel Dennett)

I began my study on artificial intelligence (AI) in the mid-1980s, and later became involved in research on swarm intelligence, evolutionary computation, and artificial life (AL) as my interests took me. Through several setbacks and good fortune, I am still able to engage in fundamental study in this field. I believe that the research so far is part of AI, and is trying to realize AI through evolution and emergence. In particular, in terms of strong AI and AL, I am interested in the co-evolution of hardware (brain) and software (language). In other words, why having a language is advantageous, why we need a bigger brain as language becomes more complex, and how animal communication leads to language emergence.

Recent advances in the practical applications of deep learning and machine learning have led to increasingly high expectations for AI. On the other hand, I feel that basic questions about AI, such as the ones above, have been forgotten. When I was a student and started my research life, my colleagues and I used to argue about strong AI and AL whenever we had time, which might have been useless. In hindsight, this has deeply contributed to the direction of my past and future research. From my experience of teaching at universities, most of the students are very active and are good at talking about deep learning and machine learning by quickly reading the latest version of articles uploaded to the archives, etc. On the other hand, I fear that there is little opportunity or motivation to consider the above-mentioned past history of AI and the nature of intelligence.

At the same time as my research life, I have also been active as an underwater naturalist, passing on my knowledge of diversity and symbiosis gained through more than 1,000 dives and underwater observations in various locations. Some of my good fortune is that I have had the opportunity to visit places and observe creatures that have become sacred for my research during the course of my work. These include the monkeys of Sachijima Island (Miyazaki, Japan), the Burgess Shale (Canada), Flores Island (Indonesia), Galapagos Islands (Ecuador), Easter Island (Chile), Hamelin Pool (Australia), handfish (Tasmania), and the sexual selection of banded pipefish (Iriomote, Japan). Seeing and thinking about these experiences with my own eyes was also the impetus for writing this book. The historical significance and research background of some of these experiences will be introduced in detail in the text.

This book describes research topics in swarm intelligence and evolutionary computation that will contribute to the realization of AI. These include my past evolutionary computation research and current deep learning applications. However, each study is not necessarily complete and may not be exhaustive of the state-of-the-art. It may also reflect some of my opinions and preferences. I was once taught by a senior researcher in AI that this field is one in which papers are presented in the form of essays. In fact, many legendary researchers who are still famous today have done so. In this sense, I hope that the readers will extend the contents of this book to their own research that will contribute to the realization of stronger AI.

Acknowledgments

To all those wonderful people, I owe a deep sense of gratitude, now that this book project has been completed. Especially, I acknowledge the pleasant research atmosphere created by colleagues and students from the research laboratory associated with the Graduate School of Information Science and Technology at the University of Tokyo.

This book is based on class notes such as "Artificial Intelligence," "System Engineering" and "Simulation Theory" that were used in my university. The assignments given to the students in my class were often unusual and considered difficult or unanswerable. However, the reports that were submitted in return often contained impressive descriptions and deep insights which I always appreciated. In this book, some examples of answers and opinions contained in the submitted reports are used after necessary corrections and refinement. Although it is impossible to acknowledge everyone by their names, I would like to express my deepest gratitude to the students who made the effort to write interesting reports.

Additionally, I deeply thank SmartRams Co. Ltd. for providing the design images for the cover of this book.

In addition, I would like to thank Mobile Internet Technology Co., LTD. and its founder, Mr. Shiratsuchi, for providing us with the interesting MindRender software and for helping us to expand it in the AI sector.

And last, but not least, I would like to thank my wife Yumiko and my sons and daughter Kohki, Hirono and Hiroto, for their patience and assistance.

Hitoshi Iba
Tokyo, Japan, 2021

Contents

Chapter 1

AI: Past and Present

I have always had some disquiet about the term "artificial intelligence" and only rarely identified myself as working primarily in that area. However, I remember the first time I met Edsger Dijkstra. He was noted not only for his pioneering contributions to computer science, but also for having strong opinions and a stinging wit. He asked me what I was working on. Perhaps just to provoke a memorable exchange I said, "AI." To that he immediately responded, "Why don't you work on I?" [143].

1.1 AI and its History

The word "artificial intelligence" (hereafter, AI) originated from the 1956 Dartmouth workshop. Many leading future researchers of AI research, including Marvin Minsky[1], John McCarthy[2], Herbert Simon[3], and[4], participated in this confer-

---

[1] Marvin Minsky (1927–2016): An American computer scientist and cognitive scientist. He is known as the "father of artificial intelligence." He is famous for his work on frame theory and the society of mind. His book [100] showed that a simple perceptron cannot identify linearly inseparable patterns, ending the first neural network boom in the 1960s and causing the "AI winter" of the 1970s.

[2] John McCarthy (1927–2011): An American computer scientist and cognitive scientist. The term "Artificial Intelligence" was invented by him for the Dartmouth workshop. He is the developer of the LISP language.

[3] Herbert Alexander Simon (1916–2001): American cognitive psychologist and information scientist. He was awarded the Nobel Prize in Economics in 1978 for his lifelong research on managerial behavior and decision-making in large organizations.

[4] Allen Newell (1927–1992): American researcher in computer science and cognitive psychology. He is well known for Logic Theory Machine (1956) and General Problem Solver (1957), early AI programs he developed with Herbert Simon.

ence. Early AI was actively studied in relation to game and theorem proving. This was followed by studies connected to the real world, such as those on machine inference, problem solving, image understanding, natural language learning, and expert systems. Moreover, academic fields connected to AI, such as cognitive science, which is the field where the mechanism of the human mind centered on "intelligence" is studied, and knowledge engineering, which is the field that aims to endow computers with human knowledge for engineering purposes, have also been established.

Broadly speaking, early AI research tended toward three main trends: the first trend was based on the theory of logical thinking from the late 1940s, which led to research on predicate logical languages, such as the Prolog; the second trend was the neural network approach (connectionism) from the 1960s; while the third trend was heuristic programing from the 1950s.

As research on AI advanced, early optimism started to wane, and many criticisms and challenges emerged. For example, the above mentioned three approaches received criticisms, such as the inability of logical methods to process the flexible thinking of humans, the difficulty of connectionism to express high-level knowledge, and the ad hoc nature of heuristics.

AI is an interdisciplinary field related to many other fields, such as psychology, engineering, information science, mathematics, philosophy, and brain science, through the keyword "intelligence," and this relationship itself is AI. The ancestors of AI in psychology are Jean Piaget[5] and Sigmund Freud[6]. Piaget conducted the pioneering study on the knowledge acquisition of children through an empirical development study. His book "The Origins of Intelligence in Children" emphasizes the role of structuring in cognition, and its influence on AI is significant. Piaget advanced the theory of staged mental development, which proposed that the development of thought is through a gradual development of structure. It was claimed that children try out logical combinations through various plays and acquire knowledge through the same to develop. This theory is called "constructivism." Meanwhile, Freud was the founder of psychoanalysis and advanced a unique theory on ego and the unconscious.

However, there are claims that the theories of Freud and Piaget have already been disproved [111]. For example, paleontologist S.J. Gould[7] views that the

---

[5]Jean Piaget (1896–1980): Swiss psychologist. He proposed "genetic epistemology." His work in developmental psychology has influenced the theory and practice of the new education.

[6]Sigmund Freud (1856–1939): Austrian psychiatrist. After working as a neuropathologist, he became a psychiatrist and conducted research on neurosis, free association, and the unconscious. He is known as the founder of psychoanalysis. He proposed the theory of psychosexual development, libido theory, and infantile sexual desire.

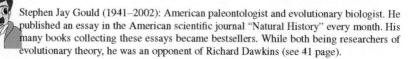

[7] Stephen Jay Gould (1941–2002): American paleontologist and evolutionary biologist. He published an essay in the American scientific journal "Natural History" every month. His many books collecting these essays became bestsellers. While both being researchers of evolutionary theory, he was an opponent of Richard Dawkins (see 41 page).

theory of Freud (i.e., interpretation of sexual developmental stage and neurosis patients) reflects the recapitulation theory[8] and Lamarckism[9] in biology. He wrote that the disproving of these two theories consequently ended the validity of the theory of Freud [51]. From the viewpoint of an evolutionary psychologist, Steven Pinker[10] also claimed that we must understand the purpose of the design of our mind in the environment we evolved in. He explained the harm of the theory of Piaget in education as follows [111]:

> Ever since the Swiss psychologist Jean Piaget likened children to little scientists, psychologists have compared the person in the street, young and old, to the person in the lab. (...) Natural selection, however, did not shape us to earn good grades in science class or to publish in refereed journals. It shaped us to master the local environment, and that led to discrepancies between how we naturally think and what is demanded in the academy.

Particularly, with the exception of the instinctual counting of small numbers and simple calculations, children will not be able to learn how to handle mathematical concepts spontaneously. Similarly, when teaching children how to read, the constructivist method postulating that "reading is a human instinct that develops naturally" (which has not been proven by evolutionary psychology) and contending that it is enough to place them in an interpersonal environment rich with texts is not correct. Moreover, in the field of evolutionally cognitive science, it is regarded that cognitive science not based on the human genome or biological function is impossible. The mechanism of human cognition is not unrelated to the evolution of the brain. Note that these views by Pinker and others have also been criticized. As one can see, the theory of intelligence has been discussed in diverse fields, and such active discussion and theoretical conflict are the essences of AI research. We will see some of these arguments in Chapter 7.

---

[8]Theory by German biologist Ernst Haeckel (1834–1919), which postulates that phylogeny repeats ontogeny. An animal repeats the path of evolution when growing from the embryo. For instance, the theory regards the gill slit seen in the human embryo to be the residue of the time when we were fish and the tail of the embryo that is later absorbed to be the residue of our amphibian ancestors. This theory has been disproven, but it persists as an urban legend.

[9]The view that acquired characters are genetically inherited. This is also disproved by the knowledge obtained through genetics. See Section 2.2.6 and 62 page.

[10] Steven Arthur Pinker (1954–): American cognitive psychologist. He is a Harvard University Professor in psychology and the author of a large number of scientific publications including "How the Mind Works," "The Blank State: The Modern Denial of Human Nature," and "The Language Instinct: How the Mind Creates Language."

In the field of AI, philosophical and psychological arguments on the definition of intelligence, expression method of knowledge, research ideology, and viability are constantly held, and we have no shortage of debaters. Famous examples include the anti-AI theory of Hubert Dreyfus[11] (which claims a limit to AI research because its premise is an incomplete understanding of humans, as was the case with traditional philosophy before the 20th century), the ethical AI critique by Joseph Weizenbaum[12] (i.e., we should not develop AI), the dispute between Terry Winograd[13] and John Perry[14] (i.e., the philosophical dispute on symbolism and pragmatism), the debate around the innateness hypothesis by Noam Chomsky[15] (the view that language skill and universal grammar exist in humans at birth), and the dispute around connectionism. The development of AI depends on the activation triggered by the heated arguments between AI researchers and anti-AI thinkers, or between AI researchers with different positions.

Recent studies on AI saw the following changes/positions regarding the question of what AI is:

1. The essence of intelligence is symbol processing.

2. The essence of intelligence is environmental recognition.

3. The essence of intelligence is the interaction with the environment.

Rodney Brooks[16] proposed an approach called SSA (subsumption architecture) for planning autonomous mobile robots [21, 22]. In this method, the problem is divided into asynchronous partial task achieving behaviors (TAB). Examples of TABs are passing through objects, wandering, searching, and object

---

[11] Hubert Lederer Dreyfus (1929–2017): American philosopher. He was an ongoing philosophical critic of artificial intelligence. His 1972 book, "What Computers Can't Do: The Limits of Artificial Intelligence," [35] was highly controversial.

[12] Joseph Weizenbaum (1923–2008): American computer scientist. In 1966, he built a simple natural language processing program called ELIZA, and showed that it could interact with humans by posing as a counselor. He was shocked at the profound effect it had on many users and how they opened up to the program. In his book "Computer Power and Human Reason: From Judgement to Calculation," [146] he criticizes AI research, keeping in mind that there are some jobs that should not be done by computers.

[13] Terry Allen Winograd (1946–): American computer scientist. Between 1968 and 1970, he developed a system called SHRDLU that could manipulate a virtual "world of building blocks" using natural language. This success gave rise to early AI optimism. However, he realized how difficult it is to create semantic memory for computers, and later became critical of the realization of artificial intelligence.

[14] John Richard Perry (1943–): American philosopher. With Jon Barwise, he proposed situational semantics [17]. The meaning of a word cannot be specified without considering the situation. For this reason, situation semantics analyzes the meaning of language by actively addressing the situation.

[15] Noam Chomsky (1928–): American philosopher of language, known as the "father of modern linguistics." He has also influenced the fields of computer science, mathematics, and psychology. He proposed that there exists a common and universal "generative grammar" for all languages, and it is innate.

[16] Rodney Allen Brooks (1954–): An artificial intelligence scientist at MIT who has been active since the 1980s. He has proposed a number of groundbreaking ideas on AI, including "Intelligence without representation." [23] He is also famous as the creator of the robot "Roomba" (founder of iRobot Corporation).

identification. These TABs operate independently and asynchronously, and each behavior is weakly related to the other. In addition, each TAB is directly coupled to the outside world and has sensors and actuators. Unlike the classical robotics approach, SSA has the following advantages:

1. Complex problems can be dealt with by increasing the number of TABs independently.

2. Even if there is an error in one part, the whole system is not affected (fault tolerant).

In classical researches on robots and AI, the problem was divided into the following parts:

1. Sensing

2. Transformation of data from sensor to model representation

3. Planning

4. Execution of task

This splits the problem vertically (Fig. 1.1(a)). The entire partition constitutes a flow of information that enters from the environment through sensing, passes through the robot, and returns to the environment through action. This is a closed feedback (each subproblem contains a different feedback inside). Each part needs to be realized so that the robot can act. If changes are made to a particular part, care must be taken to ensure that adjacent parts are not changed, or the design must allow for automatic changes in the required functionality.

Brooks did not follow the above method and divided the problem vertically, constructing the basic partition as shown in Fig. 1.1(b). Instead of dividing the problem by the internal structure used to solve it, he divided the problem based on the desirability from the perspective of the task of the robotic system.

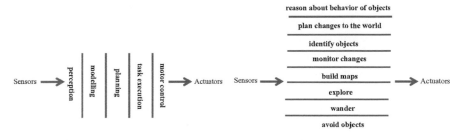

(a) Traditional division   (b) Behavior-based division

Figure 1.1: Layered structure of a mobile robot control system.

For this purpose, he defined the capability level of the robot and specified the desired actions for the robot. The higher the capability level, the more specific the action is.

In SSA, the following capability levels are used:

Level 0   Avoid contact with an object regardless of the object's state (moving/stationary). Figure 1.2 shows an example configuration.

Level 1   Move around aimlessly while avoiding objects (wandering). See Fig. 1.3.

Level 2   "Explore" the environment by observing meaningful forward objects (Fig. 1.4).

Level 3   Map the environment and plan a path to get from one place to another.

Level 4   Notice changes in a "static" environment.

Level 5   Recognize the environment based on known objects and perform tasks related to specific objects.

Level 6   Describe and execute plans that involve changes in the environment.

Level 7   Infer the behavior of objects in the environment and modify the plan accordingly.

Note that each capability level contains a subset of lower capability levels. Since capability levels specify a class of valid behaviors, higher capability levels impose additional constraints on that class. The lower layers continue to operate completely oblivious to the higher layers that occasionally interfere with the data path. As a result, a higher-order capability is achieved as shown in Fig. 1.5. Using the SSA method, a robot control system that works even in the early stages of development can be realized. This means that the system will work as soon as the lower layers are built. Additional layers can be added later, and there is no need to change the previously working system.

TABs in SSA are represented in the form of finite-state automata. Each TAB constitutes a network based on feasibility conditions and solves the problem as a whole. These are described using BL (Behavior Language), i.e., a language similar to LISP. Given this, John Koza attempted to train a robot with SSA using GP (Section 3.3). For example, he successfully evolved a wall following problem and a box moving program [79].

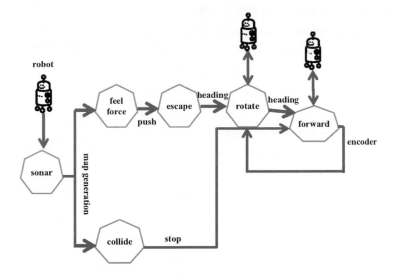

Figure 1.2: Level 0 control system.

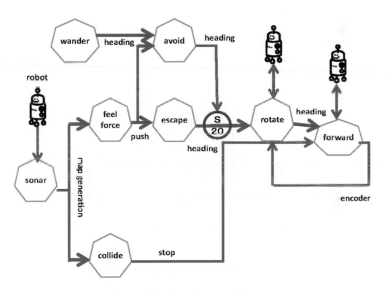

Figure 1.3: Level 1 control system.

SSA became a major trend in AI; known as "behavior-based robotics," it is referred to as "embodied cognitive science" today [109]. We humans and intelligent robots have physical existence and bodies; hence, we must interact with the environment. Particularly, because there is a body, the realization of AI must consider learning, categorization, perception, memory, and processing between

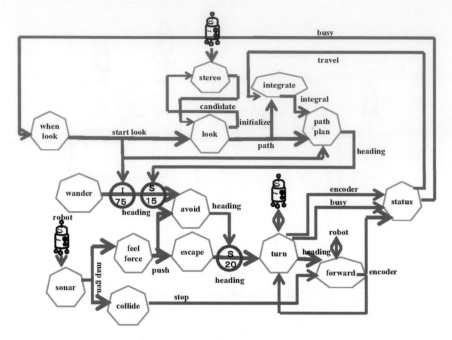

Figure 1.4: Level 2 control system.

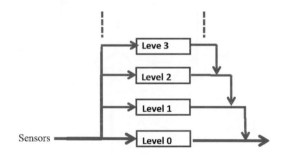

Figure 1.5: Layered structure of control.

sensors and motors from the perspective of physicality. Brooks calls such an approach "embodied intelligence." The view that intelligence can only occur in existence with a body is one of the hypotheses of embodied cognitive science.

The embodiment concept is connected to constructivist AI. The constructivist methodology is "understanding through creation" and is one of the central concepts of contemporary AI research. This is in contrast to the semiotic approach, which is the classical AI method. In classical AI, the recreation of a behavior is attempted by directly corresponding inner expressions with the observed action. However, such expressions cannot even recreate simple behaviors by robots. On the contrary, the embodied cognitive science approach includes an insight claiming that even simple brains can generate complex behaviors that can be called intelligence if used properly [110]. For instance, the mobile robot, known as the Braitenberg vehicle, has two sensors [20]. Each of these sensors is connected to the motor on the other side of its body, allowing it to move toward the light source. When light sources are attached to two vehicles, they perform extremely complex motions when they approach each other (which appear to be a courtship dance or a territorial conflict). Thus, even extremely simple Braitenberg vehicles can sometimes show surprisingly complex behaviors through their interaction with the environment. The complexity is particularly pronounced in the presence of other vehicles in the environment. The theory posited by Brooks revolutionized AI and intelligent robotics. The previous approaches to AI were such that robots were solving visual, route planning, and mapping problems that are difficult to calculate very carefully. In contrast, the SSA approach realized simple robots that move much faster. Particularly, Brooks demonstrated that intelligent behavior could be realized by repeating a process similar to that of "reflex" without involving a brain-like function.

However, this did not end the AI debate. In the recent years, collective intelligence, such as SNS and WWW, have been added to the definition of the term "environment," and new and innovative approaches to AI are currently coming into being. Moreover, the approach to deep learning that explores the semiotic expression in a neural network is reemerging.

As discussed at the beginning, AI is a field yet to be firmly established, and it exists by floating between many existing fields. A clearly defined and established field is no longer AI. A famous quote reads: "Artificial intelligence is the process of finding problems related to intelligence. When the problems to be solved become clear, it is no longer artificial intelligence." AI is perhaps an infinite attempt at presenting a definition that will be certainly disproved at one point and then trying to discover another definition. Particularly, it is an endless inquiry into the questions of "What is AI?" and "What is not AI?"

1.2   Pareto-efficiency and Human Intelligence

The word "utility" is defined in the following discussion as the value representing the degree of preference of an individual. This is regarded as the evaluation value (or fitness; see Section 3.1) of an objective function.'

Let us look at this comical anecdote from Sidney Morgenbesser[17] (see Fig. 1.6):

---

[17]Sidney Morgenbesser (1921–2004): A philosophy professor at Columbia University.

Sidney, ordering dessert, is told by a waitress after dinner that he can choose between an apple pie and a blueberry pie. He says "I want an apple pie." Shortly thereafter, the waitress comes back and says that a cherry pie is also an option. Sidney says "In that case I'll have a blueberry pie."

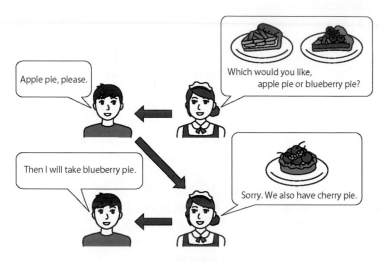

Figure 1.6: Independence from irrelevant alternatives.

Why is this story funny? It is because the independence from irrelevant alternatives was lost. It might have been simply ignored if this was not said by a famous philosopher. However, one case actually occurred. During the 1995 World Championship of female figure skating, the preliminary ranking after the performance by three skaters was: 1st: Chen Lu (China), 2nd: Bobek (USA), and 3rd: Bonaly (France). Following this, Michelle Kwan (USA) performed and ranked in fourth place. As a result, the second and third places in the ranking were swapped and became: 1st: Chen Lu (China), 2nd: Bonaly (France), and 3rd: Bobek (USA). It was understood that there was no problem with the calculation of scores by the judges [112].

It is not only humans who lose independence from irrelevant alternatives. There have been reports on an interesting behavior by a microorganism, called the slime mold [139]. A single cell of slime molds can move at the speed of a few centimeters per hour in the form of an amoeba. It can also transform into a mushroom-shaped fruiting body (plasmodium) when thousands of cells congregate. Even though this plasmodium does not have a neurotransmitter system, it reacts to various external information, such as light and feeding stations (oats), and displays unified behavior. Consequently, its ability to go through a labyrinth in the shortest route or form an optimal transportation route that ap-

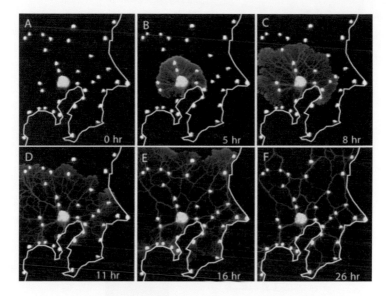

Figure 1.7: Transportation route by slime molds [139].

pears as though it was designed by a human has been reported (Fig. 1.7, see also [69]).

This slime mold was made to select how to be fed with oats [87]:

- 5*g* of oats in a bright spot, or

- 3*g* of oats in a dark spot.

Slime molds dislike bright places; hence, they chose between these two options at a 50/50 rate. Particularly, these two options were equally attractive to the slime mold. The fact that changing the amount of oats in the bright spot to 10*g* resulted in the slime mold choosing that option every time affirms this. However, when it was given the following three options, the results were odd (see Fig. 1.8):

- 5*g* of oats in a bright spot,

- 3*g* of oats in a dark spot, or

- 1*g* of oats in a dark spot.

Even in this case, if considered rationally, the top two options should be selected at a fifty-fifty ratio. However, the slime mold changed its preference and selected the 3*g* of oats in a dark spot at the rate of more than thrice that of the selection of 5*g* of oats in a bright spot. This result indicates a breakdown of independence from irrelevant alternatives.

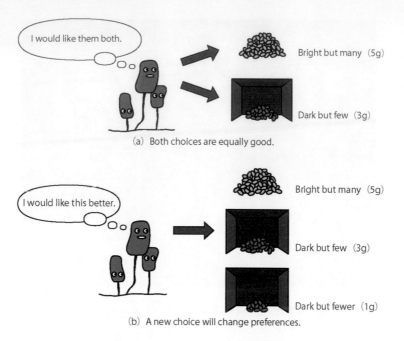

(a) Both choices are equally good.

(b) A new choice will change preferences.

Figure 1.8: Slime molds' preference.

Kenneth Arrow[18] demonstrated that the "majority rule," which is the fundamental principle of democracy, can be arbitrarily manipulated. This phenomenon, which shakes the foundation of democracy, can be considered to have emerged from the irrationality of a society composed of multiple agents. Particularly, even if each individual acts rationally, it does not necessary result in the maximum benefit to the society as a whole.

Let us introduce a mathematical paradox, which can be explained with more difficultly. There are three roulettes, as shown in Fig. 1.9. One can win the prize (integer between 1 and 6) placed at the random spot where the ball comes to rest when their wheels are turned. The small actual values are the area size of that spot. Thus, with roulette B, the probability is as follows:

■ 0.56 probability of winning two points.

■ 0.22 probability of winning six points.

■ 0.22 probability of winning four points.

Which roulette should one place one's bet on?

---

[18]Kenneth Arrow (1921–2017): American economist. One of the most important figures in the history of 20th century economics. At the age of 51, he was the youngest person ever to win the Nobel Prize in Economics in 1972.

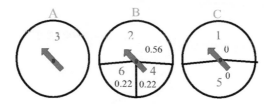

Figure 1.9: Which roulette should one place one's bet on?

B is the best bet in terms of the expected value, which is the most understandable number. On the contrary, A has a 0.56 probability of winning over B (B loses if it gets two) and a 0.51 probability of winning over C. B has a 0.617 probability of winning over C; thus, C is the worst bet. Particularly, A would be the best bet. However, if the rule was that all three roulettes are turned at the same time, and the roulette resulting in the highest number wins, C ends up being the best bet. Thus, the relative merits can significantly change according to the perspective.

The above discussion demonstrates that the preference by individuals in a group is not reflected in the preference by the group as a whole. If this is regarded to be the preference of one evaluated through three evaluation items, it becomes a problem of the evaluation of utility in multiple dimensions. In such a case, the transitivity seen above does not necessarily hold up.

The transitivity does not always hold up with regard to utility. For instance, there are cases where even though $x \succ y$ and $y \succ z$, it became $z \succ x$[19]. This can be explained if the utility function is regarded as a multidimensional vector. In the current sample, it is postulated that there are two evaluation items, and they become the utility functions u_1 and u_2 when they are considered individually. At this time, it is postulated that there are x, y, and z that are shown in Fig. 1.10. The following equation becomes true under this circumstance:

$$x \succ_{u_1} y \qquad y \succ_{u_1} z \qquad z \succ_{u_2} x, \tag{1.1}$$

where the subscripted number indicates evaluation by that utility function . The fact that the evaluator did not notice the two-dimensionality of the scale and unconsciously switched to a different utility function at each time resulted in intransitivity. This theory is called the "multidimensional utility theory."

In the multidimensional utility theory, the indifference curve is defined in a multidimensional space. The points on this curve are characteristically equivalent with each other, regardless of the position. For instance, the indifference curve shown in Fig. 1.11 is drawn in a two-dimensional space with two utility functions.

Let us consider how two opposing utilities can be optimized at once. This is a frequently occurring issue (Fig. 1.12). For example, when purchasing a car or an

---

[19]$x \succ y$ means that x is preferred to y.

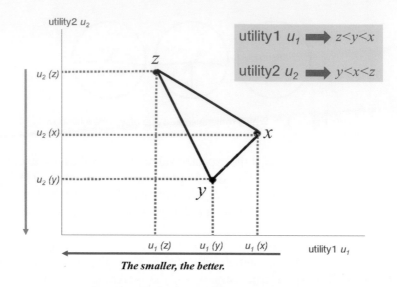

Figure 1.10: Multidimensional utility theory.

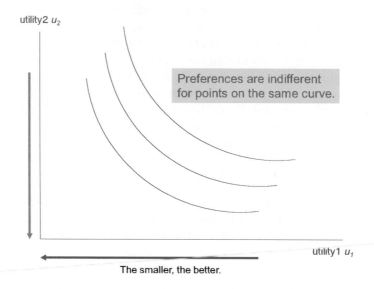

Figure 1.11: Indifference curves.

electronic product, performance and cost are normally incompatible with each other. While performance should be as good as possible, cost should be as small as possible. The incompatibility of return and risk in finance is another representative example. In asset management and investment, return is the profit gained

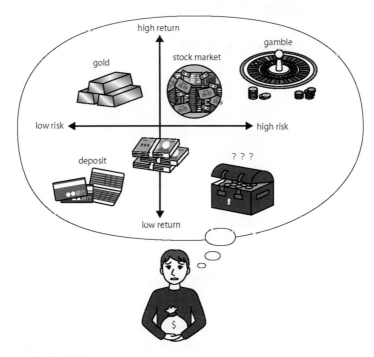

Figure 1.12: Risk vs. return.

as a result of the operation. Risk indicates the "uncertainty" and "degree of instability" involved in the operation. Particularly, it is the possibility of a given asset becoming profitable in the future. Commonly, a trade-off exists between risk and return. Ideally, financial products should be low in risk and high in return, but this is just a fantasy.

In many problems, various utilities (targets) (e.g., return vs. risk) must be simultaneously optimized. This is called multi-objective optimization. Many studies have tackled emergence from multi-objective optimization. In Sections 3.9 and 4.7, we will see how to solve this multi-objective optimization by means of evolutionary computation or swarm intelligence.

Let us see the multidimensional utility function again. Ideally, the comprehensive evaluation is represented as the sum of each dimension. In the case of two dimensions, two items X and Y exist. If the utility functions are set as u_1 and u_2, the following equation should be true:

$$X \succ Y \iff u_1(X) + u_2(X) > u_1(Y) + u_2(Y)$$

The following conditions are required to satisfy this equation:

■ Transitivity

■ Comparability

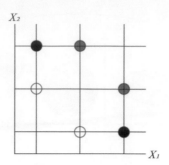

Figure 1.13: Thomsen condition.

■ Independence of preference

■ Thomsen condition

The Thomsen condition indicates that two evaluation functions X_1 and X_2 satisfy the following:

Definition 1.1   Thomsen condition

For every $a, b, c \in X_1, p, q, r \in X_2$, if $(b, p) \sim (a, q)$ and $(c, p) \sim (a, r)$, then $(c, q) \sim (b, r)$ holds true.

Note that $A \sim B \Leftrightarrow A \succeq B$ and $B \succeq A$, i.e., A and B are equally preferred. Thomsen condition represents the parallelism of the indifference curve (see Fig. 1.13). Six candidate points can be found in the figure. In this case, the Thomsen condition indicates that if two pairs with the same color are indifferent, the candidates of the remaining colors are also indifferent. For instance, if the candidates of black and white are both indifferent, the gray candidate would also be indifferent. If indifference curves can be drawn between the black points and between the gray points, an indifference curve can also be drawn between the two white candidates.

This condition is generally unsatisfied; however, the sum of each dimension is sometimes used for convenience as the overall assessment value of each item[20].

In contrast, the ways of thinking (e.g., indifference curve and Pareto optimization) have been criticized for their inability to explain human behavior well due to the fact they ignore the risk factor. The problem of the indifference curve is that it only represents the wealth and the money that is in possession at the end and does not indicate the current situation. Particularly, one cannot understand

---

[20]The simple GA of the robot motion design (see Fig. 3.28) is also based on this condition.

where humans are located from it. Demonstration experiments of selection without risk and decision making have proven that indifference curves are not given in the type of curve shown in Fig. 1.11.

Pareto efficiency and multi-objective optimization will be explained in detail in Section 3.9.

Chapter 2

Evolutionary Theories for AI

When you were a tadpole and I was a fish. (Langdon Smith, 1858–1908).

2.1   What is Evolution?

Most people are likely to picture an image like Fig. 2.1 when they hear the word "evolution." This illustration is also still used in textbooks on evolution.

In Tasmania, Australia, there is a rare fish, called the handfish. It is a family of fish related to anglerfish and is on the red list of threatened species. As its name indicates, this fish does not swim in the ocean, but crawls on the seabed using its fins (Fig. 2.2). It is regarded as evidence of fish emerging from the water to the

Figure 2.1: Wrong illustration of evolution.

Figure 2.2: Handfish @Tasmania, Australia, 2017.

ground in the evolutionary process as shown in the figure. This is said to be the missing link that connects fish and terrestrial organisms, and it is considered a relic of the coelacanths.

Tasmania is known for the Tasmanian effect of evolutionary theory. Tasmania became detached from the Australian continent due to diastrophism about 10,000 years ago. It is said that when Europeans arrived in the 18th century, Tasmanians had the simplest tools in human history. This is inferred to be due to the small population of Tasmania making the transmission of technology from the previous generations incomplete, causing the technology to be lost. The Tasmanian effect is a hypothesis based on this fact, postulating that civilization declines when the population falls below a certain threshold. Furthermore, it is known that among Tasmanian devils, a Dasyuridae endemic to Tasmania, cancer can easily be transmitted from one individual to another through biting. This does not occur normally because different lymphocytes eliminate each other. It is said that Tasmanian devils lost resistance to infectious cancer as a result of repeated breeding within a small island and the consequent decrease in the genetic diversity of their histocompatibility antigen.

The misunderstanding that evolution equates to progress (i.e., optimization) is widespread. For example, Stephen Jay Gould criticized an illustration such as Fig. 2.1 for promoting misconceptions. Humans are not the most "advanced" species; we are not the goal of evolution; and other species are not, in any way, inferior. If one must choose, the most recently evolved species are viruses and bacteria, not humans. Gould wrote that the most prosperous species in history, in an evolutionary sense, are bacteria.

Evolution is also not a purely random search. It is a construction apparatus that devises something suboptimal from past parts and its goal is robustness, not optimization. The following four conditions are necessary for evolution through natural selection:

■ There is a mutation among individuals of the same species.

■ This mutation can be inherited.

■ Enough offspring are born to make survival viable.

■ The death of an individual is not random.

For example, an ocean sunfish lays 300 million eggs, but only a few of them grow up to be adults. Among them, those with traits that are better adapted to the environment have better chances of survival. If these traits can be inherited, there will be more and more individuals with such traits. After a significant period of time, the entire species will evolve to possess these superior traits.

The following factors are important in realizing a desirable evolution:

■ Collectivity

■ Diversity

■ Coevolution

Collectivity indicates that evolution can only occur among a group. News stories claiming that an individual or a company has evolved are mistaken. Diversity indicates the variety in the members of a group. In evolution, the individual with a better group performance is more prolific and can easily survive. However, gathering only elites with better performance is not necessarily beneficial and can lead to the decline of the entire group as a result of environmental change. An elite group can only produce similar descendants, and although they perform well in the current environment, they often lack adaptability to new environments. This characteristic of weakness to changes in an environment or noise is called "the lack of robustness" in engineering , and avoiding it as much as possible is desirable. Therefore, in a sense, tolerating the existence of troublemakers and failures in a group is beneficial. While they might be useless in a normal circumstance, they could become saviors under certain situations. Particularly, evolution is not necessarily a search for optimization; instead, it aims for the robustness that makes survival in any environment more likely.

The third point is even more relevant. None of us can live alone. The value of each individual is not determined by oneself, but by our relation to others and the society, history, and culture to which we belong. Similarly, in the evolutionary system, the adaptability (survival rate) of each individual within a group is determined by the behavior of other individuals. Thus, coevolution is defined as the simultaneous evolution of two or more species through influence on each other. A famous example is the evolution of angiosperms and insects that pollinate them, which is said to have occurred to establish a more efficient interrelationship. A hawk moth (Xanthopan morganii) is said to develop its long tongue to adapt to

(a) Madagascar Stamp   (b) A hawk moth with a long proboscis

Figure 2.3: Prediction by Charles Darwin.

the corolla tube through coevolution. When Charles Darwin[1] saw an orchid with a long corolla tube (i.e., a tube filled with nectar), he predicted that a large moth would come to this flower and use its long, straw-like proboscis to feed on the nectar inside the corolla tube. Forty years later, this prediction was proven by the discovery of a hawk moth with a long proboscis (Fig. 2.3).

It is important to note that evolution is not necessarily optimization. The goal of evolution is quasi-optimization to adapt more robustly to the environment. French cultural anthropologist Claude Levi-Strauss[2] advanced a concept, called "bricolage," in his book "The Savage Mind (1962)" . He defined it as a form of intelligence humans have possessed since ancient times for assembling leftovers and off-cuts to produce useful tools that are unconnected to the original purpose of the materials. Bricolage refers to making or preparing something on one's own. Levi-Strauss contrasted it to the "cultivated mind," which is the western, engineering-oriented mind since the modern era, and contended that bricolage is a universal intelligence that can be applied to modern society. The mechanism of evolution and the evolutionary computation that will be explained later seem to be bricolage, not optimizer.

In the following sections, we will explain several theories of evolution that lead to interesting extensions of evolutionary computation.

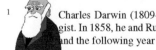

[1] Charles Darwin (1809–1882): British natural scientist. Outstanding geologist and biologist. In 1858, he and Russell Wallace (see also page 28) published their theory of evolution, and the following year Darwin published "The Origin of Species."

[2] Claude Levi-Strauss (1908–2009): French anthropologist and ethnologist. His research focused on the study of Native American mythology. He is considered the founder of "structuralism."

2.2 Neutral Molecular Evolution

2.2.1 Moran Process

Assume that there are N black or white balls in a bag. The balls are removed randomly from the bag and exchanged as directed below (see Fig. 2.4).

- Remove one ball at random, name it ball A, and record its color.

- Return ball A to the bag.

- Remove one ball at random and name it ball B.

- Return to the bag a ball of the same color as A. Do not return ball B to the bag.

This is the Moran process named after the Australian population geneticist Pat Moran (1917–1988). The Moran process is repeated a number of times. State i is defined as the number of black balls among the N balls (Fig. 2.5). The probability that state i changes to state j after an exchange process is denoted as $p_{i,j}$. The values of $p_{i,i-1}, p_{i,i}$, and $p_{i,i+1}$ are expressed using N and i in the following ways. There are three outcomes from one exchange.

- A and B are both black: The probability of this event is $(i/N)^2$, and state i does not change.

- A and B are both white: The probability of this event is $(\frac{N-i}{N})^2$, and state i does not change.

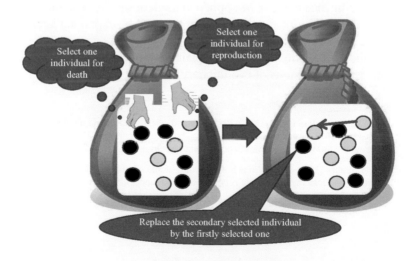

Figure 2.4: Moran process.

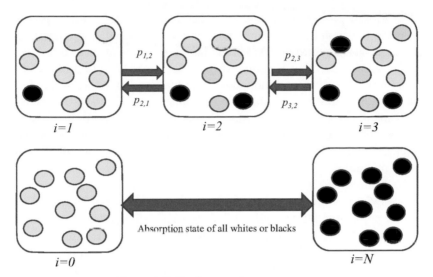

Figure 2.5: Final states of moran process.

■ A is black and B is white: The probability of this event is $\frac{i(N-i)}{N^2}$, and state i changes to state $i+1$.

■ A is white and B is black: The probability of this event is $\frac{i(N-i)}{N^2}$, and state i changes to state $i-1$.

In summary,

$$p_{i,i-1} = \frac{i(N-i)}{N^2},$$ (2.1)

$$p_{i,i} = 1 - p_{i,i-1} - p_{i,i+1}$$ (2.2)

$$p_{i,i+1} = \frac{i(N-i)}{N^2}.$$ (2.3)

The Moran process has two states that do not change further (absorbing states), which occur when balls are all black (state N) or all white (state 0). The probability of reaching absorbing states is derived as follows: Let x_i be the probability when state i ultimately becomes state N; in other words, all balls become black at the end.

$x_0 = 0$ and $x_N = 1$ is trivial. The recurrence relation of x_i using $p_{i,j}$ is given as follows:

$$x_i = p_{i,i-1} \cdot x_{i-1} + p_{i,i} \cdot x_i + p_{i,i+1} \cdot x_{i+1}.$$ (2.4)

Solving this by eqs. (2.1)~(2.3) yields the following equation:

$$x_i = \frac{i}{N}$$ (2.5)

The Moran process is a simple probabilistic model to investigate selection during the evolution of a finite population. The population consists of two species, i.e., black and white. Two individuals are chosen at every time step. One reproduces, and the other is removed (by selection). The child of the first individual replaces the second individual. The two random choices may pick the same individual; in this case, the new individual is the child of this individual. The population size is always constant. The final (absorbing) state of the Moran process is where all balls are of the same color, which corresponds to one species encompassing the entire population. No further changes are possible unless there is a new mutation.

The meaning of eq. (2.5) is explored below. This equation appears trivial at first; however, in a finite population, descendants of a certain individual occupy the entire population after a sufficiently long time. All individuals have the same possibility to be this individual if the chance of survival is the same.

Fitness is the probability that an individual survives. When fitness is the same for all individuals, the fixation probability, which is the probability that descendants of an individual survive and occupy the population, is also the same at $1/N$ if the number of individuals in the population is N. In other words, if a new individual appears in the population from mutation, the probability that the individual occupies the population is $1/N$ as long as the fitness is the same.

The term "fitness," as used here, requires further explanation. From another viewpoint, it is a measure of the reproductive success of an individual, or how many descendants the individual can produce. More descendants are equivalent to greater reproductive success and, therefore, higher fitness. The example in this section assumes that the fitness of all individuals is the same. The next section explains evolution models with more generalized fitness.

2.2.2 Genetic Drift and Fixation Probability

Assume that black balls are r times more likely than white balls to be chosen when ball A is picked during the exchange process. Here, $r \neq 1.0$. Black and white balls are picked as ball B with equal probability. In this case, $p_{i,i-1}$ and $p_{i,i}$, $p_{i,i+1}$ can be similarly expressed using N, i, and r as follows:

$$p_{i,i-1} = \frac{N-i}{r \cdot i + N - i} \cdot \frac{i}{N} \tag{2.6}$$

$$p_{i,i} = 1 - p_{i,i-1} - p_{i,i+1} \tag{2.7}$$

$$p_{i,i+1} = \frac{r \cdot i}{r \cdot i + N - i} \cdot \frac{N-i}{N} \tag{2.8}$$

The value of x_i (the probability that state i ultimately becomes state N where all balls are black) is obtained using $y_i = x_i - x_{i-1}$. The recurrence relation of y_i is given as follows:

$$y_i = \frac{p_{i,i-1}}{p_{i,i+1}} \cdot y_{i-1} = \frac{1}{r} \cdot y_{i-1} \tag{2.9}$$

Thus, $y_1 = x_1$, $y_2 = \frac{1}{r}x_1$, $y_3 = \frac{1}{r^2}x_1, \cdots$.

From the definition of y_i, $\sum_{i=1}^{N} y_i = x_N - x_0 = 1$. The equation $\sum_{i=1}^{k} y_i = x_k$ also holds and the right-hand side is

$$\left(\frac{1}{r^{i-1}} + \cdots + \frac{1}{r} + 1 \right) \times x_1 = \frac{1 - \frac{1}{r^i}}{1 - \frac{1}{r}} \times x_1. \tag{2.10}$$

From $x_1 = \frac{1-1/r}{1-1/r^N}$, we can derive the following equation:

$$x_i = \frac{1 - 1/r^i}{1 - 1/r^N}. \tag{2.11}$$

This model expresses the transition of states in a genetic population. The fitness is r for black and 1 for white balls. In this model:

■ Black is preferentially selected if $r > 1$.

■ White is preferentially selected if $r < 1$.

■ Black and white are randomly (neutrally) selected if $r = 1$.

Note that the probability of removal (death) is the same for both black and white balls.

When the fitness of black is r, as in the setup above, assume that a black individual appears through a mutation in the white population. The descendants of this mutation may either occupy the entire population or become extinct in the final state. These probabilities are as follows (Fig. 2.6):

$$\text{Fixation probability of the mutated black individual} = x_1 = \frac{1 - 1/r}{1 - 1/r^N}$$

$$\text{Probability that the black population becomes extinct} = 1 - x_1 = \frac{1/r - 1/r^N}{1 - 1/r^N}$$

The phenomenon where the fixation of genes occurs with random effects in a finite population is called "genetic drift."

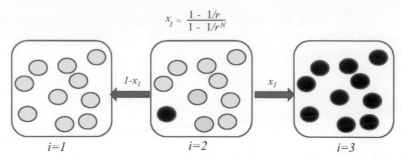

$$x_1 = \frac{1 - 1/r}{1 - 1/r^N}$$

Figure 2.6: Fixation probability.

2.2.3 Evolution Speed

Motoo Kimura[3] numerically demonstrated that mutation alone cannot drive evolution [74]. The human gene is written at approximately three billion base loci. If 3% of these loci (100 million loci) are meaningful, the possibility that the current base sequence is attained by random mutation only is an astronomically small value of $1/10^{60,000,000}$. How then did evolution occur?

Consider the process of selection in each of the 100 million loci and accumulating adaptive mutations in a step-by-step manner. If this was conducted throughout the evolution of life over the last three billion years, a change in the bases at a rate of once per 40 years per base is sufficient. This is a sufficiently realistic probability. Kimura used the metaphor of a monkey to hit a typewriter (Fig. 2.7). The chance of a monkey randomly hitting keys that consist of an alphabetic sequence from a Shakespeare play is almost zero. In contrast, if the monkey is allowed to hit the next letter once it hits a correct letter, one page could be typed in well under a year.

The fixation probability discussed earlier can be used to quantitatively understand this point. If a black ball appears in a white population by mutation, the fixation probability (ρ) that it occupies the population is given as follows:

$$\rho = x_1 = \frac{1 - 1/r}{1 - 1/r^N}. \tag{2.12}$$

Here, r is the relative fitness of the black ball versus that of a white ball. This value can be calculated using Table 2.1. The population N is assumed to be 100 in the discussion below.

A total of $\frac{\log 2}{\log(1-\rho)}$ mutations[4] result in a 50% probability that a mutated individual with relative fitness r occupies the entire population. According to Table 2.1, the number of mutations is 7 and 44 if the individual has an advantage of

---

[3]Motoo Kimura (1924–1994): Japanese population geneticist. He proposed the theory of neutral evolution.

[4]The probability of occupying once when N mutations occur is $1 - (1 - \rho)^N$. Therefore, solve for $(1 - \rho)^N = 0.5$.

Figure 2.7: A monkey typing a Shakespearean play.

Table 2.1: Fixation probability.

r	Selection	ρ, eq. (2.12)	50% prob. after mutations
2.0	100% advantageous selection	0.5	1
1.1	10% advantageous selection	0.09	7
1.01	1% advantageous selection	0.016	44
1.0	neutral selection	0.01	69
0.99	1% disadvantageous selection	0.0058	119
0.9	10% disadvantageous selection	0.000003	234,861

10% and 1%, respectively. This number is smaller than what one would expect. The most important case is a neutral mutation at $r = 1$. The entire population is occupied at a 50% probability after 69 mutations. Kimura's neutral theory, which is discussed in the next section, focuses on the size of this value.

2.2.4 Neutral Theory

Population genetics is a field in biology where the evolution of genes in a population has been studied mathematically. The neutral theory, which is a core theory, is explained below. There are two major theories, selection theory and neutral theory, which describe the mechanism of evolution by substitutions in a gene sequence. Selection theory, which originated from the concept proposed by Charles

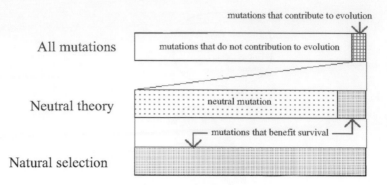

Figure 2.8: The differences between the natural selection theory and the neutral theory.

Darwin and Russel Wallace[5] in the second half of the 19th century, proposes that the evolution of life is primarily driven by natural selection. On the other hand, Kimura proposed the neutral theory in 1968 and argued that most mutations are neutral and do not affect fitness [74]. The differences in these two ideas are shown in Fig. 2.8.

Both theories agree that most mutations are localized and do not contribute to evolution. However, the view of mutations that contribute to evolution is different. Surviving mutations assist the survival of organisms in selection theory. On the other hand, the neutral theory maintains that some surviving mutations help the survival of organisms, but most have no effect.

Kimura proposed the neutral theory of molecular evolution based on these ideas, and its core is described below.

Neutral theory of molecular evolution
The mutation of DNA is fixed in the population not by natural selection but by accidental changes (genetic drift).

Changes in gene frequency easily occur simply by accident if the population is small or if an allele is very rare. This is the genetic drift explained in the previous section. Therefore, mates are not close relatives in a large population

---

5   Alfred Russel Wallace (1823–1913): British naturalist, biologist, and explorer. He identified the Wallace line, a distributional boundary that divides the distribution of animals in Indonesia into two distinct regions. He and Charles Darwin independently and almost simultaneously devised the theory of evolution by natural selection, and the paper sent by Wallace from the Malay Archipelago surprised the slow writer Darwin. Eventually, both papers were presented simultaneously in 1858 at the Linnean Society after Darwin had made "a delicate arrangement" in relevant parts of his paper [19].

with random mating. However, if the population is small for a long time, many individuals become relatives, and thus random mating becomes consanguineous mating. Random mating in a small population is anticipated to have results similar to those of inbreeding.

Therefore, genetic drift explains the survival of neutral mutations that do not affect the adaptation of organisms to the environment. The fixation probability is surprisingly high, as is clear from Table 2.1, and thus can drive evolution.

2.2.5 Neutral Evolution by Simulation

Let us see whether a mutated individual can be fixed in the population (occupy the population) by simulation. The following parameters need to be provided:

- Population size

- Mutation rate

- Fitness of the mutated individual (1.0 if neutral)

Note that when providing parameters, the mutation rate is usually very small. Changes in the time needed for fixation of the population when parameters are varied could be investigated. In particular, the dependence on population size during the time to fixation and the fixation interval is important.

Figure 2.9 illustrates the process of genetic drift. It depicts how long it takes for a neutral mutated gene to dominate the entire population. The interval of mutations follows an exponential distribution with an average of $1/(N\mu)$. In other words, mutations are likely to occur if the population size is large. Figure 2.9(a) shows a case with a large population (size 100), and Fig. 2.9(b) shows a population half this size. The mutation rate was 0.00001 in both cases, and simulations were conducted over 20,000 steps. A total of 23 and 10 mutations occurred in (a) and (b), respectively. The expected values are 20 and 10 times in (a) and (b), and the time necessary for fixation of a mutation was 5560 and 2000 steps in (a) and (b). Note that many mutations became extinct in addition to the mutation that became fixed (occupied the entire population). Previous calculations suggest that there are, on average, N extinct mutations (N is the population size) for a fixed mutation. The average time to fixation of a neutral mutation is shown in Table 2.2 and Fig. 2.10. Twenty experiments with a time step of 20,000 were conducted. The results can be fitted linearly[6].

The interval where fixed mutations appear, which is the average time interval (number of steps) between mutations that ultimately result in fixation, was analyzed. The relationship between this value and mutation rate is shown in Table 2.3. According to the figure, the average time interval is almost the same

---

[6]The coefficient is known to be approximately $4N$ in a theoretical organism model, as further discussed later; however, here, the approximate equation is different due to various constraints.

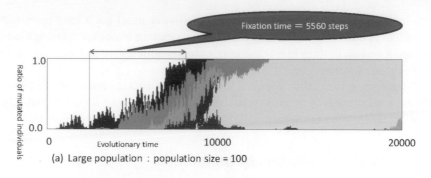

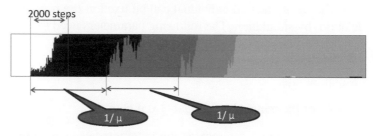

(a) Large population : population size = 100

(b) Small population : population size = 50

Figure 2.9: Evolutionary process of neural mutations.

Table 2.2: Mutation and fixation (1).

Mutation prob. (μ)	Fixation time steps			
	$N = 20$	$N = 50$	$N = 70$	$N = 100$
0.01	372.416	2308.33	4369.8	7769.96
0.005	381.663	2346.56	4359.64	7588.68
0.001	368.872	2368.71	4448.52	7584.22
0.0005	369.045	2251.25	4264.83	7592.5

Table 2.3: Mutation and fixation (2).

Mutation prob. (μ)	$1/\mu$	Fixation time steps			
		$N = 20$	$N = 50$	$N = 70$	$N = 100$
0.01	100.0	100.061	106.407	114.983	155.004
0.005	200.0	195.908	216.703	224.843	277.291
0.001	1000.0	1035.73	982.156	1138.71	1190.48
0.0005	2000.0	1971.9	1942.41	2020.43	2136.91

as the reciprocal of the mutation rate $1/\mu$ and is independent of the population size. This is the theoretical foundation of the neutral theory discussed below.

Fixation time (steps)

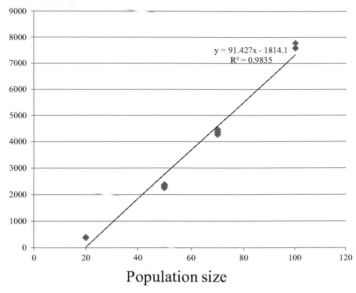

Figure 2.10: Population size vs. fixation time steps.

In summary, the time necessary for a mutation to fix is proportional to the population size, but the number of substitutions (frequency of successful mutations) is independent of the population size.

The time necessary for a neutral mutated gene to govern the entire population has been theoretically obtained [28]. Its value is approximately $4N_e$, where N_e is the effective size of the population. For example, if the number of reproducing male and female individuals is N_m and N_f, respectively, N_e is given as follows:

$$N_e = \frac{4N_mN_f}{N_m + N_f}. \tag{2.13}$$

Naturally, if the number of males and females is the same, $N_e = 2N_m = 2N_f$. On the other hand, if there is a difference in the number of reproducing males and females, the effective size depends on the smaller value. In a population where there are many more females than males, the effective size is $N_e = 4N_m$. Therefore, in a harem situation where the population is controlled by one male, $N_e = 4$. The evolution speed (speed of gene change per unit time) is obtained as follows: Assume that a black ball appears by a mutation in a population of white balls. All individuals were initially white balls in a population of size N. A black ball appears as a mutation with a very rare frequency (mutation rate μ). The speed at which a mutation occurs in a population of N individuals is $N\mu$ ($N\mu$ mutations happen per unit time); thus, the average time until a mutation occurs is $1/(N\mu)$. Setting the fixation probability of black balls as ρ from eq. (2.12), the evolution speed R, which is the elapsed time from when a population is a state with all white balls to a state with all black balls is as follows:

$$R = N\mu\rho. \tag{2.14}$$

$\rho = 1/N$ holds when black balls are neutral (see eq. (2.5)). Therefore, the neutral evolution speed is $R = \mu$ because N cancels out.

Neutral theory of molecular evolution
In the evolution of a neutral gene,

$$\text{evolution speed} = \text{mutation rate} \tag{2.15}$$

and this holds regardless of population size.

This is found in the experimental results in Table 2.3. In other words, the interval between mutations leading to fixation is the same regardless of population size and changes such that $1/\mu$ is the expected value (μ is the mutation rate). This relation holds even when the population size changes with time.

Moreover, if the mutation rate is the same, neutral mutations accumulate at a certain rate; therefore, they can be used as a molecular clock. This is the principle behind molecular phylogenetic tree derivation (see Section 6.1).

The neutral theory of molecular evolution, which was proposed by Motoo Kimura in the 1960s, resulted in an unexpected consequence. Kimura and his coworkers vigorously argued that most molecular changes during evolution are intrinsically neutral and are an accumulation of mutations and genetic drift. Although there are doubts regarding whether complete evidence was obtained, the number of supporters has increased after this theory was first presented. On the other hand, genes that evolve through natural selection have been detected, and the debate is ongoing.

2.2.6 Baldwinian Evolution

Lamarck[7] proposed the following theory. This is called the "use and disuse theory."

> Depending on the environment, the organs that are used most frequently will develop over time, while those that are no longer used will gradually shrink or degenerate.

---

[7] Jean-Baptiste Pierre Antoine de Monet, Chevalier de Lamarck (17441–1829): Famous 19th century naturalist. He was one of the first people to use the word "biology" in its modern sense.

A famous example is the giraffe (see Fig. 2.11). The giraffe stretches out its neck in search of young leaves to feed on at increasingly higher altitudes. As a result of this behavior being repeated over a long period of time by all individuals of the species, the forelimbs and neck of the giraffe gradually lengthened. Lamarck's theory of evolution is based on the "inheritance of acquired traits." However, with the subsequent development of genetics, the inheritance of acquired traits was completely rejected. Although Lamarck is second only to Darwin as the most important biologist who clearly considered the fact that organisms evolve, his theory itself was not correct. Nonetheless, Lamarck's theory has been considered by many scholars. This may mean that the idea of inheritance of acquired traits appeals to our intuition.

Even if the acquired traits themselves are not inherited, it is hard to imagine that learning, which is an important factor for organisms, is completely unrelated to evolution (heredity). The Baldwin effect is a theory that refers to this fact. In the following, the relationship between learning and heredity will be explained with the Baldwin effect as the axis, and the method of applying it to evolutionary computation will be described in Section 3.5.

In 1896, Baldwinian evolution and the Baldwin effect were proposed independently by James Baldwin[8] [7], Morgan [102] and Orsborn [108], also known as ontogenic evolution. Later in 1942, Waddington [144] reviewed the theory and presented the term "genetic assimilation" or "canalization." In this theory, acquired traits cannot transfer phenotypic information directly back to the genotype. Instead, when an individual learns good traits in its lifetime, it is rewarded in the selection. Therefore, the selection priority is automatically assessed to the genotypes, inherently easier to acquire good traits. It is denoted that the children of a neck-stretching animal do not necessarily receive long necks, but the good ability in the stretching. The children of such a parent will be excellent in various activities (see Fig. 2.11). The Baldwin effect has always been controversial in biology, as in the complex natural world it is too difficult to verify it.

Baldwinian evolution is illustrated in Fig. 2.12. First the individual translates its initial genotype to the phenotype. The phenotype is adapted through a learning process, and improves its fitness. Selection is performed based on the adapted fitness. Mating is performed using the initial genotype. While the traits acquired during learning are not transferred back to the genotype, it has the potential to develop good or bad final phenotypes based on learning.

For many problems, the search for an optimum can be likened to finding a needle in a haystack. There will be an acute fitness decrease after leaving the optimum, such as in Fig. 2.13. In situations like these, even if an individual is near a local optimum, it will not be able to detect the local optimum and thus will not find it.

---

[8]James Mark Baldwin (1861–1934): American philosopher and psychologist.

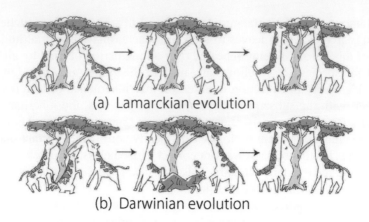

(a) Lamarckian evolution

(b) Darwinian evolution

Figure 2.11: Different types of evolution.

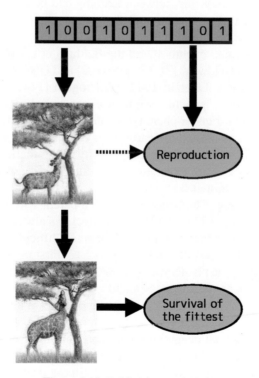

Figure 2.12: Baldwinian evolution.

If we give the individuals in the evolutionary process the ability to learn, so that they can search in a neighborhood around its initial position, the ability to find a local optimum will be broadened. The learning process can be implemented by constructing an analytic model of the local area, by a stochastic search

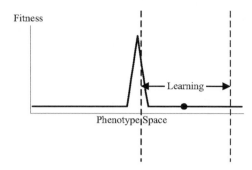

Figure 2.13: Learning enables more individuals to find a needle.

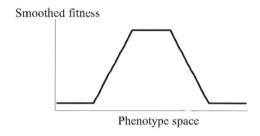

Figure 2.14: Equivalent fitness landscape smoothed by learning.

method, or by some random trials. In this case (see Fig. 2.13), only if the point is not so far from the spike, it may be possible to reach the spike by learning, that is, by receiving some fitness bonus and calling attention to the area. With learning, it is possible to search in an equivalently smoothed landscape, just as in the curve in Fig. 2.14.

However, learning always incurs in a cost. This is true of evolutionary computation as well as in the natural world. If this learning cost is included in the selection mechanism, we can transform it in a second drive for approaching the optimum [141]. More traits learned by the individual will become fixed to the genotype as the evolution proceeds. This mechanism is named as "genetic assimilation," or "canalization" [137].

By chance, possibly affected by mutation, certain genius individuals may be born with good traits that its ancestors spent much time learning. These individuals have a higher starting point, thus cost less to learn what their ancestors learned, Under the selection pressure, such genius individuals will win in the selection and the species is allowed to obtain even better phenotypes as a result of learning. As shown in Fig. 2.15, we can reach the top of the hill by learning form both points A and B. However, due to the low cost in learning, individuals starting from B will beat those from A in the selection. Although Baldwinian evolution does not transfer acquired traits back to the genotype, it can be ob-

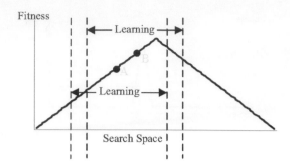

Figure 2.15: Genetic assimilation.

served that evolution follows the indication of learning. Waddington [144] noted the process by which a phenotypic character, which initially is produced only in response to some environmental influence, becomes, through a process of selection, taken over by the genotype, so that it is formed even in the absence of the environmental influence which had at first been necessary.

Affected by these two basic mechanisms, the Baldwin effect acts as a two phase process in the search, as shown in Fig. 2.16. In the whole process, the learning cost is adapted by the selection pressure automatically. The two phases are described as follows:

Phase1 Individuals which have gained an advantage from a learned adaptive trait proliferate throughout the population.

Phase2 Individuals with a lower cost of learning, that is, those which innately acquire the adaptive trait, proliferate throughout the population.

In the first phase, the individuals do not fit the environment well when directly determined by genotypes. The individuals with more potentials in learning, or more parts left to learning, are likely to attain higher fitness in its lifetime. The learning cost grows, but not as fast as the increase of fitness. As a result, such individuals will survive, and the learning-assisted search may dominate the whole population. This search explores different areas in the search space and fitness grows remarkably, while learning costs rise and keep high.

In the second phase called "genetic assimilation," most individuals can reach a similar level of fitness after lifetime learning. At this stage, increasing cost in learning helps little in improving final fitness, while more punishment is imposed because of such high cost. As a result, individuals with less learning costs to reach the optima will survive so that the genetic assimilation will dominate. This search concentrates on the exploitation and the fitness increases steadily, while learning costs decrease, even to zero in some situations.

In summary, the Baldwin effect is essentially as follows: Acquired traits themselves are not inherited; rather, ostensibly acquired traits are inherited

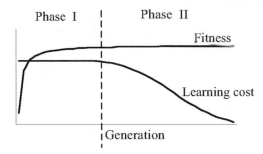

Figure 2.16: Two-phase process of the Baldwin effect.

through the accumulation of small mutations and learning in combination with changes in the environment, giving the appearance that a specific capability has been acquired without learning. It is thus an argument concerning the effect of the balance between learning advantage and cost during evolution.

2.3   Introns and Selfish Genes

2.3.1   Basics of DNA and RNA

An interesting fact arises from the comparison of genome sizes of various organisms. Genome size is the number of characters (bases) in DNA. *Phages* have a few thousand to a few tens of thousands of characters, whereas humans have a huge number, constituting three billion characters. *Escherichia coli* has a few million characters, yeast a few tens of millions of characters, and fruit flies, with a few hundred million characters between them. However, there is no complete correlation between the complexity of the organism and the number of characters. For example, mice have approximately the same number of characters as humans, but salamanders have many more characters than humans do.

The amount of DNA per monoploid genome depends on the organism species and is called the C-value [91]. The C-value may also be chemically measured as the amount of DNA in picograms (pg). Figure 2.17 shows the "C-values" for various organisms. The minimum genome size clearly increases as the organism becomes more complex. The genomes of single-celled *eukaryotes* are larger than those of bacteria, but not significantly larger. Eukaryotes do not necessarily have a larger genome size. The complexity of DNA is more profound in complete multicellular organisms. For instance, the amount of DNA in *Caenorhabditis elegans* is 8×10^7 bp (bp is the unit of base pairs[9]). The relationship between complexity and the amount of DNA in higher organisms is not clear. Insect genomes have at least 10^8 bp, *echinoderms* at least 4×10^8 bp, birds and amphibia at least 8×10^8

---

[9]Bases are major components of DNA, and there are four types: adenine (A), thymine (T), guanine (G), and cytosine (C).

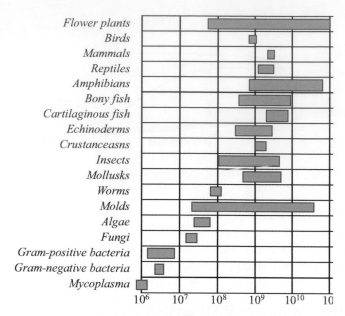

Figure 2.17: C-value paradox.

bp, and mammals at least 2×10^9 bp. The genome size spread is relatively smaller in birds, reptiles, and mammals; the spread is within a range of approximately 2-fold. However, the spread exceeds 10-fold in some cases. The number of known functions and the amount of DNA per genome does not correlate; this is called the "C-value paradox." Interestingly, although the C-value may fluctuate widely in a species, the fluctuation in the apparent complexity is not reflected in the C-value fluctuation.

The C-value spread is very large in amphibia; the minimum is less than 10^9 bp and the maximum reaches 10^{11} bp. It is unthinkable that this spread of a factor of 100 in the amount of DNA is necessary to determine the species in amphibia. Moreover, there are cases in which very similar species have surprisingly different genome sizes, and there are examples where the amount of DNA differs by a factor of 10 in species that are morphologically very similar. If the number of genes does not differ much, most of the DNA with large-sized genomes does not code proteins. What is the purpose of such large amounts of uncoded DNA? The genes of eukaryotes contain a considerably higher amount of DNA than the base sequences necessary to code proteins. Therefore, the C-value paradox is closely related to the presence of excessively higher amounts of DNA than is necessary to code proteins.

The meaning of a DNA sequence is very complex. A specific base sequence in a DNA molecule corresponds to a gene, which is a physical and functional unit in heredity. These genes become the structural unit of the body or contain information on the amino acid sequences of proteins involved in biosynthesis.

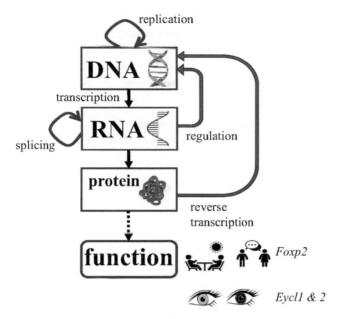

Figure 2.18: DNA, RNA and proteins.

However, some portions are clearly not genes, and there are many DNA sequences with no clear meaning. The entire human DNA is thought to contain 100 thousand genes. Approximately 10% (which some claim to be 3%) of human genes actually code proteins; however, the meaning of most of the genes has not been clarified. Single-celled organisms with small amounts of DNA are converted, with almost no waste, into amino acid sequences. In contrast, only a few percent are converted into higher organisms, including humans. Many portions do not correspond to amino acid sequences, including sequences with no known meaning. Salamanders contain vastly more DNA than humans, probably because the ratio of DNA sequences corresponding to proteins is much lower.

Figure 2.18 shows the relationship between DNA, RNA, and proteins. DNA replicates during cell division. During the replication process, the double helix unwinds, the two DNA strands become casts for the synthesis of complementary DNA, and two identical double helixes are obtained. Transcription to an RNA is similar to the replication of DNA; however, transcription differs in the following aspects; therefore, it is more complex:

■ Only part of the long DNA gene is transcribed.

■ There exists a process to edit information (splicing).

DNA is used as a cast to make complementary RNA in the initial stage of transcription. DNA and RNA are almost the same in terms of molecular species,

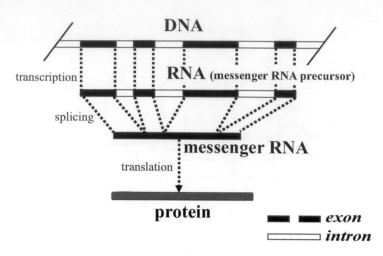

Figure 2.19: Splicing process.

and the base pairs are complementary in both. However, among the four bases, thymine in DNA changes to uracil in RNA. The resulting RNA consists of two parts, exons and introns, that alternate in a sequence. Introns are selectively removed in the subsequent splicing process, and a messenger RNA in which only exons are joined is obtained. Figure 2.19 shows a schematic of the splicing process.

Organisms elaborated the transcription process, probably because it has some benefits. Transcription to RNA separates where the genetic information is stocked (nucleus) and the status of biosynthesis (cytoplasm). Two very complex processes can be conducted independently in this manner, and errors and confusion can be minimized. Moreover, the emergence of proteins can be controlled by the synthesis and decomposition of RNA. Such control is impossible, particularly when directly translating proteins from DNA because DNA cannot be decomposed. The meaning of splicing is discussed in relation to the evolutionary process. Each exon corresponds to a protein structure unit (module), and various proteins are designed by combining these modules.

Gould considered selection as a force for retention instead of change. Supporting evidence from this view is that the mutation rate in exons is lower than that in introns. This is because mutations in introns are not affected by selection, but mutations in exons are generally harmful and do not survive selection [50].

2.3.2 Selfish Genes

Richard Dawkins[10] proposed the idea of the "selfish gene" [29], where genes behave cleverly to succeed in reproduction and leave as many descendants as possible. Increasing the copy number among descendants is important for genes. Males fighting fiercely for territories and females, and touching maternal love, could be actions caused by genes. From the point of view of a gene, the individual in which the gene lives does not need to live forever, as long as the individual creates and ensures the maturation of its children. Some genes, such as cancer genes, only emerge after the individual matures, have created children, and the cancer gene is passed onto the children. Although the individual dies from its emergence, the copy of the gene has certainly been passed on to the children. This line of thought suggests that we are vehicles for the survival of genes that live within us.

This idea explains many life phenomena. The "selfish gene" theory, which led to Neo-Darwinism (the viewpoint that all life's phenomena can be explained by evolution), is very powerful and difficult to confute.

As discussed later, the bloat phenomenon in genetic programming (GP) is expected to arise from a substructure in the code that behaves selfishly as does a gene. Bloating is a result of adding redundancy and hoarding introns to prevent destruction from crossover and mutation.

2.4 Gene Duplication

The bar of Drosophila melanogaster (fruit fly) is an eye mutation caused by the duplication of a small segment in a chromosome (the following discussion is based on [28]). Observation of a normal salivary gland X-chromosome reveals a segment with four horizontal stripes, but a bar-eye chromosome has eight horizontal stripes in the same region because of duplication of this segment. This segment may be tripled; in this case, the bar-eye is further pronounced. The discovered position effect is related to the duplication of genes that form bar eyes in fruit flies. Denoting R as the duplicate segment, the following correspondence relationship with the phenotype is found:

---

10 Richard Dawkins (1941–): English evolutionary biologist, who has written many general books and general introductions to biology and, as a result, espoused thinking on the selfish gene, meme (cultural information replicators, see Section 7.1), and expanded phenotypes (host operation due to the parasites, dams made by beavers, and mounds of white ants can be seen as phenotypes). His revolutionary ideas and provocative comments about evolution are still causing many discussions. He is a famous atheist.

	Phenotype	Chromosome config.	#. of facets
1.	Normal	R/R	750
2.	Heterozygous bar-eye	RR/R	360
3.	Homozygous bar-eye	RR/RR	68
4.	Heterozygous super bar-eye	RRR/R	45
5.	Homozygous super bar-eye	RRR/RRR	25

Here, RR/R shows that one of the diploid chromosomes has two genes and the other has one. The position effect is demonstrated by the difference in eye size between genotypes 3 and 4. The amount of the chromosome matter is the same when added, but the eye size is smaller when one chromosome has three genes and the other has one than when both chromosomes have two. The following reasons for gene duplication have been proposed (see [96] for details).

1. Unequal crossover

   Figure 2.20 shows that the copies of the same DNA sequence, which are positioned in tandem, can be obtained by unequal crossover. A in the figure shows the first step in forming a DNA sequence where abcde is positioned in tandem. In B, the two chromosomes each have nine copies of the same sequence in tandem. These pairs become misaligned, and crossover results in the formation of chromosomes with six and 12 copies. There is evidence in the hemoglobin gene family that such tandem sequences exist. Unequal crossover can also form repetitive segments in a gene. Once crossover forms tandem repetition, chromosomes can come out of alignment and pair, and further gene duplication is facilitated.

2. Transfer

   A DNA sequence is replicated, and its copy is inserted into a new position on the chromosome. This process may include transcription of RNA before insertion and reverse transcription to its DNA.

3. Polyploidization

   A tetraploid forms if replication of a chromosome occurs without cell division. A tetraploid with high reproductive power is likely to form if polyploidization occurs on a crossbreed of a diploid species.

The duplicated locus is considered to become one of the following in the future.

1. One copy will be deactivated.

2. As in the hemoglobin gene family, two loci maintain the same basic functionality, but branch during the evolution process. The two loci gain different functionalities while retaining the homologies in the three-dimensional structure and amino acids to some extent.

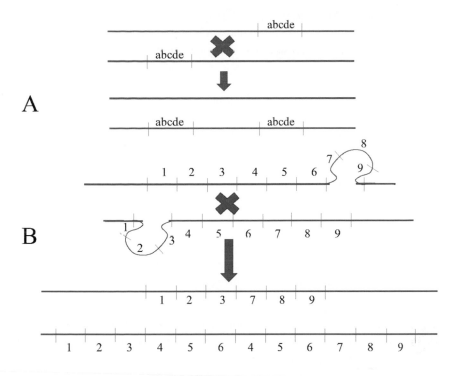

Figure 2.20: Duplication process.

3. One of the duplicated genes gained new functionality through mutation. The homology of amino acids and similarity in the three-dimensional structure are both lost between the old and new gene products. This type of evolution process has not been found as of now.

How can duplications be fixed? A frequently used general explanation is that when a pair of dominant alleles, A1 and A2, exist on a locus, an advantageous chromosome that simultaneously has both loci A1 and A2 can be gained by duplication. Note that the crossover between homologous chromosomes plays an important role. Incorporation of heterozygote-favoring duplication in a species, as discussed above, has been shown from the viewpoint of population genetics [74].

Susumu Ohno[11] uncovered many of the creative roles of gene duplication in evolution and discussed new evidence based on current molecular, cellular, and paleontological studies. He proposed a bold hypothesis in which the ancestors of vertebrates underwent two tetraploidizations at the fish stage before beginning to live on land. This polyploidization should have existed before a rigid sex determination mechanism using chromosomes was established. When a gene becomes

---

[11] Susumu Ohno (1928–2000): Japanese-American geneticist and evolutionary biologist.

duplicated, one is unnecessary and therefore can be freely mutated into a new genotype [74]. This is considered to play an important role in gene duplication.

For example, the human hemoglobin gene family is thought to have arisen as a result of gene duplication. Hemoglobin proteins are responsible for transporting oxygen through blood vessels. The primitive hemoglobin genes were duplicated to form α-globulin and β-globulin. Each globulin underwent further duplication to form the current four kinds of α-globulin variants and five kinds of β-globulin variants. During human development, combinations of these different genes are expressed, resulting in a variety of hemoglobin genes with different binding properties to oxygen.

In this way, organisms have benefited from gene copying in many ways. The following genetic traits can be considered:

1. Acquisition of lethal mutations
   Suppose that there exist two copies of a gene and that one of them fails due to a mutation. If there is a second copy, the negative effects of such harmful mutations can be minimized.

2. Evolution of new functions
   If the mutation is desirable, it will produce a protein with a new function. If the genes are duplicated, this can be done without interfering with the protein synthesis of the original gene.

3. Production of more proteins
   If the protein of a gene is desired, duplication can produce more protein.

Section 3.11 describes the extensions to GP (genetic programming) based on the properties of these duplicated genes.

Chapter 3

Evolutionary
Computation

> Natural selection is a miserly economist, invisibly counting the pennies, the nuances of cost and benefit too subtle for us, the observing scientists to notice. (Richard Dawkins [31])

3.1   Introduction to GA

The objective of a genetic algorithm (GA) is to search for the solution to a problem. A number of ways to do this have been proposed in addition to GA. In this chapter, first we will look at what it means to search, and then we will look at what kinds of situations comprise problems.

Information handled using GA comprises a two-layer data structure consisting of GTYPE and PTYPE. The PTYPE results from the expression of the GTYPE. The operators of genetic algorithms (GA operators, see Fig. 3.1) act on the GTYPE, and the fitness value is determined from the PTYPE, based on the environment. For the time being, let us assume that the larger the fitness value, the better. At the moment, let us also use the target function values for the fitness value.

For the time being, we will think of a one-dimensional bit string (a string of 0s and 1s) as the GTYPE of GA, and take the result of the binary conversion of this string as the PTYPE. The location of the gene on the chromosome is called the "locus" in biology. With GA, as well, we use the word "locus" to specify the

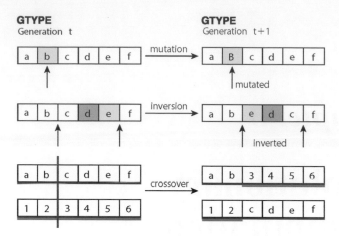

Figure 3.1: GA operators.

location of the GTYPE. For example, for GTYPE 010, the genes would be as follows:

- Gene of the 1st locus → 0

- Gene of the 2nd locus → 1

- Gene of the 3rd locus → 0

Before going any further, let us take a brief look at the process of selection. With GA, selection takes place in such a way that the larger the fitness value of an organism, the higher the probability for it to reproduce. On the other hand, the organisms with smaller fitness values are more likely to die out. The simplest way of achieving this is to create a roulette wheel of all individuals. Each individual gets a surface area in the roulette proportional to its fitness value, hence it is called a "weighted roulette." Selection is performed by rotating this roulette wheel and choosing the individual in the place where the roulette wheel stops. This is called the "fitness proportionate strategy" (as will be described in detail in page 47).

When reproduction occurs, the operators shown in Fig. 3.1 are applied to the selected GTYPE to generate new GTYPE for the subsequent generation. These operators are called GA operators. To keep the explanation simple, we express the GTYPE as a one-dimensional array here. Each operator is analogous to the recombination or mutation of a gene in a biological organism. Generally, the frequency with which these operators are applied, as well as the sites at which they are applied, are determined randomly. In more precise terms, the crossover shown in Fig. 3.1 has one crossover point, so it is called a one-point crossover. Following are some methods for performing the crossover operation:

1. One-point crossover (hereafter abbreviated as 1X)

2. Multi-point crossover (*n*-point crossover, hereafter abbreviated as nX)

3. Uniform crossover (hereafter abbreviated as UX)

The *n*-point crossover operation has *n* crossover points, so if $n = 1$, this is equivalent to the one-point crossover operation (Fig. 3.2(a)). With this crossover method, genes are carried over from one parent alternately between crossover points. A case in which $n = 3$ is shown in Fig. 3.2(b). Two-point crossovers, in which $n = 2$, are often used. Uniform crossovers are a crossover method in which any desired number of crossover points can be identified, so these are realized using a mask for a bit string consisting of $0, 1$. First, let us randomly generate a character string of 0s and 1s for this mask. The crossover is carried out as follows. Suppose the two selected parents are designated as Parent *A* and Parent *B*, and the offspring to be created are designated as Child *A* and Child *B*. At this point, the genes for offspring Child *A* are carried over from Parent *A* when the corresponding mask is 1, and are carried over from Parent *B* when the mask is 0. Conversely, the genes for offspring Child *B* are carried over from Parent *A* when the corresponding mask is 0, and are carried over from Parent *B* when the mask is 1 (Fig. 3.2(c)).

The basic flow of GA can be summarized as follows (Fig. 3.3). Let us say that the GTYPE $\{g_t(i)\}$ is a group of individuals at generation t.

For the phenotype $p_t(i)$ of each $g_t(i)$, a fitness value $f_t(i)$ is calculated in the environment. The GA operators are generally applied to GTYPEs with a larger fitness value, and the newly bred GTYPE is substituted for a GTYPE with a smaller fitness value. Based on the above, selection is carried out based on fitness values, and the group $\{g_{t+1}(i)\}$ for the next generation $(t + 1)$ is generated. The process described above is repeated generation after generation.

There are many selection strategies in GA. Basically, candidates must be selected for reproduction in such a way that the larger (better) the fitness value, the more offspring the parent will be able to reproduce. There are a number of ways to do this and the following two are the most commonly used.

Fitness-proportionate Strategy (Roulette Wheel Selection)

With this method, candidates are selected at a percentage proportional to the fitness value. The simplest way of doing this is to use a weighted roulette wheel.

A roulette wheel that has fields that are proportional to individuals' fitness values is rotated, and the individuals in the field in which the roulette ball lands are selected.

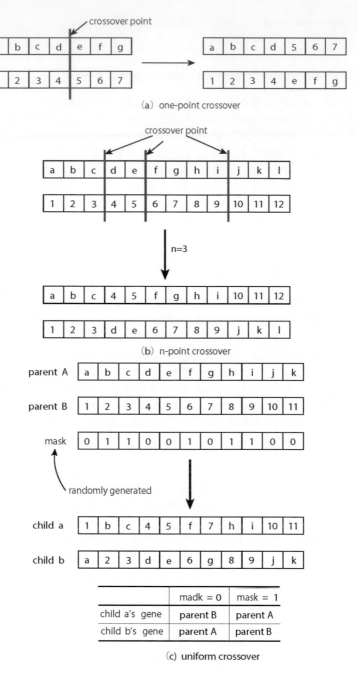

Figure 3.2: GA crossovers: (a) one-point crossover, (b) *n*-point crossover, (c) uniform crossover.

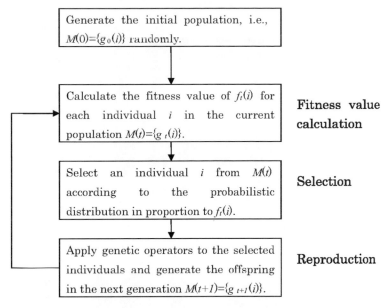

Figure 3.3: Flow chart of GA.

Tournament Strategy

This is a strategy in which a certain number (tournament size) of individuals are randomly selected from a population, and the best of these individuals is finally chosen. This process is repeated until the size of the population is reached.

Elite Strategy

With the above selection methods, the parent candidates are always selected on a probabilistic basis, so the best individual will not necessarily remain in the next generation. Even if they survive the selection process as parent candidates, mutations and crossovers could occur in those candidates. As a result, the outcome will not necessarily improve over successive generations. There is another method, however, by which the best individual (or several individuals with the highest scores) will definitely be carried over to the next generation. This is called the "elite strategy." In this strategy, genes are simply copied, without crossovers or mutations being applied. Consequently, as long as the fitness value functions are the same, the outcome of the current generation is minimally guaranteed at the next generation.

Summarizing the above, the alteration of generations with GA will be as shown in Fig. 3.4. In this figure, G represents the elite ratio (i.e., the percentage of individuals with highest scores that will be copied and carried over to the next generation).

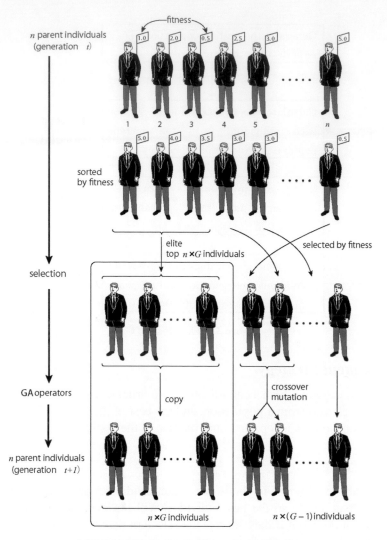

Figure 3.4: Selection and reproduction of GA.

3.2 Covariance Matrix Adaptation Evolution Strategy (CMA-ES)

Evolutionary strategies (ESs) are real-valued optimization algorithms for searching better solutions iteratively by improving individuals using mutations. Among them, the covariance matrix adaptation ES (CMA-ES) [55, 56] is widely used in various fields of real number searching as it is highly efficient.

In CMA-ES, using μ individuals (solution candidates) as the parent, λ ($\lambda > \mu$) children are generated, and μ better individuals are selected, becoming the next generation, in a repetitive cycle. The child $x_k \in \mathbb{R}^n$ at k-th generation is generated based on the following multivariate normal distribution $N(0, C)$:

$$x_k = \langle x_{\text{parents}} \rangle_w + \sigma z_k,$$

$$z_k \sim N(0, C),$$

$$\langle x_{\text{parents}} \rangle_w = \sum_{i=1}^{\mu} w_i x_{i\text{th}-\text{best}-\text{parent}}$$

$$\sum_{i=1}^{\mu} w_i = 1, \; 0 \le w_i \le 1$$

Here, the weight coefficient w_i denotes the weight of the i-th best parent $x_{i\text{th}-\text{best}-\text{parent}}$ and is set so that $w_1 \ge w_2 \ge \cdots \ge w_\mu > 0$. When $w_i = 1/\mu$, it is set to the average of μ parent individuals. Generally, it is recommended to set high weights in correspondence with good individuals such that $w_i \propto \ln(\mu + 1) - \ln(i)$.

In CMA-ES, n-dimensional covariance matrix C and step size σ are adapted simultaneously. Reaching a quick and optimal solution can be expected when using covariance matrix C, which is updated using vector p that determines the direction of evolution. p and C are updated according to the following rules:

$$p \leftarrow \eta_1 p + \eta_2 (\langle x_{\text{newparents}} \rangle - \langle x_{\text{oldparents}} \rangle),$$

$$C \leftarrow \eta_3 C + \eta_4 p p^T,$$

where $\eta_1, \ldots, \eta_4$ denote the learning rates and are determined in advance; step size σ is increased when the success rate (i.e., when the child is better than the parent) is high and decreased when the success rate is low.

3.3 Introduction to GP

The aim of Genetic Programming (GP) is to extend genetic forms from Genetic Algorithm (GA) to the expression of trees and graphs and to apply them to the synthesis of programs and the formation of hypotheses or concepts. Researchers are using GP to attempt to improve their software for the design of control systems and structures for robots.

The original concept of GP was conceived by John Koza of Stanford University and his associates [80]. GP is one of the fields of evolutionary computation. When the concepts of GP are applied in AI (Artificial Intelligence), the processes of learning, hypothesis formation and problem solving are called "evolutionary learning" or Genetic-Based Machine Learning (GBML). This learning method is based on fitness and involves transformation of knowledge and elimination of unfit solutions by a process of selection to preserve appropriate solutions in the subsequent generation.

The procedures of GA are extended in GP in order to handle graph structures (in particular, tree structures). Tree structures are generally well described by

S-expressions in LISP. Thus, it is quite common to handle LISP programs as "genes" in GP. As long as the user understands that the program is expressed in a tree format, then he or she should have little trouble reading a LISP program (the user should recall the principles of flow charts). The explanations below have been presented so as to be quickly understood by a reader who does not know LISP.

A tree is a graph with a structure as follows, incorporating no cycles:

More precisely, a tree is an acyclical connected graph, with one node defined as the root of the tree. A tree structure can be expressed as an expression with parentheses. The above tree would be written as follows:

```
(A (B)
   (C (D)))
```

In addition, the above can be simplified to the following expression:

```
(A B
   (C D))
```

This notation is called an "S-expression" in LISP. Hereinafter, a tree structure will be identified with its corresponding S-expression. The following terms will be used for the tree structure:

- Node: Symbolized with A, B, C, D, etc.

- Root: A

- Terminal node: B, D (also called a "terminal symbol" or "leaf node")

- Non-terminal node: A, C (also called a "non-terminal symbol" and an "argument of the S-expression")

- Child: From the viewpoint of A, nodes B and C are children (also, "arguments of function A")

- Parent: The parent of C is A

Other common phrases will also be used as convenient, including "number of children", "number of arguments", "grandchild", "descendant", and "ancestor." These are not explained here, as their meanings should be clear from the context.

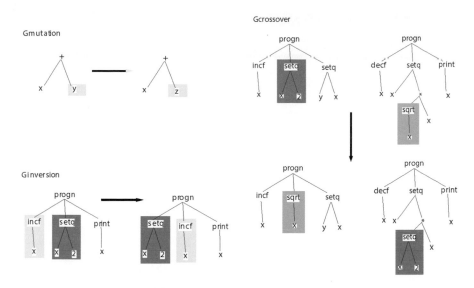

Figure 3.5: Genetic operators in GP.

The following genetic operators acting on the tree structure will be incorporated:

1. **Gmutation** Alteration of the node label

2. **Ginversion** Reordering of siblings

3. **Gcrossover** Exchange of a subtree

These are natural extensions of existing GA operators and act on sequences of bits. These operators are shown below in examples where they have been applied in LISP expression trees (S-expressions) (see Fig. 3.5). The underlined portion of the statement is the expression that is acted upon:

Gmutation Parent: $(+ \, x \, \underline{y})$
$\Downarrow$
Child: $(+ \, x \, \underline{z})$

Ginversion Parent: $(\text{progn } \underline{(\text{incf } x) \, (\text{setq } x \, 2)} \, (\text{print } x))$
$\Downarrow$
Child: $(\text{progn } \underline{(\text{setq } x \, 2) \, (\text{incf } x)} \, (\text{print } x))$

Gcrossover Parent$_1$: $(\text{progn } (\text{incf } x) \, \underline{(\text{setq } x \, 2)} \, (\text{setq } y \, x))$
Parent$_2$: $(\text{progn } (\text{decf } x) \, (\text{setq } x \, (* \, \underline{(\text{sqrt } x)} \, x)) \, (\text{print } x))$
$\Downarrow$
Child$_1$: $(\text{progn } (\text{incf } x) \, \underline{(\text{sqrt } x)} \, (\text{setq } y \, x))$
Child$_2$: $(\text{progn } (\text{decf } x) \, (\text{setq } x \, (* \, \underline{(\text{setq } x \, 2)} \, x)) \, (\text{print } x))$

Table 3.1: Program changes due to GP operators.

Operator	Program before operation	Program after operation
Mutation	Add x and y.	Add x and z.
Inversion	1. Add 1 to x. 2. Set $x = 2$ 3. Print $x(=2)$ and return 2.	1. Set $x = 2$. 2. Add 1 to x. 3. Print $x(=3)$ and return 3. ·
Crossover	Parent$_1$: 1. Add 1 to x. 2. Set $x = 2$. 3. Set $y = x(= 2)$ and return 2. Parent$_2$: 1. Subtract 1 from x. 2. Set $x = \sqrt{x} \times x$. 3. Print x and return the value.	Child$_1$: 1. Add 1 to x. 2. Take square root of x. 3. Set $y = x$ and return the value. Child$_2$: 1. Subtract 1 from x. 2. Set $x = 2$ and its value $(=2)$ is multiplied by $x(=2)$. The result value $(=4)$ is set to x again. 3. Print $x(=4)$ and return 4.

Table 3.1 provides a summary of how the program was changed as a result of these operators. "progn" is a function acting on the arguments in the order of their presentation and returns the value of the final argument. The function "setq" sets the value of the first argument to the evaluated value of the second argument. It is apparent on examining this table that mutation has caused a slight change to the action of the program, and that crossover has caused replacement of the actions in parts of the programs of all of the parents. The actions of the genetic operators have produced programs that are individual children but that have inherited the traits of the parent programs.

More strictly, we use the following kinds of Gmutation: (Fig. 3.6).

1. Mutations that change a terminal node to a non-terminal node, corresponding to the creation of a subtree (Fig. 3.6(a)).

2. Mutations that change a terminal node to another terminal node, changing only the node label (Fig. 3.6(b)).

3. Mutations that change a non-terminal node to a terminal node, corresponding to the deletion of a subtree (Fig. 3.6(c)).

4. Mutations that change a non-terminal node to another non-terminal node.

    Case 1   The new non-terminal node has the same number of children as the old non-terminal node (Fig. 3.6(d)).
        ⇒ Only the node label is changed.

    Case 2   The new non-terminal node has a different number of children from the old non-terminal node (Fig. 3.6(e)).
        ⇒ A subtree is created or deleted.

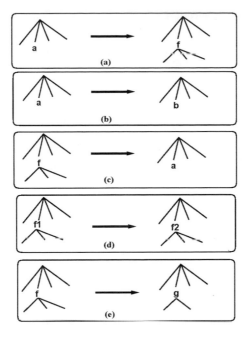

Figure 3.6: Gmutation operators.

The application of the above genetic operators is controlled stochastically.

Except for the aspect that the genetic operator acts on the structural representation, the GP employs a standard GA process (see Fig. 3.4). The original program (the structural representation) changes a little at a time under the action of the genetic operators illustrated in Table 3.1. The GP searches for the desired program by the same process of selection operations.

ADF (Automatically Defined Function) has been proposed in GP [81]. ADF is a method to define functions by oneself and use them efficiently. The purpose of this is to prevent the trees (S-expressions in LISP) from becoming too large during the search process and degrading the search efficiency.

Figure 3.7 shows an example of a program that has one automatically defined function ADF0 with two arguments (ARG0 and ARG1). The numbers attached to the nodes are labels for explanation. The structure of this program is as follows.

1. A PROGN (node with label 400) that appears at the top of the entire program.

2. DEFUN (label 410) at the top of the branch of the automatically defined function.

3. The name of the automatically defined function branch ADF0 (label 411) that appears as the first argument under DEFUN.

4. The function LIST (label 412) that appears as the second argument under DEFUN. The list of arguments comes below this list.

5. Argument variables that appear below LIST (node ARG0 with label 413 and node ARG1 with label 414).

6. The function VALUES (label 419) that appears as the third argument of DEFUN. The main body of the ADF0 definition appears below this.

7. The body function VALUES (label 470) appears as the last argument of PROGN. The definition of the body comes under this.

The definition of the body function is as follows:

```
(AND (ADF0 D1 D2)
     (NAND D0 (ADF0 D3 (NOR D4 D0))))
```

The definition part of the automatically defined function ADF0 is as follows:

```
(OR ARG1 (AND ARG1 ARG0))
```

In case of the body evaluation, each time ADF0 is called, the argument is substituted to obtain the value of the function.

In fact, when the left ADF0 (label 481) is executed,

```
(ADF0 D1 D2) --> (OR D2 (AND D2 D1))
```

is assigned.

When the right ADF0 (label 487) is executed,

```
(ADF0 D3 (NOR D4 D0))
        --> (OR (NOR D4 D0) (AND (NOR D4 D0) D3))
```

is assigned. As a result, the body is the same as the execution of the following function:

```
(AND (OR D2 (AND D2 D1))
     (NAND D0 (OR (NOR D4 D0) (AND (NOR D4 D0) D3))))
```

From this, it can be seen that using ADF saves many function codes. ADFs can be used in the same way as ordinary GP functions. For ADFs, genetic operators (crossover, mutation, etc.) are applied, just as in the usual GP functions. However, crossover is done between ADFs, and the termination and function symbols for mutation are usually prepared specifically for ADFs.

The improvement of GP search efficiency by using ADFs is described in detail in [81].

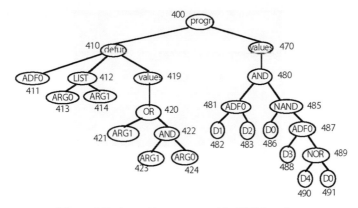

Figure 3.7: A genetic program with ADF functions.

3.4 Why GA and GP?

As we will see the need for predictive models in later chapters, the question of why GA and GP should be used needs to be answered.

In the author's experience, the answer depends on the questioner's background and experience.

If the questioner has little knowledge of GA and GP (and particularly the difference between the two) and other AI methods, the answer can be given as follows:

- GA and GP methods enable automatic performance of the process of trial and error.

- Obtaining the best solution from among many candidates tends to be extremely time consuming, and some means of abbreviating the process is essential.

- To eliminate wasted time from the computation, the evolutionary methodology of GA and GP is appropriate.

- The need for GA and GP may be seen from the period of several billion years that has been required for the natural evolution of present-day living organisms by trial and error.

- By effectively applying the power of the computer to the evolutionary process, it is possible to obtain practical solutions for many real-world applications.

- These applications include such areas as the design of the Japanese "Shinkansen N700 series" bullet trains (see Fig. 3.8) and the development of car navigation or elevator controls.

Figure 3.8: Japanese "Shinkansen N700 series" bullet trains.

GA and GP do not involve spending long periods in an attempt to obtain a perfect score of 100 (perfectly correct). Rather, they make it possible to obtain scores of 80 or 90 in a practical time period. They are, in short, highly appropriate for financial engineering, robotics, and other extremely complex problems, which require the acquisition of satisfactory solutions within reasonable time frames.

In cases where the questioner has some knowledge of GA and GP and other AI methods, the primary focus of the answer is how evolutionary computation differs from other methods, and the ways in which it is superior. This is essentially as follows:

- GA and GP searching has advantages that are quite different from those of other AI methods and classical optimization methods (e.g., operations research, OR).

- In population-based searches, they enable simultaneous searching among many individuals in the population. This is appropriate for highly parallel applications, as it enables full usage of the computer's power.

- Search facilitation: These algorithms do not presume a deep knowledge of the search spaces (such as differentiability and gradient computation).

- Diversity: These algorithms are excellent for solving problems involving dynamic change or a noisy environment, which is usually the case with a population that includes a large variety of individuals, and still provide robust solutions. They can therefore be expected to fully demonstrate their advantages in applications relating to financial markets and other complex systems.

- They can readily incorporate new and promising insights from biological research, such as coevolution, memes (Section 7.1), and sharing.

Given their general search possibilities, the use of GA and GP requires the selection of just three basic elements:

- Mapping from GTYPE to PTYPE

- Fitness functions

- Genetic operators

Little work is required to start these methods. They are excellent for scheduling and searching complex data structures. Following their application, modifications can be readily performed to increase their performance as the need arises. "Look before you leap" is a common saying that applies here, but "from the beginning, let it evolve" is most appropriate. The memetic algorithm (MA) is a prime example of the methods used in these modifications (see Section 7.1). Unlike "hill-climbing" and neural networks, GA and GP allow combined structure searching that may lead to unforeseen solutions. This is a highly attractive characteristic of using evolutionary computation. It is important to note that neural networks and reinforcement learning require sequential backpropagation and reward, which are difficult to perform in some applications because appropriate teaching signals often cannot be obtained when short-term (local) results are insufficient for effective evaluation. On the other hand, with GA/GP, evolution can readily proceed once the ultimate return is taken as the fitness criterion.

Finally, in response to a questioner who is quite familiar with GA and GP, the answer essentially proceeds as follows:

- GA and GP have been found effective in practical use as a method of solving optimization problems and generating profitable structures.

- However, no complete theoretical proof for their search effectiveness has been accomplished.

- As shown by the NFL ("no free lunch") theorem (see Section 7.3), moreover, no universal search method exists for all search spaces. In short, no methods can be regarded as a panacea.

- Nevertheless, theoretical research on extension of their statistical search approach is widespread and rapidly growing.

In their application to the field of finance, GA and GP are inherently more appropriate for the solution of constrained problems than for prediction. This does not mean that other methods and techniques may apply, particularly in the light of the NFL theorem. Rather, it is important to try to increase GA and GP performance through their integration with other methods.

Ultimately, the answer to the question of whether to use GA and GP may be more philosophical and turn on whether the user understands the concept of evolution and has an intuitive feel for its methodology. Evolution is not simply optimization. For a population, rather, it is a method of building a robust configuration that adapts to the environment. In short, it may turn on the question of whether you accept the concepts of diversity and symbiosis. It is on this basis that this section should be concluded with the message "Use GA and GP with confidence."

3.5 How to Pack a Knapsack?

Let us consider the following problem (see Fig. 3.9):

> You are going on an excursion tomorrow, and you are packing now. There are many things you want to take, but you cannot take everything because the knapsack is small. You cannot take too heavy a knapsack. What should you take?

People frequently encounter similar situations in daily life. The knapsack problem can be formulated as follows:

> There are N items, and the weight w_i and the value p_i of each item are known. The knapsack has a weight limit W, and the weight of items cannot exceed it. Find a method to decide what items to put in the knapsack, such that the sum of the values is maximized.

Figure 3.9: Knapsack problem.

Table 3.2: Example of knapsack problems.

Problem		
P07	weight	70, 73, 77, 80, 82, 87, 90, 94, 98, 106, 110, 113, 115, 118, 120
	value	135, 139, 149, 150, 156, 163, 173, 184, 192, 201, 210, 214, 221, 229, 240
	capacity	750
	optimum	1458 (1,0,1,0,1,0,1,1,1,0,0,0,0,1,1)
P08	weight	382745, 799601, 909247, 729069, 467902, 44328, 34610, 698150, 823460, 903959, 853665, 551830, 610856, 670702, 488960, 951111, 323046, 446298, 931161, 31385, 496951, 264724, 224916, 169684
	value	825594, 1677009, 1676628, 1523970, 943972, 97426, 69666, 1296457, 1679693, 1902996, 1844992, 1049289, 1252836, 1319836, 953277, 2067538, 675367, 853655, 1826027, 65731, 901489, 577243, 466257, 369261
	capacity	6404180
	optimum	13549094
		(1,1,0,1,1,1,0,0,0,1,1,0,1,0,0,1,0,0,0,0,0,1,1,1)

More formally, the goal is to find T, which is a subset of $\{1, 2, \cdots, N\}$, that which maximizes $\sum_{i \in T} p_i$, under the following condition:

$$T \subseteq \{1, 2, \cdots, N\} \tag{3.1}$$

$$\sum_{i \in T} w_i \leq W \tag{3.2}$$

One way to obtain the optimum solution is to generate all solution candidates and then derive the maximum of the total sum of values. This method is called "finding all solutions" or the enumeration method. The correct solution is always found in the enumeration method; however, it is not realistic because the number of solution candidates becomes enormous in practical problems. If there are $N = 10$ items, the number of solution candidates is $2^{10} - 1,024 \approx 10^3$. For $N = 100$, $2^{100} = 1,024^{10} \approx 10^{30}$. Searching for 10^{30} solution candidates is difficult even for the fastest computer. For example, if 10^5 solutions can be evaluated in a second, the total time is $10^{30}/10^5 = 10^{25}$ seconds $\approx 3.17 \times 10^{17}$ years. Therefore, a more efficient solution method is necessary. In the theory of computation, the knapsack problem is known to be an NP-complete problem, which is a difficult problem.

Table 3.2 shows an example of knapsack problems[1].

The GTYPE (genotype) in a GA is a simple sequence of 0s and 1s (binary sequence). An order is assigned to items that may be included in the knapsack. If the corresponding GTYPE element is 1(0), this means that the item is included (not included) in the knapsack.

---

[1]KNAPSACK_01 Data for the 01 Knapsack Problem homepage: https://people.sc.fsu.edu/~jburkardt/datasets/knapsack_01/knapsack_01.html.

Fitness is the total value of the items in the knapsack, but set to 0 if the weight exceeds the limit of the knapsack. The parameters in the following experiment were population size 50, number of elites 2, and mutation rate of 0.05. The tournament method and two-point crossover were adopted.

Learning (local search) in Lamarck and Baldwin-type GA were implemented as follows:

■ Randomly select an item whose GTYPE is 0.

■ Change GTYPE to 1 if the total weight after adding the item does not exceed the limit.

■ Repeat the above procedure several times. Finish if no GTYPE can be changed from 0 to 1.

This procedure selects items at random and, therefore, does not necessarily repack items for optimization. Therefore, this is a local search.

In Baldwin-type learning, the fitness of GTYPE of individuals is the total sum of values in the local optimum solution found above, and the GTYPE is not changed (acquired traits are not inherited). On the other hand, in Lamarck-type GA, the fitness is obtained as in the Baldwin-type GA, and the GTYPE is changed to the local optimum solution found during learning (acquired traits are inherited).

Figure 3.10 shows how the P08 problem is solved through each evolutionary process. The best fitness in each generation is shown. Lamarck-type GA was the fastest to reach the optimum solution (4,840 generations), followed by Baldwin-type GA. Darwin-type GA did not reach the optimum solution in 500 generations. Therefore, the Lamarck-type GA had the best efficiency in this problem.

The performance of different evolutions on the P07 problem is compared next. Table 3.3 shows the difference from the optimal value of the solution candidate within 50 generations when the population size was 50 or 500. The result is the average when evolution was repeated 100 times from a different initial population set. The number in brackets is the average run time in seconds. Baldwin-type GA had the best performance in a small population (50) because searching is faster compared to standard GA and is less likely to be trapped in a local solution than the Lamarck-type GA. The computation time of the standard GA was approximately 10 times faster than that of the Baldwin and Lamarck-type GAs, which is natural because there is no learning related to local solution searching. When the population size was increased to 500, the performance of the Baldwin-type GA improved, whereas the Lamarck-type and standard GAs were trapped in a local solution, and the performance deteriorated.

The right column in the figure is the average number of generations needed to obtain the maximum solution. The superiority of the Lamarck-type GA is underway. The computation time required by the Lamarck-type GA to reach the

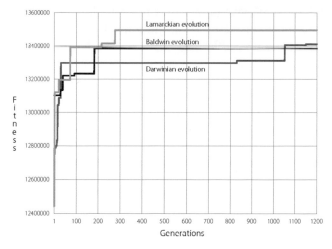

Figure 3.10: Solving knapsack problems by different types of GAs.

Table 3.3: Comparison of different types of evolution.

Evolution	Difference from the optimal value				Avg. success gen.	
	Maximum generation = 50					
	Pop. size = 50		Pop. size = 500			
Darwinian	22.77	(1.26 s)	37.33	(14.03 s)	2187.84	(1.88 s)
Baldwin	11.99	(11.43 s)	9.24	(121.08 s)	2217.71	(3.42 s)
Lamarckian	13.71	(11.32 s)	17.18	(115.29 s)	681.76	(0.95 s)

optimum solution was 0.5 and 0.27 times that of Darwin and the Baldwin-type GA, respectively. Baldwin-type GA actually needed a longer time.

The above experiments show that differences in evolution and learning result in a difference in performance. The results depend on the problem and design of the local search. Lamarck-type GA is not necessarily the best method.

3.6 GA Convergence

3.6.1 *Wright-Fisher Model*

A search in a GA converges when all individuals in a population become the same and diversity is lost. This is desirable if the optimum solution is found, but should be avoided during a search because the chance of obtaining a better solution candidate decreases, which is called "premature convergence."

The convergence process can be modeled as "genetic drift" in population genetics. A theoretical study on GAs founded on genetic drift, based on [106], is discussed below.

Most analyses in population genetics use a limit approximation, where the number of individuals increases toward infinity. This provides a good approximation if the population is sufficiently large, as in biology. However, GAs mostly handle populations that are not very large, and the approximation is often not good.

The population size is set to a constant N, regardless of the generation. Assume that each individual has a genotype of length one, the number of alleles is two, and there is no difference in the fitness of each gene. The generation change is discrete, and N individuals out of N individuals are chosen where the same individual may be chosen multiple times. The state-transition matrix Q, which uses the number of each gene in the population as the state, is as follows [74]:

$$Q_{ij} = {}_NC_j \left(\frac{i}{N}\right)^j \left(1 - \frac{i}{N}\right)^{N-j}$$

Here, Q_{ij} is the transition probability, where the number of genes changes to j from i. This model is called the Wright-Fisher model and is the subject of various analyses. The state-transition matrix Q' when mutations (alleles are exchanged with probability μ) are added to Q, is

$$Q'_{ij} = {}_NC_j \left(\frac{1-2\mu}{N}i + \mu\right)^j \left(1 - \frac{1-2\mu}{N}i - \mu\right)^{N-j}$$

The eigenvalue of Q', $\lambda_k (k = 0, 1, \cdots, N)$, is

$$\lambda_k = \frac{N!}{(N-k)!} \left(\frac{1-2\mu}{N}\right)^k$$

and the distribution of the steady state is given as the eigenvector for $\lambda_0 = 1$. When the population size N is sufficiently large, the distribution of the steady state has been proven as

$$\frac{\Gamma(4N\mu)}{\{\Gamma(2N\mu)\}^2} \left\{\frac{i}{N}\left(1 - \frac{i}{N}\right)\right\}^{2N\mu - 1}.$$

The behavior of this approximation is shown in Fig. 3.11(a)[2]. The z-axis in this figure shows the probability density of the steady state. The x-axis is the frequency of each gene, and the y-axis is the mutation rate multiplied by the population size ($\mu \times N$). The frequency of each gene is the number of genes of interest divided by N. Therefore, it is 0.0 and 1.0 if the number of genes is 0 and N, respectively. The density function is a cross-section when this figure is cut by a plane parallel to the xz-plane ($\mu \times N$ =constant). The approximation equation for $N = 10$ is shown in Fig. 3.11(b). These results show that the limit approximation is a very good approximation.

---

[2]Γ function is a generalization of factorials. The definition is $\Gamma(z) = \int_0^\infty t^{z-1}e^{-t}dt$. Note that $\Gamma(n+1) = n!$ if n is an integer.

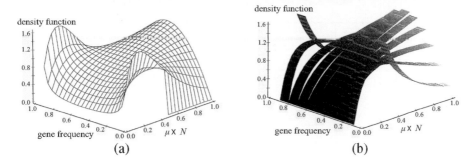

Figure 3.11: Density function of gene frequency [106].

3.6.2 Genetic Drift and Mutation Rate

The Wright-Fisher model calculates the average time until one gene becomes extinct from the population (mean absorption time), τ, as follows: The matrix where the 0-th row, 0-th column, N-th row, and N-th column are removed from the state-transition matrix Q is denoted as $\tilde{Q}$. Using a vector ξ where all elements are 1, and the unit matrix I, $(I - \tilde{Q})^{-1}\xi$ is calculated. The mean absorption time, based on a continuous approximation of the population size N, is:

$$\tau \approx \sum_{j=0}^{\infty} \frac{P_{2j}(1-2p) - P_{2j+2}(1-2p)}{(j+1)(2j+1)} N$$

according to [74]. Here, P_j is the Legendre polynomial[3], and p is the component ratio at the initial state.

This becomes $1.386N$ when $p = 1/2$, which almost matches the value of $1.4N$ (see [46] and [5]) from the numerical simulation. Table 3.4 shows the value calculated from the above equation and the numerical experiment in [5], including other cases of p values. Numerical calculations also showed that the mean absorption time is proportional to the population size.

Genes that become extinct can reappear when there is a mutation. However, an excessively large mutation rate results in a biased distribution, and convergence becomes difficult. Figure 3.11 shows that the steady-state distribution becomes uniform when the mutation rate μ satisfies $N\mu = 1/2$. Niwa et al. speculated that this value serves as a reference when determining an appropriate mutation rate in a GA search (see [106]).

Figure 3.12 shows a cross-section of Fig. 3.11 at $N\mu = 1/2$. The $N \to \infty$ limit approximation is a completely uniform distribution (dashed line), but slight shifts are found when N is finite (the $N = 10$ case is shown with a solid line).

---

[3] $P_j(x) = 2^j \sum_{k=0}^{j} x^k \binom{j}{k} \binom{\frac{j+k-1}{2}}{j}$.

Table 3.4: Comparison of mean absorption times.

Initial state	Predicted by τ approx.	Predicted by numerical calc. [5]
$p = 1/2$	1.386N	1.4N
$p = 1/4$	1.125N	1.0N
$p = 1/8$	0.754N	0.7N

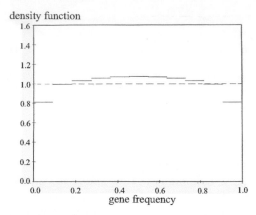

Figure 3.12: Cross-section at $N\mu = \frac{1}{2}$ [106].

3.6.3 Long Genotypes

GAs typically handle long genotypes, but mathematical analysis that considers the effects of crossover becomes difficult because the number of states increases tremendously. However, each locus independently transitions in the case of uniform crossover; thus, analysis of the Wright-Fisher model is applicable.

Consider the case where the population size is $N = 2$ and the genotype length is ℓ. The probability that all loci are in an absorbing state by time t is $(1 - 1/2^t)^\ell$. Therefore, the probability of the situation where all loci reach an absorbing state, which is attained at time t, is as follows:

$$\left(1 - \frac{1}{2^t}\right)^\ell - \left(1 - \frac{1}{2^{t-1}}\right)^\ell.$$

The mean absorption (convergence) time E is

$$
\begin{aligned}
E &= \sum_{t=1}^{\infty} t \left\{ \left(1 - \frac{1}{2^t}\right)^\ell - \left(1 - \frac{1}{2^{t-1}}\right)^\ell \right\} \\
&= \sum_{t=0}^{\infty} \left\{ 1 - \left(1 - \frac{1}{2^t}\right)^\ell \right\}.
\end{aligned}
$$

Table 3.5: Comparison of mean absorption times for long genes.

Gene length	Actual values	Predicted values [5]
1	2.0000	2.00
2	2.6667	2.67
4	3.5048	3.50
8	4.4211	4.42
16	5.3774	5.37
32	6.3552	6.36
64	7.3440	7.34
128	8.3384	8.34
256	9.3356	9.34
512	10.3341	10.33
1024	11.3335	11.33

The following successive approximation is used to approximate E with $\tilde{E}$.

$$
\begin{aligned}
\tilde{E} &= \int_0^\infty \left\{ 1 - \left(1 - \frac{1}{2^t} \right)^\ell \right\} dt + \frac{1}{2} \\
&= \frac{1}{\log 2} \sum_{i=1}^\ell \frac{1}{i} + \frac{1}{2}.
\end{aligned}
$$

Note that

$$
\begin{aligned}
\sum_{i=1}^\ell \frac{1}{i} &= \psi(\ell) + \frac{1}{\ell} + \gamma \\
&\simeq \log \ell + \gamma + \frac{1}{2\ell} - \sum_{i=1}^\infty \frac{B_{2i}}{2i\ell^{2i}},
\end{aligned}
$$

where γ is the Euler constant, ψ is the digamma function,[4] and B_i is the Bernoulli number[5]. Then, the following equation holds:

$$
\tilde{E} \simeq \frac{1}{\log 2} \left(\log \ell + \gamma + \frac{1}{2\ell} - \frac{1}{12\ell^2} + \frac{1}{120\ell^4} + \cdots \right) + \frac{1}{2}.
$$

Therefore, $E \simeq \tilde{E}$ is proportional to $\log \ell$ when ℓ is sufficiently large. Table 3.5 compares the precise and numerically calculated values [5]. Therefore, the correctness of the prediction from numerical calculations is confirmed. Analysis of convergence time E is difficult when the population size is larger thant two.

---

[4] Defined as the logarithmic derivative of the gamma function, i.e., $\psi(z) = \frac{d}{dz} \ln \Gamma(z) = \frac{\Gamma'(z)}{\Gamma(z)}$.

[5] $B_0 = 1, \ B_n = -\frac{1}{n+1} \sum_{k=0}^{n-1} \binom{n+1}{k} B_k$.

3.6.4 Mutation Rate and GA Search

The frequency distribution of states (number of genes in a population) is uniform when the mutation rate μ and population size N satisfy $N\mu = 1/2$. GA searches are conducted below to confirm that this value can be used as a reference mutation rate.

Two-bit genotypes are considered here. The fitness is $f_{11} = 1.1, f_{01} = 1.05, f_{00} = 1.0$ and $f_{10} = 0.0$, as indicated by the black circles in Fig. 3.13(a). This is a type of deceptive function (type I, see [46]). Statistics are taken for each generation when a GA is run, and the frequency distribution is observed. Figure 3.13(b) shows the frequency distributions for a GA with $\mu = 1/(2N)$ up to 1,000,000 generations. A uniform crossover (crossover probability of $1/2$) was adopted, and the population size was 10. Although the frequency distribution is along a curve connecting the four black dots in Fig. 3.13(a), the frequency distribution stresses the differences between the fitness values. Figure 3.13(c) shows a GA search result when the mutation rate is smaller than $1/(2N)$. The difference between the fitness values is greater. On the other hand, the steady state did not reflect the fitness function when the mutation rate was larger than $1/(2N)$ (see Fig. 3.13(d)). Figure 3.14 is the result of a type II deceptive function, i.e., $f_{11} = 1.1, f_{00} = 1.0, f_{01} = 0.9$ and $f_{10} = 0.5$. The result was similar to that from a type I deceptive function.

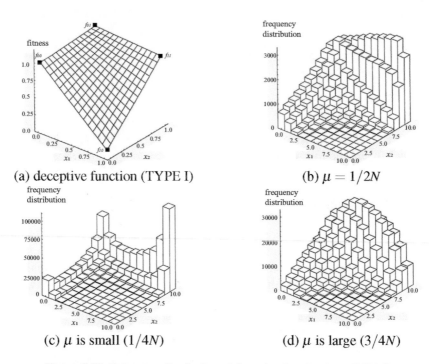

(a) deceptive function (TYPE I)

(b) $\mu = 1/2N$

(c) μ is small ($1/4N$)

(d) μ is large ($3/4N$)

Figure 3.13: Frequency distribution of deceptive function (type I) [106].

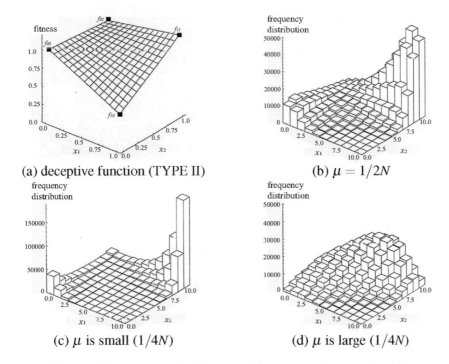

(a) deceptive function (TYPE II)

(b) $\mu = 1/2N$

(c) μ is small $(1/4N)$

(d) μ is large $(1/4N)$

Figure 3.14: Frequency distribution of deceptive function (type II) [106].

3.7 Introns and GA

3.7.1 *How to Evolve a Bird?*

What is beneficial when introducing the concept of introns to GAs and GP? In this section, we discuss the relationship between introns and GA search efficiency, according to [90] and [149].

Consider the problem of five exons (A, B, C, D, and E), each of which has six binary bits (0 or 1). The exon emerges if all six bits are 1. The gene contains 30 bits when the five exons are placed in the order A, B, C, D, and E. For example, only A and E exons emerge in

```
111111 001100 101010 000001 111111
```

Fitness is determined as in the following table based on the emergence of the five exons.

Phenotype	Fitness
none	1
A or B or C or D or E	5
D and E	50
A and B and C	100
A and B and C and D and E	1000

The optimum fitness is when all exons, A to E, emerge (1000). This situation can be understood through this example. The evolution of an animal that can fly is considered (e.g., evolution from dinosaurs to birds; see Fig 3.15), and the meaning of each exon is given in the following table.

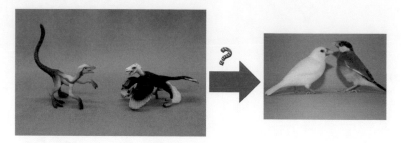

Figure 3.15: Feathered dinosaurs; Velociraptor (left), Microraptor (right). They apparently had feathers but could not fly.

Exon	Phenotype	Benefit
A	Elongation of finger bones	Able to catch food from the finger crevices
B	Feathers growing	Warm up
C	Skin formation between fingers	Warm up
D	Rear feet formation, allowing small jumps	Able to catch food more easily
E	Finger formation on feet	Able to grasp food

Genes A to E each carry its benefits. The emergence of both D and E would be more advantageous because the animal can fly from branch to branch and can also grasp. On the other hand, the emergence of A, B, and C is more advantageous because the animal can cover itself or its children with feathered wings and can fly over a great distance. The emergence of A to E allows flying, which results in maximum fitness.

Introns are introduced into this genotype. A 7-bit non-coding region is inserted between each block (A, B, C, D, and E) when there are introns and, to make the condition identical, a 28-bit non-coding region is appended at the end when there are no introns. The gene length was 58 bits in both cases.

```
Genotype with introns:
    aaaaaaiiiiiiibbbbbbiiiiiiicccccciiiiiiiddddddiiiiiiieeeee

Genotype without introns:
    aaaaaabbbbbbccccccddddddeeeeeeiiiiiiiiiiiiiiiiiiiiiiiiiiii
```

Here, exons are expressed such as aaaaaa, and introns as iiiiiii. For comparison, GA was run on four different population sizes (16, 64, 256, and 1024)

Table 3.6: Successful evolutions of a flying creature (ABCDE).

	Population size						
	16		64		256		1024	
Repro.	introns?		introns?		introns?		introns?	
Rate	no	yes	no	yes	no	yes	no	yes
10%	0	0	0	2	3	22	4	48
30%	0	0	0	2	2	16	4	28
50%	0	0	0	1	1	9	3	23
70%	0	0	0	0	0	8	1	11
90%	0	0	0	1	0	4	1	12

and five different reproduction rates (10, 30, 50, 70, and 90%). Here, the reproduction rate is the generation gap. New individuals were generated by crossover and mutation. The mutation rate was 0.003 for each bit. Runs were conducted until 20000 individuals were evaluated or the optimum individual was detected. Fifty runs were performed for each combination.

The effect of introns in the GA search is discussed below. Table 3.6 shows the results of the experiments. The number of times that the optimum individual (ABCDE) was found (number of successes) among the 50 GA runs is shown in the table. The following is deduced from the results:

1. The number of successes increases with increasing population size.

2. The number of successes decreases with increasing reproduction rate.

3. The number of successes increased approximately 10-fold (187:19) when introns were inserted.

The reasons are explained below:

1. The following two conditions must be satisfied for ABCDE to evolve.

   ■ All genes are present in the population.
   ■ All genes are combined to form one individual.

   The latter is difficult to achieve without the former. The probability that the former occurs increases non-linearly with increasing population size. For example, this probability is 0.103256, 0.91436, and 0.9999995 for population sizes of 64, 256, and 1024, respectively. This relationship is shown in Fig. 3.16. Here, the probability P that at least one of the five six-bit exons emerges in a population of size N is given.

2. Even if all five exons are in the initial population, there is no guarantee that the GA can combine them appropriately. Convergence to, for example, a combination of ABC and DE may occur. A low reproduction rate helps

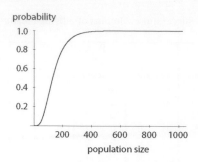

Figure 3.16: Probability that at least one of five exons emerges in a population.

to suppress premature convergence. On the other hand, a high reproduction rate can more easily remove character sequences with only one exon. These sequences survive for a long time when the reproduction rate is low.

3. Insertion of introns increases crossover with crossover points that preserve the schema of the genotype. If there are no introns, there are only four crossover points, such as between A and B, that do not destroy the gene. On the other hand, there are 32 such points if there are seven-bit introns between exons.

The importance of the order of exons (ABCDE) is investigated next. The problem in which the order of exons is set to ADBEC is discussed, which is clearly more difficult than the previous problem. For instance, the chance of formation of ADBEC through (single-point) crossover of moderately good individuals, such as DE and ABC, is low. Table 3.7 shows the results when the exon order was ADBEC. The number of successful GA runs, among 50, that found the optimum individual is given. The population size was 256 or 1024, and the reproduction rate (generation gap) varied between 1% and 90%. The "yes" and "no" regarding replacement mean that the same individual can or cannot be chosen as both parents. GA without replacement allows the generation of at most one child per individual per generation.

Table 3.7 implies that the performance is affected by whether the replacement is allowed. The performance is better, with a ratio of 9:1 when replacement is not allowed compared to when it is allowed. The reason for this is premature convergence to DE. The fitness of DE is sufficiently high and generates many descendants. As a result, genes including ABC are shut out. Parents generate at most one individual when there is no replacement; hence, the diversity of the population is sustained for a longer time, leading to better performance.

What happens if the "fitness of D and E" is set smaller than the "fitness of A or B or C or D or E?" Does performance improve because premature convergence to DE is decreased? Simulations were performed after changing the fitness values to those in the following table.

Table 3.7: Successful evolutions of a flying creature (ADBEC).

	Population size							
	256				1024			
	replacement				replacement			
	yes		no		yes		no	
Repro.	introns?		introns?		introns?		introns?	
Rate	no	yes	no	yes	no	yes	no	yes
1%	0	0	0	6	1	8	1	12
3%	0	0	0	12	1	8	3	14
5%	1	1	0	7	2	16	0	21
10%	0	1	0	12	3	17	2	27
30%	0	0	0	30	2	23	5	48
50%	0	1	0	32	4	31	9	47
70%	0	0	2	38	5	37	6	50
90%	0	4	10	37	5	38	13	46

Table 3.8: Successful evolutions (ADBEC) with lower fitness for DE.

	Population size							
	256				1024			
	replacement				replacement			
	yes		no		yes		no	
Repro.	introns?		introns?		introns?		introns?	
Rate	no	yes	no	yes	no	yes	no	yes
10%	0	9	3	6	1	23	0	24
30%	0	12	4	18	1	27	4	40
50%	0	12	2	17	1	21	4	44
70%	1	10	0	31	2	26	12	36
90%	0	6	4	32	6	17	6	28

Phenotype	Fitness
none	1
A or B or C or D or E	1.01
D and E	5
A and B and C	10
A and B and C and D and E	1000

The results of the experiment are shown in Table 3.8. As expected, the difference in the performance with and without replacement decreased to a factor of less than 2. The effectiveness of the introns was 9:1 compared to when there was no replacement.

3.7.2 Royal Road Function

The royal road function was designed by John Holland,[6] and Melanie Mitchell to investigate details of schema processing and formation in GAs. This function is widely used as an objective function for search analyses using GAs. The fitness of the royal road function (R_1) is defined using the schema set $s_i (i = 1, \cdots, 8)$.

```
s1 = 1111******************* ; c1 = 8
s2 = ****1111**************** ; c2 = 8
s3 = ********1111************ ; c3 = 8
s4 = ************1111******** ; c4 = 8
s5 = ****************1111**** ; c5 = 8
s6 = ********************1111 ; c6 = 8
```

Here, the genotype of R_1 consists of 24 bits. Cost c_i is assigned to s_i, and the fitness $R_1(x)$ of the character string x is as follows:

$$R_1(x) = \sum_i c_i \delta_i(x) \quad \text{where} \quad \delta_i(x) = \begin{cases} 1 & (x \in s_i) \\ 0 & (x \notin s_i). \end{cases} \tag{3.3}$$

For example, if x is an instance of two fourth-order schemas, $R_1(x) = 16$. Similarly, $R_1(111 \cdots 1) = 48$. The optimum solution $111 \cdots 1$ assumes a search for the maximum value. The order of a schema is the number of 0 and 1 characters (not *).

The meaning of this function is that a "royal road" (easy road) will be paved for a GA to reach the optimum character string according to the building block hypothesis. The building block hypothesis is a theoretical background for an effective search in GAs. According to this hypothesis, GA searches by forming beneficial substructures, which are building blocks (schemas), through crossovers. The building blocks in the above function are combinations of s_i.

The building block hypothesis implies that GA searches are hopeful when the following schemas exist [101]:

■ Schemas with low order and high fitness.

■ Intermediate-size "stepping stones" (schemas with intermediate-sized order and high fitness).

The second guarantees that high fitness schemas can be obtained in succession from low-order schemas. The royal road is a fitness function with such characteristics. In particular, changes from low-order schemas (such as $1111**\cdots*$) to high-order, intermediate-size schema (for instance, $1111********1111*$ $*\cdots*$) can occur in many loci simultaneously; thus, GA should be better than a simple hill-climbing method. However, this is not the case.

---

[6]John Holland (1929–2015): American computer scientist and the founder of the genetic algorithm. He is best known for his pioneering work in complex systems and nonlinear science.

Comparison experiments showed that GAs are often poorer than the simple hill-climbing method. This function was originally designed to be a "royal road" for GAs; if this is true, then we ask why.

One reason is "hitchhiking". Once a high-order schema instance is found, it will rapidly become widespread in the population because its fitness is high. 0s in other positions hitchhike to 1s in the defining section of the schema and spread together. As a result, finding schema in other positions, particularly those in positions near the defining section of the high fitness schema, will be delayed. Note that hitchhiking most frequently happens close to the defining section of the high fitness schema because hitchhikers are, after crossover, more likely to come together with the defining section of the schema.

3.7.3 Royal Road Function and Introns

The effectiveness of introns was investigated using the royal road function.
Consider the following royal road function *RR2*:

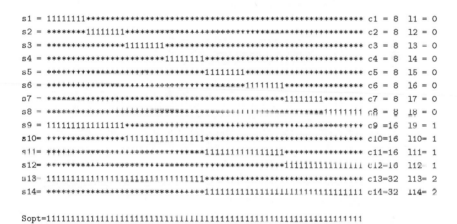

For a binary string x, the fitness for $RR2$ is given as follows:

$$RR2(x) = \sum_i C_i \delta_i(x), \quad \text{where} \quad \delta_i(x) = \begin{cases} 1 & (x \in S_i) \\ 0 & (x \notin S_i). \end{cases} \quad (3.4)$$

Here, C_i is the fitness contribution of schema S_i, and l_i is the number of levels. In this problem, C_i is the order of S_i and hence C_i increases exponentially. Therefore, this royal road function is exponential $RR2_{exponential}$. 0th-level building blocks $(S1, S2, \cdots, S8)$ are called base schemas and are the smallest building blocks that contribute to fitness. This problem has intermediate schemas of two levels between base schemas and the optimum individual (genotype consisting of 1s only).

Extra bits are inserted between the base schema when an intron is inserted.

The number of inserted bits is the intron length. Examples of genotypes with and without introns are as follows:

```
Genotype when there are no introns:
11111111 11111111 11111111 11111111 11111111 11111111 11111111 11111111

Genotype when there are introns:
** 11111111 **** 11111111 **** 11111111 **** (Continued below)
   11111111 **** 11111111 **** 11111111 **** 11111111 **
```

Here, * is the intron gene. There are eight base schemas in this problem, and eight intron regions are added. Each intron region is cut into halves and added to both ends of the individual. Therefore, when the intron region length is four, the length of an individual increases by

$$(8 \text{ base schema}) \times (4\text{-bit introns}) = 32 \text{ bits.} \tag{3.5}$$

An experiment on *RR*2 is explained below. The effect of introns is compared with the four coefficient types given below.

Type	Scheme fitness
Exponential	Scheme order
Flat	1
Power	$base^{level+1}$

Recall that coefficients C_i determine the contribution to the fitness of each building block (schema). The coefficient types are investigated by varying the intron length from zero to 300 bits. The GA parameters are shown in Table 3.9.

One hundred GA runs were conducted, and the average was compared.

Table 3.9: GA parameters (Royal road function).

Parameter	Value
population size	128
#. of bits in exon	64
level no.	4
#. of basic schemes	8(8-bit lenght each)
total no. of schemes	15
crossover	0.7(one-point crossover)
mutation ratio	0.005(no. of bits)
generation gap (reproduction ratio)	1.0
selection	roulette strategy with replacement
expected no. of children per. individual	0 to 2
terminal condition	5000 generations

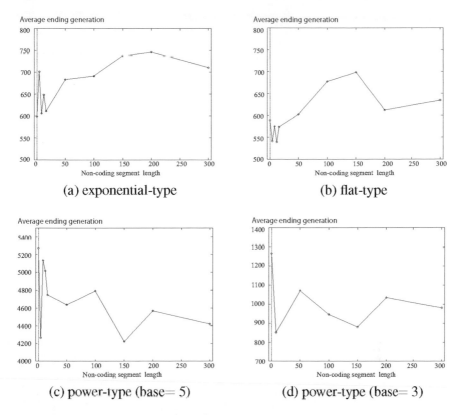

(a) exponential-type (b) flat-type

(c) power-type (base= 5) (d) power-type (base= 3)

Figure 3.17: The average number of successful generations vs. non-coding segment length [149].

Figure 3.17 shows the average number of generations until the GA finds the optimum solution. The considered coefficient types were exponential, flat, and two power types (the base was five and three). Experiments showed that the performance did not improve using exponential-type coefficients; instead, more time (GA search time) was necessary to find the optimum value. Using flat-type coefficients was not, in general, beneficial, although some improvements were found when the introns were short, being 20 bits or less. When power-type coefficients were used, the simulation times were reduced by the addition of introns. Overall, the average number of generations until success was always smaller when introns were added.

Figure 3.18 shows the stability of schemas by coefficient type. The stability is defined as

$$S_{basic} = \sum_{i=1}^{\#basicBL} s_i \; ; \; S_{all} = \sum_{i=1}^{\#BL} s_i. \tag{3.6}$$

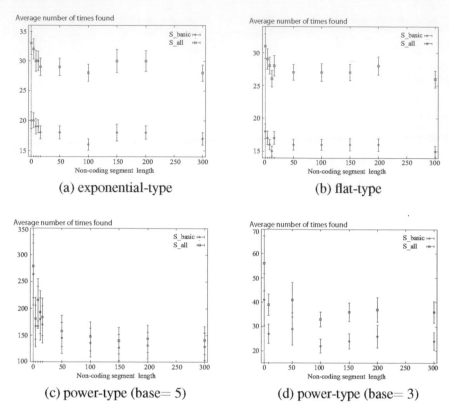

Figure 3.18: The average number times building blocks are found before the optimal solution is discovered [149].

Here, s_i is the number of times that schema i is found. #*basicBL* and #*BL* are the number of base schemas and all schemas, respectively. Therefore, S_{basic} is the number of times that the base schemas were found, and S_{all} is when all schemas were found. The vertical bars represent the 95% confidence interval with respect to the average. Inserting introns reduced the average number of times a schema was found, but the stability increased (a schema is less likely to be lost). This effect was more profound in introns with 50 or more bits. In most cases, the 95% confidence intervals with and without introns did not overlap. When the introns have 50 or fewer bits, the average number of times that a schema is found was still lower than when there were no introns, but the 95% confidence interval overlapped.

Figure 3.19 shows the average number of generations until schemas at each level were found. Needless to say, a smaller value is a better value. In low-level schemas, the average number of generations until a schema was found was almost the same even when the intron length was changed. There was a significant change in the maximum level schema, but the order was arbitrary. There seemed

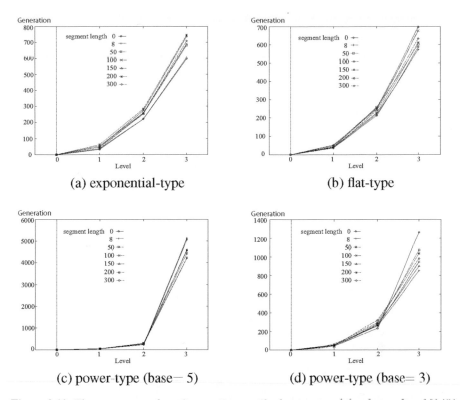

(a) exponential-type

(b) flat-type

(c) power-type (base= 5)

(d) power-type (base= 3)

Figure 3.19. The average number of generations until schemas at each level were found [149].

to be no relationship between intron length and the number of generations until discovery. When power-type coefficients were used, introns larger than 50 bits clearly demonstrated better performance than shorter or no introns.

The effect of introns depends on the fitness landscape of the problem. For example, the addition of introns when exponential or flat coefficients were used worsened the performance (Fig. 3.17(a),(b)). On the other hand, adding introns improved the results with the power-type coefficients (Fig. 3.17(c)(d)). The larger the fitness increase when a new-level schema was found, the larger the performance enhancement when introns were added. In other words, the effect of hitchhiking was more significant, and introns were more effective when the increase in fitness between levels was larger.

3.7.3.1 *Effectiveness of Introns*

There are several reasons why introns are beneficial to GA searches. Wu et al. pointed out the following [149]:

1. Introns promote genetic combinations of the current building blocks. Introns provide extra bits between building blocks; therefore, the crossover

point is more likely to occur between building blocks. Thus, adding introns has the same effect as changing the crossover rate; in other words, a different crossover rate is set depending on the position of the gene [50].

2. Introns decrease the effect of hitchhiking, making space between building blocks; therefore, hitchhikers are more likely to be included in introns adjacent to high fitness schemas. Consequently, the discovery of nearby building blocks is less likely to be hindered.

3. Introns retain changes in an individual. Changes are vital to the exploration of search space. Mutations are likely to accumulate in introns because they are irrelevant to selection. Such changes are beneficial when the environment is dynamic. If introns are to become building blocks, changes in such regions will prevent premature convergence to a local solution.

4. Introns reduce the chances of crossover that destroy current building blocks.

The number of times that a building block is found may decrease by the insertion of introns, as seen in the experiments discussed above. On the other hand, introns stabilize GA searches, which means that building blocks will not be lost once found.

The above is analyzed using *RR2*. The genotype in this problem has a 64-bit exon consisting of eight building blocks. All genes were chosen because the crossover point had the same probability. Eight crossover points did not destroy building blocks (both ends were considered the same position) when there were no introns. In other words, the probability that a crossover point did not destroy building blocks was $\frac{8}{64} = 0.125$, whereas $1 - 0.125 = 0.875$ was the probability that a crossover destroyed a building block. When introns with length n were inserted between building blocks, the total gene length became $64 + 8n$, and $8(n+1)$ crossover points did not destroy the building blocks. Therefore, the probability that building blocks were not and were destroyed among all crossover points was $\frac{8n+8}{64+8n} = \frac{n+1}{n+8}$ and $1 - \frac{n+1}{n+8} = \frac{7}{8+n}$, respectively. The two inequations $\frac{n+1}{n+8} > \frac{1}{8} = 0.125$ and $\frac{7}{8+n} < \frac{7}{8} = 0.875$ hold because $n > 0$. The first inequality shows that the ratio of crossovers that did not destroy building blocks increased when introns were inserted. The second inequality implied that the probability of crossovers destroying building blocks decreased with the insertion of introns.

3.7.4 Introns in GP and Bloating

3.7.4.1 Introns in GP

This section discusses the introns in GP. The following discussion is based on [10].

Angeline found that most solutions obtained by evolution through GP contained a nonessential code. Such codes are irrelevant because removing these codes does not affect the final result. These codes are called GP introns and can be split into two types [2].

1. Semantic introns
   Code that is executed, but does not affect fitness

   ```
   Eg.  (+ 0 a)
        (not (not x))
   ```

2. Syntactic introns
   Code that is not reached

   ```
   Eg.  (if true A B)   --> B not executed
        (and true x)    --> x not executed
   ```

These introns emerge spontaneously during the evolution process because the GP structure has a variable length. The emergence characteristics are thought to be important for successful evolution.

GP experiments tend to bloat, which means that individuals obtained by evolution grow indefinitely until the maximum allowed tree length is reached. Bloating in GP is caused by a code block that has almost no value by itself but coincidentally happens to be close to a high fitness code block and this is called phenomenon hitchhiking.

Bloating is the accumulation of apparently unnecessary code in a population, that is, a phenomenon where part of the code is not concisely expressed. The number 4 is expressed as, for example,

```
(* (+ 4 0) 1)
(+ (+ (+ 1 1) 1) 1)
```

in a bloat. Note that these codes do not necessarily contain introns. Bloating strongly depends on the behavior and semantics of the programming language.

Many studies confirmed that bloating in GP is actually caused by introns. Angeline claimed that extra code coincidentally forms, but further studies revealed that introns are cumbersome portions that form during a GP search process. For instance, introns are shown to be made up of 40%–60% of the total code in the early to middle stages of a GP run. Emerging introns exponentially increase during the latter half of a run, dominating almost all of the entire code in the total population. These reasons strongly indicate that evolution selects the survival of introns in the GP.

Bloating is a serious problem in GPs. GP runs become almost stagnant and chances of further evolution diminish once bloating (exponential growth of introns) occurs. On the other hand, Angeline stated that emerging introns have an important effect on GP evolution [2]. Which claim should be deemed correct?

Introns are beneficial in the initial and middle stages of a run. Theoretical and experimental evidence shows that introns can protect good building blocks from the destructive effects of crossover. On the other hand, exponential growth (bloat) of introns at the end of a run is probably harmful. The following methods for controlling bloating are proposed: However, inappropriate use may hinder GP searches.

3.7.5 Improvement of GP using Introns

Nordin et al. discussed that introns improve GP searches from at least these two aspects [107].

1. Protection of the structure
   High fitness building blocks (scheme) in the population are preserved.

2. Protection globally
   Protection of individuals from destructive actions of crossover.

The two effects are double-edged swords, as is discussed afterward.

Let us consider the following two introns:

1. Explicitly defined intron (EDI)
   These do not affect the fitness calculation but influence the probability of crossover between adjacent codes. This is an analogy of introns in biology.

2. Implicit intron (II)
   These introns emerge during the GP run process.

An example of an EDI is shown below. Figure 3.20 shows a program without introns (GP individual). The node denoted as E in the figure is a functional code that affects the fitness calculation. If crossover and mutation are both destructive with a high probability, the chance that the individual in Fig. 3.20 can have a child with high fitness would be very low. In contrast, Fig. 3.21 shows the same program code; however, this individual has 14 introns (node denoted as I). There are four and 14 crossover points that do and do not destroy the functional code, respectively. Even if the fitness values of the two individuals in GP are the same, and the possibility of being chosen during selection is also the same, Fig. 3.21 is clearly more likely to pass on its functional code to descendants.

The experiment by Nordin et al. [107] demonstrated the effectiveness of introns in these aspects.

1. Fitness, generalization capability, and CPU time are often improved by the introduction of EDIs.

2. IIs and EDIs often work together, and IIs help chains of EDIs.

3. EDIs may be replaced completely by IIs in certain conditions.

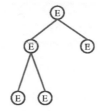

Figure 3.20: A tree without introns.

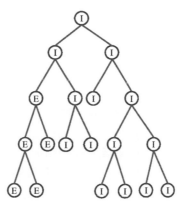

Figure 3.21: A tree with introns.

4. As in IIs, EDIs often protect part of, or the entire, individual from a destructive crossover.

5. Using EDI and a parsimony fitness function (see page 90) together allows the population to use the structural role of IIs without being subject to overhead during runs.

3.7.5.1 Code Growth in GP

The growth of introns and codes in GP are discussed based on research by Soule [132]. Introns and exons are denoted as functional and non-functional codes, respectively, in the following discussion.

A problem is considered in which a robot is controlled using GP. The objective of this problem is to precisely lead a robot in a room with obstacles. The layout of the room is shown in Fig. 3.22. The initial position and direction of the robot are shown with an arrow. The symbol X represents a wall or obstacle. The fitness of a program is the distance of the horizontal movement of the robot. Therefore, the fitness can vary between one and 18 (width of the room), and a better program can move the robot further to the right. Fitness is one when there is no horizontal movement. There is no penalty from a collision with a wall,

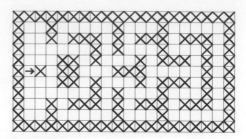

Figure 3.22: A robot in a room with obstacles.

but with too many collisions, the robot cannot move far away, and therefore the fitness indirectly decreases. The robot can move up to 3000 steps, which is a sufficient number of moves to reach the right end. The terminal symbols of the GP are as follows:

```
left, right, forward, back, no-op
```

The first four literally changes the position and direction of the robot, whereas the last does nothing. This symbol was added because it can remove and/or exchange non-functional code without destroying the structure. Function symbols are as follows:

```
progn, if, while
```

Here, `progn` runs two arguments in sequence, whereas `if` and `while` take either `wall_ahead` or `no_wall_ahead` as the predicate. These judge whether there is a wall right ahead, respectively. The statement executes the first and second arguments if the predicate is true and false, respectively, whereas the statement repeatedly executes the first and second arguments, and the predicate is true. A code based on these symbols forms a binary tree (predicates are considered to be appended to function symbols). Let us consider the following program for example: .

```
progn(left, while(no_wall_ahead, forward, right))
```

The corresponding binary tree is shown at the top of Fig. 3.23. Executing this tree from 0 (position and direction) in the environment at the bottom of Fig. 3.23 results in movement to 5 (position and direction) and stopping against a south-facing wall. The fitness of this code was 2.

The GP was run under the following conditions: population size 500, crossover rate 0.6667, mutation rate 0.001, and random initial population. Runs were compared for the following four cases:

1. Simple GP (control)

2. GP where non-functional code is edited and removed in each generation (edited programs)

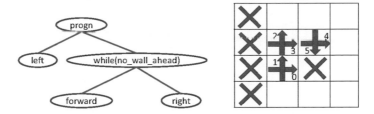

Figure 3.23: An example binary tree and its movement.

3. GP, where non-functional code is edited and removed in the initial population only (edited initially).

4. GP, where a penalty is applied to long code, and the fitness function is changed (selective pressure).

There are two types of non-functional code.

1. Code that does not execute anything.
   For example,

   - `if` and `while` statements where both are arguments of `no-op`
   - `progn` statements containing `no-op`
   - combination of `left` and `right`

2. Nested conditional expression that is not executed
   For instance, X and Y are never executed in the following statement:

   `if(wall_ahead, while(no_wall_ahead, X, Y) Z)`

   Therefore, the `while` statement is replaced by `no-op`, resulting in a change to

   `if(wall_ahead, no-op, Z)`

   Z may be non-functional in this statement. For instance, Z is not executed if the robot is facing a wall. However, this is dependent on the running environment; thus, it is not considered a non-functional code.

Determining all non-functional codes is equivalent to the equivalence problem of programs, which is known to be non-recursive and generally not solvable.

The following experimental results were averaged over 50 runs. Figure 3.24 shows the program length of the fittest individual, whereas Fig. 3.25 shows the average program length. The fittest individual is generally larger than the average in the early generations (up to approximately 20 generations). Afterward, the

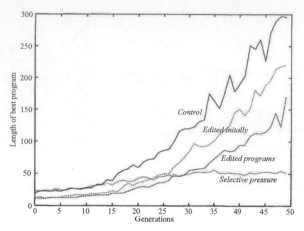

Figure 3.24: The program length of the fittest individual [132].

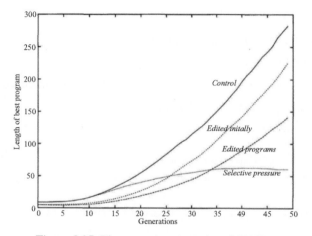

Figure 3.25: The average program length [132].

fittest and average individuals have similar sizes, which means that the efficiency of long programs is almost the same as short codes once programs reach a certain minimum size. The sole exception is when the length is penalized (selective pressure), where the fittest individual is marginally smaller than the average. The reason is that a penalty is imposed when the size is large (long).

Approximately 50% of initial random programs are non-functional codes. When programs that were edited and not edited were compared, removing non-functional codes in the initial generation had a significant effect on the code size. However, there was no effect on the basic behavior of tree growth.

Non-functional code is the cause of bloating in standard GP (control). The functional code grows much more slowly. In contrast to the overall code size, functional code growth hits a ceiling. Consequently, removing non-functional

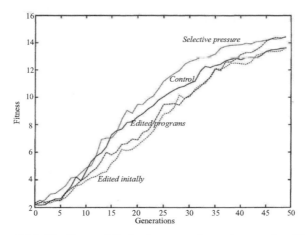

Figure 3.26: The fitness of the best program for each generation [132].

code in each generation may be able to limit the overall growth of programs. However, the results of the edited GP show that this has not occurred. The code continues to grow even when the programs are edited in every generation. When non-functional code is removed, GP reacts by generating large programs consisting of potentially functional code. However, most of these codes are not executed because they are in branches that are not reached when run. Therefore, such codes are called potentially functional codes. This is the reason for code growth in edited GPs, and the actually executed code is still relatively small.

GP that penalizes long code (selective pressure) has a profound effect on decreasing code length. This method also limits the total amount of code growth. Figure 3.26 shows the fitness of the best program for each generation. The performance is almost the same in all cases, which means that a sudden growth of programs is unnecessary to generate efficient programs. The figure also shows that successes in programs hit a ceiling in later generations. This phenomenon implies convergence of the population to a particular solution and that further improvement cannot be expected.

Even if the obtained code is no longer improving (in most cases, the optimum solution has been found and improvement of fitness cannot be achieved), GP continues to make even larger programs. Soule claimed that the reason is crossover. Assume that there are two identical in high fitness programs, p1 and p2, chosen for crossover. A relatively small substructure was removed from p1 and replaced with a larger substructure from p2. On the other hand, p2 lost a large substructure and gained a small substructure. After crossover, p1 appears to have a high chance of being a fitter individual because a small part is lost and a large program is gained from p2. On the other hand, p2 loses more than what is gained, and its fitness is more likely to decrease. The larger individual from crossover is advantageous, although slightly; thus, code growth continues even

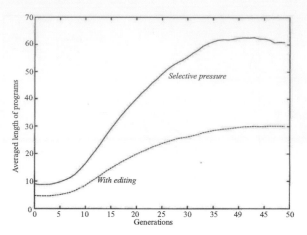

Figure 3.27: The ratios of introns [132].

after the optimum solution is found. The size continues to grow, as before, even if the program performance reached a limit. Removing the non-functional code is not sufficient to stop this growth. The code size was successfully suppressed, thus limiting the code size, only when the penalty function was used (selective pressure). Figure 3.27 shows, by generation,

1. Average program length with penalty function (selective pressure).

2. The average length, after edition, of the original program.

The program clearly contains many non-functional codes. However, using a penalty function can sufficiently prevent the amount of such code from infinitely increasing.

3.7.6 Why do GP Introns Emerge

Introns, by definition, do not affect the fitness of the GP individual. One may think that strong selection pressure does not act on gene structures that do not affect the fitness of the individual. Why do introns emerge? The following is a simple answer: Introns are irrelevant to the fitness of an individual, but can affect the survival of its descendants. This new viewpoint of fitness is denoted hereafter as effective fitness, which includes information on the survival of descendants of the individual.

Effective fitness is a function of not only the current fitness of the individual, but also includes the fitness of the children of the individual. From this standpoint, the capability for an individual to have high fitness children is important, as is the capability to be selected through crossover and mutation in the first place, for its genes to spread in the population. If an individual has very high fitness, but the fitness of its child is low, selection for crossover and mutation is not fruitful. Therefore, individuals compete to have children with higher fitness.

After crossover, the child has a lower fitness than the parent. The same holds true for mutations. A parent that has an advantageous edge in either of these effects is superior in terms of evolution compared to other parents. This is where introns come in. In the proposed hypothesis, introns emerge in response to genetic operators that are often destructive. The effective fitness of a parent increases with an increasing capability to protect its children from destructive genetic operators. Introns help parents in this aspect.

Introns almost always exponentially increase at the end of a run because introns protect from a destructive crossover. This means that this protection is global for all individuals. The reason for this phenomenon is that individuals are close to, or already at, the best performance in the final stages of a run. A further increase in fitness by solving the problem better is difficult for these individuals. Therefore, the optimal survival strategy changes, thereby preventing negative impacts or alterations on the existing solution by destructive genetic operators.

The effect of explosive growth of introns is very dramatic. Typically, a crossover of more than 75% is considered destructive. However, most crossovers become almost neutral when introns occupy most of the population. This is because at this point, individuals simply exchange introns at a high probability. Exchanging codes without any effect between individuals have absolutely no effect as a whole. Therefore, neutral crossovers become dominant with the explosive growth of introns.

The above-introduced theories regard why introns exponentially increase. These theories have sufficient support, and there is experimental evidence. An additional prediction from this theory is that exponential growth comes from (a set of) introns that are actually terminal symbols. The crossover of introns in the center of a functional code block is rarely neutral. This is because there is a functional code on both sides of the intron, which are exchanged between individuals.

3.7.7 Merits and Demerits of Introns

Researchers have clarified some of the problems that may be caused by introns, namely stagnation during a run, degradation of results, and over-utilization of digital memory or CPU time. Stagnation during a run is partially caused by bloating (exponential growth of introns). This effect is not desired. Once the population starts exchanging introns by crossover, the improvement of the best individual and other individuals cannot be expected. All effective growth is terminated.

Distinguishing the structural and global effects (the effect of explosive intron growth discussed above) is important. The two effects of introns should cause different results and appear differently.

1. Global effects typically have high adversity against a GP run. Global effects protect the entire individual against the destructive effects of crossover. In practice, this happens when intron groups that act as terminal symbols are exchanged by crossover.

2. On the other hand, structural effects tend to protect effective code blocks from the destructive effects of crossover. If the emergence of building blocks is allowed despite the destructive effects of crossover and mutation, structural protection will be very beneficial.

Several methods are proposed to control and utilize introns.

1. Reduction of destructive effects
   The reduction of destructive crossover suppresses the emergence of introns. At least, the onset of exponential growth will be delayed. For instance, the following types of edit operation are used:

   ```
   Eg.  (+  1  1)  ->  2
        (AND FALSE x) -> x
   ```

2. Parsimony
   The effect of parsimony pressure is to apply a penalty to the program length. Consequently, longer solutions have lower fitness than shorter solutions. This prevents an exponential increase in introns; however, the point of evolution where introns are suppressed depends on the strength of the penalty.

3. Changing the fitness function
   Changing the fitness function during a run suppresses the explosive growth of introns. GP individuals that may have stagnated in a fixed fitness function may improve their fitness if the fitness function is made variable.

4. Minimum description length (MDL) fitness
   An evaluation function that considers errors in the code and complexity of the model is useful (see [66] for details).

The reader is referred to [10], for details on the above studies.

3.8   Estimation of Distribution Algorithm

EDAs (Estimation of Distribution Algorithms) are stochastic optimization algorithms, also known as Probabilistic Model-Building Genetic Algorithms (PMB-GAs).

In EDAs, as in genetic algorithms, promising solution candidates (i.e., parents) are selected from a set of individuals and new solution candidates (i.e., children) are generated based on them. By repeating this operation, a population of

---

Algorithm 1 Estimation of Distribution Algorithm

$t \leftarrow 0$

Randomly initialize the initial set P_0.   ▷ Initial generation.

while $t < MaxGeneration$ **do**

Select the individuals with high fitness values from P_t and generate the candidate set Q_t.   ▷ Parent selection.

Build a probabilistic model M_t using Q_t.

Generate a next set P_{t+1} by generating individuals from M_t.   ▷ Next generation.

     $t \leftarrow t + 1$

end while

---

individuals with high fitness is generated. The distinctive feature of EDAs is the method of generating children. The set of parents is assumed to have been sampled according to some unknown probability distribution. The unknown probability distribution is estimated from the set of parents, and children are generated from the estimated probability distribution. This allows us to efficiently search for the part of the space where promising solution candidates are likely to exist. Since the search is performed without using information such as the gradient or symmetry of the function to be optimized, it can be applied to a wide range of problems.

The EDA algorithm is shown in **Algorithm 1**.

One of the simplest EDAs is PBIL (Population Based Incremental Learning, [9]). This algorithm deals with solutions expressed in binary and assumes that there is no dependency between the variables of the solution. It estimates a probability vector $\vec{p} = (p_1, p_2, \cdots)$, where p_i is the probability that the i-th bit occurs. Here, since there is no dependency between each bit, we learn each bit independently.

There are many other EDAs that use various probability models. For instance, MIMIC (Mutual Information-Maximizing Input Clustering) [14], which can take into account the dependency between two variables by using conditional probabilities, ECGA (Extended Compact Genetic Algorithm) [57], which incorporates the dependency between multiple variables into the model, and BOA (Bayesian Optimization Algorithm), in which gene relationships are described by conditional probabilities of Bayesian networks, and complex dependencies can be handled. As models that handle more practical solutions, PBIL and UMDA (Univariate Marginal Distribution Algorithm) have been proposed for real-valued domains (see [85] and [126]).

It is necessary to use an appropriate model depending on the characteristics of the problem, especially the complexity of the dependencies among the variables. The more complex the dependencies between variables are, the more complex the model needs to be.

For more information on EDA, the reader is referred to [67].

3.9 Evolutionary Multi-objective Optimization: EMO

Many studies have tackled emergence from multi-objective optimization. In this section, we introduce an approach based on evolutionary computation.

Before that, we will explain the motion generation of robots as an example of its application. For the motion generation of humanoid robots, the stability of motion is important, together with the accomplishment of the task that is its goal. Let us consider the design for the motion of kicking a ball. If the objective is to simply kick a ball as far as possible, an unstable motion that would result in the robot falling after the kick is enough. However, this will be problematic for the real robot usage. Thus, the trade-off between the ball distance and the motion stability should be considered. Figure 3.28 shows the result of designing the kicking motion by means of evolutionary computation. The plot in the lower figure shows the robot motion stability obtained through the evolution and the distance the ball flew. The stability is shown as the inverse of the maximum value of the link speed of the hip. The larger these values are, the more desirable they become. Thus, this multi-objective optimization aims for the maximization of two value functions. In the multi-objective evolutionary computation, the solutions on the Pareto front (the upper polyline in the figure) are simultaneously found. The figure shows an example of the representative motion of the solutions. The upper left solution represents a short movement distance of the ball and a stable motion, whereas the lower right solution represents a long movement distance and an unstable motion, where the robot is almost falling. The upper right solution represents moderate results in both movement distance and stability. In conventional optimization, one of them may be obtained by devising an objective function to be optimized. For instance, the lower polyline in the figure represents an example of the solution obtained through simple GA. Note that, in multi-objective optimization, different motions on the Pareto front are simultaneously discovered.

Pareto optimality is defined more formally as follows. Let two points $x = (x_1, \cdots, x_n)$ and $y = (y_1, \cdots, y_n)$ exist in an n-dimensional search space, with each dimension representing an objective (an evaluation) function, and with the objective being a minimization of each to the degree possible. The domination of y by x (written as $x <_p y$) are defined as

$$x <_p y \iff (\forall i)(x_i \leq y_i) \wedge (\exists i)(x_i < y_i). \tag{3.7}$$

In the following, we will refer to n (the number of different evaluation functions) as the "dimension number." Any point that is not inferior to any other point will be called "non-dominated" or "non-inferior," and the curve (or curved surface) formed by the set of Pareto optimal solutions will be called the "Pareto front".

On this basis, it is possible to apply GA to multi-objective optimization. In the following example, we use the VEGA (Vector Evaluated Genetic Algorithms) system of Schaffer et al. [123, 122]. Selection with VEGA is performed as fol-

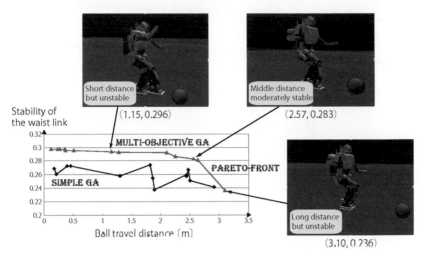

Figure 3.28: The motion generation of humanoid robots.

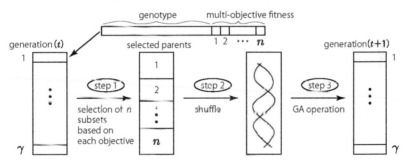

Figure 3.29: VEGA (Vector Evaluated Genetic Algorithms) algorithm.

lows (see Fig. 3.29), where n is the evaluation dimension number (the number of different evaluation functions).

1. Let the n subsets be Sub_i ($i = 1, \cdots, n$).

2. In Sub_i, retain the individual selected only by evaluation function i.

3. Mix $Sub_1, Sub_2, \cdots, Sub_n$ and shuffle.

4. Produce the next-generation offspring, using the genetic operator on these sets.

Note that the selection is based upon every evaluation function (i.e., the function value in every dimension). In contrast, reproduction is performed not for each subset but rather for the complete set. In other words, crossover is performed for the individuals in Sub_i and $Sub_j (i \neq j)$. In this way, we preserve the superior

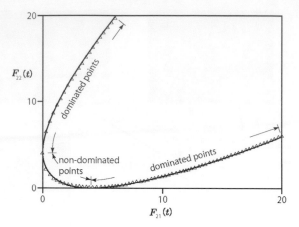

Figure 3.30: Pareto maps.

individuals in each dimension and at the same time select the individuals that are superior to the average in one or more dimensions.

Let us now consider the following multi-objective optimization:

$$F_{21}(t) = t^2,$$
$$F_{22}(t) = (t-2)^2,$$

where t is the only independent variable. The graphical appearance of this function is shown in Fig. 3.30 (i.e., a "Pareto map"). The objective is to select non-dominated points, such as those shown in the figure.

Figure 3.31 shows the results for generations 0 and 3. The population size is set to 30 individuals in each dimension, and a crossover ratio of 0.95 and a mutation ratio of 0.01 is applied. As shown, the VEGA can effectively find a front (a Pareto front) containing no dominated points. However, it has lost several intermediate points.

VEGA selection, as may be seen in this example, involves a problem that may be described as follows. The selection pressure (in biological terms, the degree of selectivity applied to the survival and proliferation of the organism's population) on the optimum values in at least one dimension (evaluation function) works as desired. In the unlikely event that a utopian individual (an individual superior in all dimensions) exists, it may be possible to find it through genetic operation on the superior parents in only one dimension. In most cases, however, no utopian individual exists. It is then necessary to obtain the Pareto optimal points, some of which are intermediate in all dimensions.

In an ideal GA, it is desirable to have the same selection pressure applied on all of these. With VEGA selection, however, an intermediate point cannot survive. In effect, species differentiation occurs within the population, with dimension-specific superiority of each species. The danger of this is more preva-

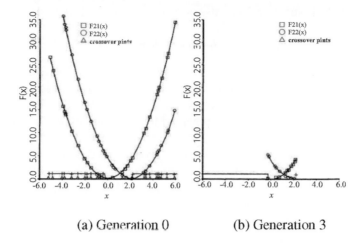

(a) Generation 0   (b) Generation 3

Figure 3.31: Results of multi-objective optimization [122].

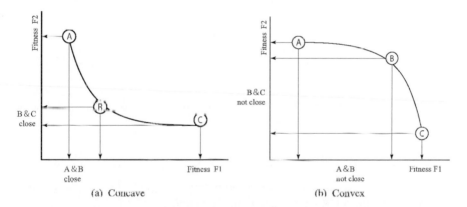

(a) Concave   (b) Convex

Figure 3.32: Pareto fronts.

lent when the Pareto optimal region is convex rather than concave (see Fig. 3.32).
Two modifications have been proposed to resolve this difficulty. One is to apply
an excess of heuristic selection pressure on the non-dominant individuals in each
generation. The other is to increase interspecies crossbreeding. Although ordinary GA selection is random, this is effective because utopian individuals are
more readily produced by interspecies than intraspecies' crossover.

A Pareto GA simulator is provided for the sake of Pareto optimization. The
simulator details are given in the appendix (Section A.2).

In addition to VEGA, other methods have been proposed for Pareto optimization. For example, the ranking method assigns a rank $rank_i$ to each individual i
as an evaluation criterion. Let n_i be the number of other individuals over which

an individual i is superior. Then the rank of i is given as follows:

$$rank_i = 1 + n_i. \tag{3.8}$$

In VEGA, the evaluation criterion is a single function value, which has the disadvantage of bias in the solution. In particular, it is difficult to find a solution that has intermediate values in each objective function with VEGA. On the other hand, the ranking method has the potential to search for such solutions.

Another method is to consider niching. In this method, the degree of crowding around each individual is taken into account in the evaluation. Basically, while using the ranking method, the method gives priority to the one with the smaller niching (lower congestion) for individuals of the same rank. Alternatively, this is achieved by penalizing individuals that are dense in the objective function value space. The penalty is based upon the number of individuals within a certain distance, and reduces the rank by that amount.

The distance $dist(x, y)$ between two individuals x and y is defined in the following way by using the maximum value f_i^{max} and the minimum value f_i^{min} of each objective function $f_1, \cdots, f_n$ in the population:

$$dist(x,y) = \sqrt{\left(\frac{f_1(x) - f_1(y)}{f_1^{max} - f_1^{min}} \right)^2 + \left(\frac{f_2(x) - f_2(y)}{f_2^{max} - f_2^{min}} \right)^2 + \cdots + \left(\frac{f_n(x) - f_n(y)}{f_n^{max} - f_n^{min}} \right)^2},$$

$$\tag{3.9}$$

where the values of each objective function $f_1, \cdots, f_n$ for x and y are $f_1(x), \cdots, f_n(x)$ and $f_1(y), \cdots, f_n(y)$.

3.10 Interactive Evolutionary Computation (IEC)

Let us consider the application of evolutionary computation (EC) to problems such as designing tables that match the atmosphere of a room or composing unobtrusive ringtones for mobile phones.

EC might seem applicable to these problems if they are considered in terms of optimizing the size and color of the boards in the case of the tables, or the frequencies, filters, and other parameters in the case of the synthesizers. However, the problem in this situation is how to evaluate each unit. An evolutionary system based on the survival of the fittest must include a method for evaluating whether individual units are suitable for their environment; in other words, how close they are to the optimal solution. For example, when using GA to evolve a solution to the shortest path for the traveling salesman problem (TSP[7]), the solution represented by each unit is assigned a degree of fitness in terms of path length. Is it possible to use a computer in the same manner to determine whether a table

---

[7]An optimization problem for a salesman who travels between multiple cities, visiting all cities exactly once, and finding the path with the lowest total travel cost. It is one of the NP-complete problems, and enumeration methods are impractical, making it difficult to find the optimal solution.

matches the atmosphere of a room? Unfortunately, modeling a subjective evaluation process based on human preferences and feelings, and then implementing such a model on a computer, is an extremely difficult task.

For instance, consider the fitness function in the case of a computer drawing a portrait. Conceivably, the first step is to compute the Euclidean distance between the structural information of a face extracted from a photograph and the portrait drawn by the computer. However, drawing a portrait is not the same as creating a photorealistic representation of a face—rather, drawing a portrait involves the more interesting process of capturing the unique features of the face and then drawing them in a stylized manner. However, can a computer determine whether a person is identical in a facial photograph and a portrait in which specific facial features are captured and stylized? This fitness problem is considered to be extremely difficult to implement using the existing level of technology.

Nevertheless, there is something close to all of us that is capable of performing such evaluations instantaneously: the brain. Humans have evolved a method for direct evaluation of individual units, and in this regard, the human evaluation system can be incorporated into an optimization system as an evaluation function. Thus, when EC is employed for optimization based on human subjective evaluation, this process is then referred to as interactive evolutionary computation (IEC) [11].

Put simply, IEC is EC in which a human is substituted for the fitness function. In IEC, the person using the system (the user) directly evaluates each unit, and the viability (fitness) of subsequent generations is derived depending on the user preferences (Fig. 3.33). When implementing this system, personal preferences and sensations are not modeled, and evaluation based on user subjectivity is incorporated into the system as a black box. In contrast to conventional EC, where evolution is modeled as the result of a struggle for survival, IEC is inspired by

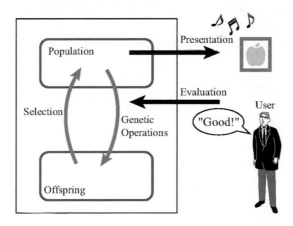

Figure 3.33: IEC overview.

the process undertaken by humans of intentionally breeding agricultural products and domestic animals.

Modern keywords such as "emotional (kansei) engineering" and "humanized technology" reveal the increasing tendency for technology to make use of human subjectivity. As part of this trend, IEC is beginning to attract attention as a method able to incorporate the user's subjective evaluation system.

Various types of human evaluation scales are used in IEC. For example, psychological experiments often use a scale with at most 7 grades, although a scale with 10 or 100 grades would certainly increase clarity in everyday situations. In contrast, for two-step evaluation, members of the population can be either selected (or not) as a parent for the next generation. This process is referred to as "simulated breeding" [142], since it is analogous to artificial breeding, in which desirable features are selected and then bred.

In his 1986 book *The Blind Watchmaker* [30], Richard Dawkins describes how images created according to simple rules can evolve into extremely complex and intriguing images as a result of rule mutation and user selection. These image sequences were called *biomorphs*, since they appear to resemble animals (e.g., insects) at first sight (see Fig. 3.34). Biomorphs can be regarded as the first example of IEC; specifically, evolution artificially created with a computer through selection based on human subjective preferences.

3.11 Gene Duplication in GP

Gene duplication has been used in research applications of evolutionary computation. For example, John Koza extended GP with the idea of gene duplication [82]. He devised the following eight operators in addition to the conventional genetic operators of GP. These operators change the structure of a function and are called "architecture-altering operators."

1. Branch duplication
   Duplicates an ADF branch and makes the necessary changes to create the children.

2. Argument duplication
   Duplicates one argument in an ADF branch and makes the necessary changes to generate the children.

3. Branch deletion
   Delete an ADF branch and makes the necessary changes to generate a child.

4. Argument deletion
   Removes one argument in an ADF branch and creates a child with the necessary changes.

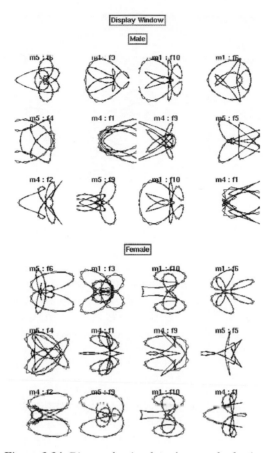

Figure 3.34: Biomorphs simulator by sexual selection.

5. Branch creation

   Add an ADF branch that contains part of the current ADF branch. A child is created with a pointer to the new branch.

6. Argument creation

   Appends a new argument to the argument list of the current ADF branch and creates a child by appending a popinter to the new argument as appropriate.

7. Iteration branch creation

   Add a new iteration branch that contains a portion of the current iteration-performing branch and create a child with a pointer to the new branch.

8. Iteration group creation

   Create a new iteration group that contains a portion of the current iteration-performing branch and add a pointer to it to generate a child.

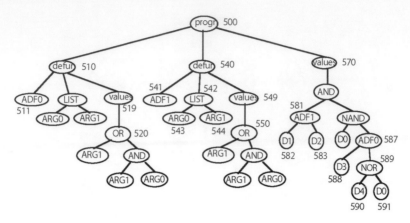

Figure 3.35: A genetic program as a result of branch duplication.

Now let us take a closer look at how the branch duplication and argument duplication operators work. For example, the result of applying this operator to Fig. 3.7 is shown in Fig. 3.35. In this case, ADF0 (label 410 or 510) is duplicated and a new ADF branch ADF1 (label 540) is created. ADF1 has the same arguments (ARG0, ARG1) as ADF0. In addition, the two function definition bodies are the same as follows:

```
(OR ARG1 (AND ARG1 ARG0))
```

In the original definition of the body, there were two references to ADF0 (labels 481, 487). As a result of these random changes, one of them is now a reference to ADF1 (label 581). Note that even after the above changes, the result of the function execution is the same as the original program. This is due to the fact that ADF1 has the same definition as ADF0.

Next, let us look at the effect of the duplicate argument operator. This is done as follows:

1. Select individuals from the population to apply the operator to.

2. Randomly select one of the automatically defined function branches ADFi.

3. Randomly select one argument from ADFi. Let this be ARGk.

4. Add the new argument ARGn to the list of arguments.

5. If ARGk appears in the function definition of ADFi, change it to ARGn with a certain probability.

6. If there is a pointer to ADFi in the entire program (function definition body and automatic function definition), increase the argument by one. This is done by overlapping the argument value to ARGk.

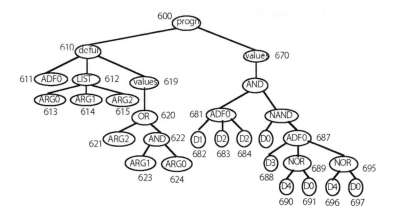

Figure 3.36: A genetic program as a result of argument duplication.

7. Add ARGn to the terminal symbol of the branch of ADFi (this is for the use of the mutation operator).

Figure 3.36 shows the result of executing this operator on the program shown in Fig. 3.7. Here, among the two arguments of ADF0, ARG1 is duplicated and ARG2 (label 615) is added. This makes the new ADF0 have three arguments (ARG0, ARG1, and ARG2). As a result, one ARG1 in the definition of ADF0 has been changed to ARG2 (label 621). Also, when ADF0 is referenced in the definition of the body of the function, the number of arguments is increased. In this case, the argument value of ARG1 (the second argument value) is copied and added as the argument value of ARG2 (the third argument value).

For example, in the following pointer of ADF0 (label 481) on the left side of the original definition:

```
(ADF0 D1 D2)
```

is now a pointer to the new ADF0 (label 681):

```
(ADF0 D1 D2 D2).
```

Also, the pointer to ADF0 (label 487) on the right

```
(ADF0 D3 (NOR D4 D0))
```

now becomes

```
(ADF0 D3 (NOR D4 D0) (NOR D4 D0))
```

as a pointer to the new ADF0 (label 687).

Table 3.10: Experimental results with gene duplication.

Experimental condition		Computation cost	execution time	Program complexity
ADF	Duplication operators			
none	none	5,025,000	36,950	469.1
yes	none	4,263,000	66,667	180.9
yes	yes	1,789,500	13,594	88.8

Note that the application of these operators does not affect the overall execution result of the program. It is expected that the effect of evolution will be accelerated by additional genetic operators acting on the overlapping parts. Koza [82] reported the experiments with even-5-parity problem[8]. In this study, the following three methods are compared.

1. GP without ADF

2. GP with ADF

3. GP with ADF and with duplication operators

Table 3.10 shows the results of the experiment. This is based on the average data of 25 runs with a population of 96,000. The table shows the computational cost[9], execution time (i.e., wall-clock time) and the average number of nodes in the final solution program. The results of these comparisons show that the use of duplication operators leads to an improvement in search efficiency. In addition, the size of the resulting program can be reduced.

Koza et al. have confirmed the effectiveness of the gene duplication on various other problems (genetic analysis, evolving hardware, analog circuit synthesis, etc.). For more details, the reader is referred to [82].

3.12 Selfish Genes: Revisited

In the previous section, the effect of gene duplication was explained based on the GP. Table 3.10 shows that the complexity of the program does not necessarily increase with gene duplication. However, we should not forget that this is a double-edged sword. In some cases, it has been observed that bloats can occur.

Let us remember the idea of selfish genes as explained in Section 2.3.2. The following is a quote from Richard Dawkins.

---

[8]This problem is to find a Boolean function that outputs 1 only if the number of 1's is 1, 3, or 5, and outputs 0 otherwise.

[9]Number of individuals to be processed to guarantee a 99% success rate, assuming the most efficient generation of solutions [82].

They (=Selfish genes) are in you and in me; they created us, body and mind; and their preservation is the ultimate rationale for our existence. They have come a long way, those replicators. Now they go by the name of genes, and we are their survival machines [29].

The discussion so far illustrates that the GP code (substructure) sometimes behaves in a very selfish way. This may have led to the clever use of introns to protect the region (exon) being encoded. In the search for GPs, it works for better or worse.

Chapter 4

Swarm Intelligence

Scatter some sugar near an ant's nest on a warm day and then sit back and watch. What will unfold will soon seem an appropriate subject for a life's work. (E.O. Wilson; when he was asked by a young man how a person could spend his entire research career studying something as straightforward as prosaic and as small as ants [8]).

4.1 Ant Colony Optimization (ACO)

4.1.1 Collective Behaviors of Ants

Ants march in a long line. There is food at one end, a nest at the other. This is a familiar scene in gardens and on roads, but the sophisticated distributed control by these small insects was recognized by humans only a few decades ago.

Ants established their life in groups, or colonies, more than a hundred million years before humans appeared on Earth. They formed a society that handles complex tasks such as food collection, nest building, and division of labor through primitive methods of communication. As a result, ants have a high level of fitness among species, and can adapt to harsh environments. New ideas including routing, agents, and distributed control in robotics have developed based on simple models of ant behavior. Applications of the ant behavior model have been used in many papers, and are becoming a field of research rather than a fad.

Marching is a cooperative ant behavior that can be explained by the pheromone trail model. Cooperative behavior is frequently seen in ant colonies, and has attracted the interest of entomologists and behavioral scientists (see

Figure 4.1: Photo of an ant mound with the author. Ant mounds appear only when the ant colony reaches a certain size.

Fig. 4.1). Pheromones are volatile chemicals synthesized within the insect, and are used to communicate with other insects of the same species. Examples are sex pheromones that attract the opposite sex, alarm pheromones that alert group members, and trail pheromones that are used in ant marches.

However, recent research indicates that pheromones are effective within a distance of only about 1 m from the female. Therefore, it is still not known if males are attracted only because of the pheromones.

Many species of ants leave a trail of pheromones when carrying food to the nest. Ants follow the trails left by other ants when searching for food. Pheromones are volatile matter that is secreted while returning from the food source to the nest. Experiments shown in Fig. 4.2 by Deneubourg and Goss using Argentine ants linked this behavior to the search for the shortest path [49]. They connected bridge-shaped paths (two connected paths) between the nest and the food source, and counted the number of ants that used each path. This seems like a simple problem, but because ants are almost blind they have difficulty recognizing junctions, and cannot use complex methods to communicate the position of the food. Furthermore, all the ants must take the shorter path to increase the efficiency of the group. Ants handle this task by using pheromones to guide the other ants.

Figure 4.3 shows the ratio of ants that used the shorter path [49]. Almost every ant used the shorter path as time passed. Many of the ants return to the shorter path, secreting additional pheromones; therefore, the ants that followed also take the shorter path. This model can be applied to the search for the shortest path, and is used to solve the traveling salesman problem (TSP) and routing of networks. There are many unknown factors about the pheromones of actual ants; however, the volatility of pheromones can be utilized to build a model that

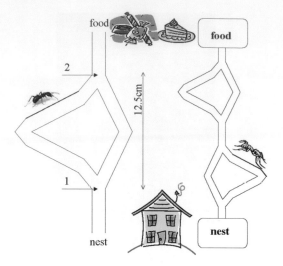

Figure 4.2: Bridge-shaped paths.

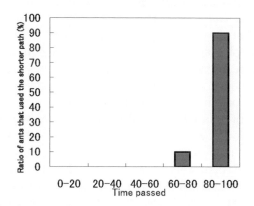

Figure 4.3: The ratio of ants that used the shorter path.

maintains the shortest path while adapting to rapidly changing traffic. The path with a greater accumulation of pheromones is chosen at junctions, but random factors are inserted to avoid inflexible solutions in a dynamic environment.

4.1.2 Simulating the Pheromone Trails of Ants

An easy model can describe the actions of ants as follows:

■ In case of nothing, random search is done.

■ If the food is found, takes it back to the hive. Homing ant knows the position of the hive, and returns almost straight back.

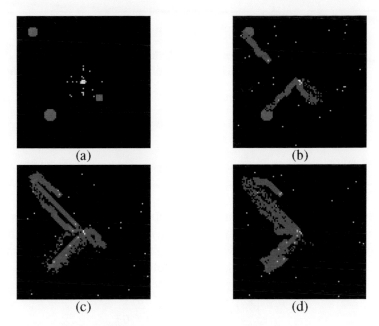

(a) (b)

(c) (d)

Figure 4.4: Pheromone trails of ants.

- Ants that take the food back to hive drop their pheromone. Pheromones are volatile.

- Ants not having the food have the habit of being attracted to the pheromone.

Figure 4.4 shows the simulation of the pheromone trails. Here, the hives are placed in the center, and there are three (lower right, upper left, lower left) food sources. (a) is the first random search phase. In (b), the closer lower right and lower left food are found, and the pheromone trail is formed. Upper left is in the middle of formation. In (c), pheromone trails are formed for all three sources, and makes the transport more efficient. The lower right source is almost exhaustively picked. In (d), the lower right food source finishes, and the pheromone trail is already dissipated. As a result, a vigorous transportation for the two sources on the left is being done. After this, all the sources finish, and the ants returns to random search again.

4.1.3 *ACO using a Pheromone Trail Model*

Optimization algorithms based on the collective behavior of ants are called ant colony optimization (ACO) [34].

ACO using a pheromone trail model for the TSP uses the following algorithm to optimize the travel path:

1. Ants are placed randomly in each city.

2. Ants move to the next city. The destination is probabilistically determined based on the information on pheromones and given conditions.

3. Repeat until all cities are visited.

4. Ants that make one full cycle secrete pheromones on the route according to the length of the route.

5. Return to 1 if a satisfactory solution has not been obtained.

The ant colony optimization (ACO) algorithm can be outlined as follows. Take η_{ij} as the distance between cities i and j. The probability $p_{ij}^k(t)$ that an ant k in city i will move to city j is determined by the reciprocal of the distance $1/\eta_{ij}$ and the amount of pheromone $\tau_{ij}(t)$ in the following way:

$$p_{ij}^k(t) = \frac{\tau_{ij}(t) \times \eta_{ij}^{\alpha}}{\sum_{h \in J_i^k} \tau_{ih}(t) \times \eta_{ih}^{\alpha}}. \tag{4.1}$$

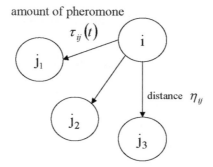

Figure 4.5: Path selection rules of ants.

Here, J_i^k is the set of all cities that the ant k in city i can move to (has not visited). The condition that ants are more likely to select a route with more pheromone reflects the positive feedback from past searches as well as a heuristic for searching for a shorter path. The ACO can thereby include an appropriate amount of knowledge unique to the problem.

The length and pheromone accumulation of paths between cities are stored in a Table (Fig. 4.5). Ants can recognize information on their surroundings, and probabilistically decide the next city to visit. The amount of pheromones added to each path after every cycle is inversely proportional to the length of the cycle path.

Table 4.1: Comparison between ACO and metaheuristics.

TSP	ACO	GA	EP	SA	Optimal
Oliver 30	420 [830]	421 [3200]	420 [40,000]	424 [24,617]	420
Eil 50	425 [1,830]	428 [25,000]	426 [100,000]	443 [68,512]	425
Eil 75	535 [3,480]	545 [80,000]	542 [325,000]	580 [173,250]	535
KroA 100	21,282 [4,820]	21,761 [103,00]	N/A [N/A]	N/A [N/A]	21,282

More formally, the pheromone table is updated by the following equations:

$$Q(k) \quad - \quad \text{the reciprocal of the path that the ant } k \text{ found}, \quad (4.2)$$

$$\Delta\tau_{ij}(t) \quad = \quad \sum_{k \in A_{ij}} Q(k), \quad (4.3)$$

$$\tau_{ij}(t+1) \quad = \quad (1-\rho) \cdot \tau_{ij}(t) + \Delta\tau_{ij}(t). \quad (4.4)$$

The amount of pheromone added to each path after one iteration is inversely proportional to the length of the paths that the ants found (eq. (4.2)). The results for all ants that moved through a path are reflected in the path (eq. (4.3)). Here, A_{ij} is the set of all ants that moved on a path from city i to city j. Negative feedback to avoid local solutions is given as an evaporation coefficient (eq. (4.4)), where the amount of pheromone in the paths, or information from the past, is reduced by a fixed factor (ρ).

The ACO is an effective method to solve the traveling salesman problem (TSP) compared to other search strategies. Table 4.1 shows the optimized values for four benchmark problems and various minima found using other methods (smaller is better, obviously) [34]. The numbers in brackets indicate the number of candidates investigated. The ACO is more suitable for this problem compared to methods such as genetic algorithm (GA, Section 3.1), simulated annealing (SA) and evolutionary programming (EP). However, it is inferior to the Lee-Kernighan method (the current TSP champion code). The characteristic that specialized methods perform better in static problems is shared by many metaheuristics (high-level strategies which guide an underlying heuristic to increase their performance). Complicated problems, such as TSPs where the distances between cities are asymmetric or where the cities change dynamically, do not have established programs and the ACO is considered to be one of the most promising methods.

4.2   Particle Swarm Optimization (PSO)

4.2.1   *Collective Behavior of Boids*

Many scientists have attempted to express the group behavior of flocks of birds and schools of fish, using a variety of methods. Two of the most well-known of these scientists are Craig Reynolds and Frank Heppner, who simulated the movements of birds. Reynolds was fascinated by the beauty of bird flocks [117], and Heppner, a zoologist, had an interest in finding the hidden rules in the instantaneous stops and dispersions of flocks [60]. These two shared a keen understanding of the unpredictable movements of birds; at the microscopic level, the movements were extremely simple, as seen in cellular automata, while at the macroscopic level, the motions were very complicated and appeared chaotic. This is what is called an "emergent property" in the field of Artificial Life (Alife). Their model places a very high weight on the influence of individuals on each other. Similarly, it is known that an "optimal distance" is maintained among individual fish in a fish school (see Fig. 4.6).

Figure 4.6: Do the movements of a school of fish follow a certain set of rules? (@Coral Sea in 2003).

This approach is probably not far from the mark as the basis for the social behavior of groups of birds, fish, animals and, for that matter, human beings. The sociobiologist E.O.Wilson made an interesting suggestion with respect to schools of fish (see the quote at the beginning of this chapter)[1].

---

[1]Edward Osborn Wilson (1929–): American entomologist. Researcher of sociobiology and biodiversity. In the last chapter of his book [148], he included a human as "Man: From Sociobiology to Sociology." Regardless of his intentions, he was criticized as an eugenicist and debate on social biology came about. The controversy gradually escalated emotionally and water was poured on Wilson during one of his lectures.

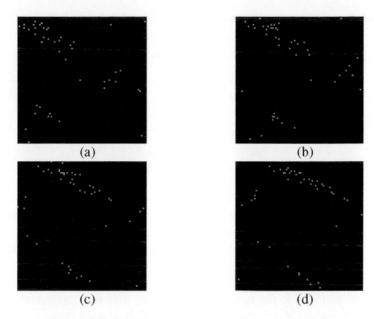

Figure 4.7: Simple behavior of boids ((a)⇒(b)⇒(c)⇒(d)).

Figure 4.8: Boids in a situation with obstacles (MindRender simulation, see Appendix A.3).

As one can understand from this quote, the most useful information to an individual is what is shared from other members of the same group. This hypothesis forms the basis for the PSO method, which will be explained in Section 4.2.2.

The collective behavior of a flock of birds emphasized the rules for keeping the optimum distance between an individual and its neighbors.

The CG video by Reynolds features a group of agents called "boids." Each boid moves according to the sum of three vectors: (1) force to move away from the nearest individual or obstacle, (2) force to move toward the center of the flock, and (3) force to move toward its destination. Adjusting coefficients in this summation results in many behavioral patterns. This technique is often used in special effects and videos in films. Figure 4.7 (simple behavior of flocks) and Fig. 4.8 (situation with obstacles) are examples of simulations of boids.

The following are the details of the algorithm that boids follow. Many individuals (boids) move around in space, and each individual has a velocity vector. The three factors below result in a flock of boids.

1. Avoid collision: attempt to avoid collision with nearby individuals.

2. Match pace: attempt to match velocity of nearby individuals.

3. Move to center: attempt to be surrounded by nearby individuals.

Each boid has an "optimum distance" to avoid collision, and behaves so as to maintain this distance with its nearest neighbor [120]. Collision becomes a concern if the distance between nearby boids becomes shorter than the "optimum distance." Therefore, to avoid collision, each boid slows down if the nearest boid is ahead, and speeds up if the nearest boid is behind (Fig. 4.9).

The "optimum distance" is also used to prevent the risk of straying from the flock. If the distance to the nearest boid is larger than the "optimum distance", each boid speeds up if the nearest boid is ahead, and slows down if it is behind (Fig. 4.10).

Here, "ahead" ("behind") are defined as ahead (behind) a line that crosses the boid's eyes and is perpendicular to the direction in which the boid is moving (Fig. 4.11). Boids try to move parallel to (with the same vector as) their nearest neighbor. Here, there is no change in speed. Furthermore, boids change velocity so as to always move toward the center of the flock (center of gravity of all boids).

In summary, the velocity vector ($\vec{v}_i(t)$) of the i-th boid is updated at time t as follows (see Fig. 4.12):

$$\vec{v}_i(t) = \vec{v}_i(t-1) + \vec{Next}_i(t-1) + \vec{G}_i(t-1), \tag{4.5}$$

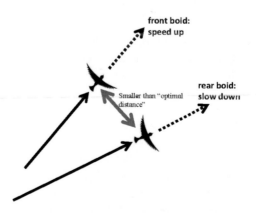

Figure 4.9: Avoid collision (1).

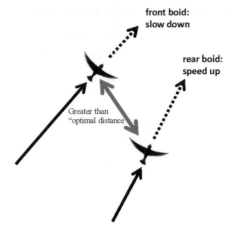

Figure 4.10: Avoid collision (2).

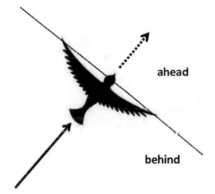

Figure 4.11: Ahead or behind a line that crosses the boid's eyes.

where $\vec{Next}_i(t-1)$ is the velocity vector of the nearest boid to individual i, and $\vec{G}_i(t-1)$ is the vector from individual i to the center of gravity. The velocity at one step before, i.e., $\vec{v}_i(t-1)$, is added to take inertia into account.

Each boid has its own field of view (Fig. 4.13) and considers boids within its view when finding the nearest neighbor. However, the coordinates of all boids, including those out of view, are used to calculate the center of gravity.

It is interesting to see how close the collective motion of such boids is to the real thing. Hausknecht et al. [61] studied this topic using the Turing test[2]. In this study, a real school of fish and a simulated school[3] were shown to the partici-

---

[2] A test proposed by Alan Turing, the father of computers, to distinguish between human and artificial intelligence. It is considered one of the criteria for determining whether AI is truly intelligent or not. For more detailed discussion, refer to [69].

[3] In this study, a different self-propelled particle model was used instead of Boid.

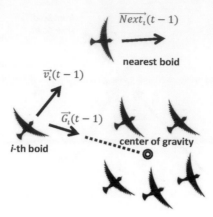

Figure 4.12: Updating the velocity vector.

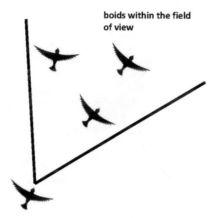

Figure 4.13: Each boid has its own field of view.

pants (fish experts and novices), who had to answer which one was the real fish. As a result, the fish experts were able to answer correctly, but the general participants (those who had been collected through an online game) could hardly tell the difference. On the other hand, the general participants improved their correct answer rate the second time. The participants who answered correctly explained that they had noticed that the spatial organization and smoothness of trajectories were different between the real and simulated fish. This kind of research shows that "citizen science" can be used to refine biological models and adjust AI techniques.

Kennedy et al. designed an effective optimization algorithm using the mechanism behind boids [72]. This is called "Particle Swarm Optimization (PSO)," and numerous applications are reported. The details are provided in Section 4.2.2.

4.2.2   PSO Algorithm

The classic PSO was intended to be applied to optimization problems. It simulates the motion of a large number of individuals (or "particles") moving in a multi-dimensional space [72]. Each individual stores its own location vector ($\vec{x}_i$), velocity vector ($\vec{v}_i$), and the position at which the individual obtained the highest fitness value ($\vec{p}_i$). All individuals also share information regarding the position with the highest fitness value for the group ($\vec{p}_g$).

As generations progress, the velocity of each individual is updated using the best overall location obtained up to the current time for the entire group and the best locations obtained up to the current time for that individual. This update is performed using the following formula:

$$\vec{v}_i = \chi(\omega\vec{v}_i + \phi_1 \cdot (\vec{p}_i - \vec{x}_i) + \phi_2 \cdot (\vec{p}_g - \vec{x}_i)) \qquad (4.6)$$

The coefficients employed here are the convergence coefficient χ (a random value between 0.9 and 1.0) and the attenuation coefficient ω, while ϕ_1 and ϕ_2 are random values unique to each individual and the dimension, with a maximum value of 2. When the calculated velocity exceeds some limit, it is replaced by a maximum velocity V_{max}. This procedure allows us to hold the individuals within the search region during the search.

The locations of each of the individuals are updated at each generation by the following formula:

$$\vec{x}_i = \vec{x}_i + \vec{v}_i. \qquad (4.7)$$

The overall flow of the PSO is as shown in Fig. 4.14. Let us now consider the specific movements of each individual (see Fig. 4.15). A flock consisting of

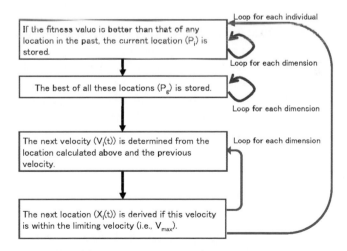

Figure 4.14: Flow chart of the PSO algorithm.

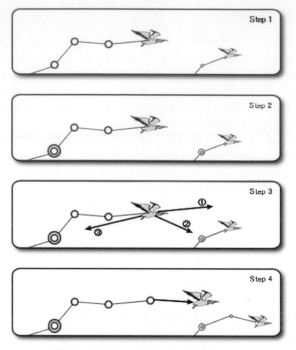

Figure 4.15: In which way do birds fly?

a number of birds is assumed to be in flight. We focus on one of the individuals (Step 1). In the figure, the ○ symbols and linking line segments indicate the positions and paths of the bird. The nearby ⊙ symbol (on its path) indicates the position with the highest fitness value on the individual's path (Step 2). The distant ⊙ symbol (on the other bird's path) marks the position with the highest fitness value for the flock (Step 2). One would expect that the next state will be reached in the direction shown by the arrows in Step 3. Vector ① shows the direction followed in the previous steps; vector ② is directed towards the position with the highest fitness for the flock; and vector ③ points to the location where the individual obtained its highest fitness value so far. Thus, all these vectors, ①, ② and ③, in Step 3 are summed to obtain the actual direction of movement in the subsequent step (see Step 4).

The efficiency of this type of PSO search is certainly high because focused searching is available near optimal solutions in a relatively simple search space. However, the canonical PSO algorithm often gets trapped in local optimum in multimodal problems. Because of that, some sort of adaptation is necessary in order to apply PSO to problems with multiple sharp peaks.

To overcome the above limitation, a GA-like mutation can be integrated with PSO [62]. This hybrid PSO does not follow the process by which every individual of the simple PSO moves to another position inside the search area with a

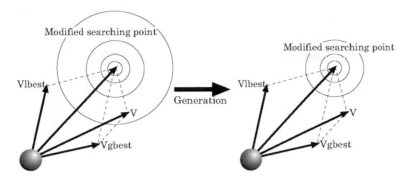

Figure 4.16: Concept of searching process by PSO with Gaussian mutation.

predetermined probability without being affected by other individuals, but leaves a certain ambiguity in the transition to the next generation due to Gaussian mutation. This technique employs the following equation:

$$mut(\vec{x}) = \vec{x} \times (1 + gaussian(\sigma)), \qquad (4.8)$$

where σ is set to be 0.1 times the length of the search space in one dimension. The individuals are selected at a predetermined probability and their positions are determined at the probability under the Gaussian distribution. Wide-ranging searches are possible at the initial search stage and search efficiency is improved at the middle and final stages by gradually reducing the appearance ratio of Gaussian mutation at the initial stage. Figure 4.16 shows the PSO search process with Gaussian mutation. In the figure, V_{lbest} represents the velocity based on the local best, i.e., $\vec{p}_i - \vec{x}_i$ in eq. (4.6), whereas V_{gbest} represents the velocity based on the global best, i.e., $\vec{p}_g - \vec{x}_i$.

4.2.3 Comparison with GA

Let us turn to a comparison of the performance of the PSO with that of the GA using benchmark functions, to examine the effectiveness of PSO.

For the comparison, $F8$ (Rastrigin function) and $F9$ (Griewank function) are employed. These are defined as:

$$F8(x_1, x_2) = 20 + x_1^2 - 10\cos(2\pi x_1) + x_2^2 - 10\cos(2\pi x_2) - (-5.11 \le x_i \le 5.11)$$

$$F9(x_1, x_2) = \frac{1}{4000} \sum_{i=1}^{2} (x_i - 100)^2 - \prod_{i=1}^{2} \cos\left(\frac{x_i - 100}{\sqrt{i}}\right) + 1(-10 \le x_i \le 10)$$

Figure 4.17 shows the shapes of $F8$ and $F9$, respectively. $F8$ and $F9$ seek the minimum value. $F8$ contains a large number of peaks so that its optimization is particularly difficult.

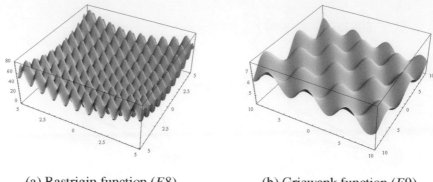

(a) Rastrigin function ($F8$) (b) Griewank function ($F9$)

Figure 4.17: Benchmark functions.

Table 4.2: Search space for test functions.

Function	Search space
$F8$	$-65.535 \leq x_i < 65.536$
$F9$	$-10 \leq x_i \leq 10$

Comparative experiments were conducted with PSO and GA using the above benchmark functions. PSO and GA were repeatedly run 100 times. Search space ranges for the experiments are listed in Table 4.2. PSO and GA parameters are given in Table 4.3. BLX-α (Blend Crossover) is a crossover method proposed by Esheleman [40]. The method finds the interval where the real-valued vectors of parent individuals exist, and extends it by α to both sides. From this interval, a child is randomly generated according to a uniform random number.

The performance results are shown in Fig. 4.18 which plots the fitness values against the generations. Table 4.4 shows the averaged best fitness values over 100 runs. As can be seen from the table and the figures, the combination of

Table 4.3: PSO and GA parameters.

Parameters	PSO,PSO with Gaussian	Real-valued GA
Population	200	200
V_{max}	1	
Generation	50	50
ϕ_1, ϕ_2	upper limits = 2.0	
Inertia weight	0.9	
Crossover ratio		0.7(BLX-α)
Mutation	0.01	0.01
Elite		0.05
Selection		tournament (size=6)

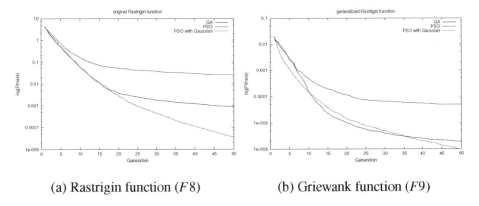

(a) Rastrigin function ($F8$)   (b) Griewank function ($F9$)

Figure 4.18: Standard PSO versus PSO with Gaussian mutation.

Table 4.4: Average best fitness of 100 runs for experiments.

	Gen	GA	PSO	PSO with mutation
$F8$	1	4.290568	3.936564	3.913959
	10	0.05674	0.16096	0.057193
	20	0.003755	0.052005	0.002797
	30	0.001759	0.037106	0.000454
	40	0.001226	0.029099	0.000113
	50	0.000916	0.02492	3.61E-05
$F9$	1	0.018524	0.015017	0.019726
	10	0.000161	0.000484	0.000145
	20	1.02E-05	0.000118	1.43E-05
	30	3.87E-06	6.54E-05	4.92E-06
	40	2.55E-06	5.50E-05	2.04E-06
	50	1.93E-06	4.95E-05	1.00E-06

PSO with Gaussian mutation allows us to achieve a performance that is almost equal to that of the canonical PSO for the unimodals, and a better performance than the canonical PSO for the multimodals. The experimental results with other benchmark functions are further discussed in [67].

PSO is a stochastic search method, as are GA and GP, and its method of adjustment of $\vec{p}_i$ and $\vec{p}_g$ resembles crossover in GA. It also employs the concept of fitness, as in evolutionary computation. Thus, the PSO algorithm is strongly related to evolutionary computation (EC) methods.

However, PSO has certain characteristics that other EC techniques do not have. GA operators directly operate on the search points in a multi-dimensional search space, while PSO operates on the motion vectors of particles which in turn update the search points (i.e., particle positions). In other words, GA operators are position specific and the PSO operators are direction specific. One of the reasons PSO has gathered so much attention was the tendency of its individuals to proceed directly towards the target.

In the chapter "The Optimal Allocation of Trials" in his book [65], John Holland ascribes the success of EC on the balance of "exploitation," through search of known regions, with "exploration," through search, at finite risks, of unknown regions. PSO is adept at managing such subtle balances. These stochastic factors enable PSO to make thorough searches of the relatively promising regions and, due to the momentum of speed, also allows effective searches of unknown regions (see [27, 73] for the details of theoretical research).

4.3 Firefly Algorithms

Fireflies glow owing to a luminous organ and fly around. This glow is meant to attract females. The light generated by each firefly differs depending on the individual insect, and it is considered that they attract others following the rules described below:

■ The extent of attractiveness is in proportion to the luminosity.

■ Female fireflies are more strongly attracted by males that produce a strong glow.

■ Luminosity decreases as a function of distance.

The firefly algorithm (FA) is a search method based on blinking fireflies [152]. This does not discriminate between gender. That is, all fireflies are attracted to each other. In this case, the luminosity is determined by an objective function. To solve the minimization problem, fireflies at a lower functional value (with a better adaptability) glow much more strongly. The most glowing firefly moves around at random.

Algorithm 2 describes the outline of the FA. The moving formula for a firefly i attracted by firefly j is as follows:

$$\vec{x}_i^{new} = \vec{x}_i^{old} + \beta_{i,j}(\vec{x}_j - \vec{x}_i^{old}) + \vec{\alpha}(rand(0,1) - \frac{1}{2}), \qquad (4.9)$$

where $rand(0,1)$ is a uniform random number between 0 and 1. $\vec{\alpha}$ is a parameter vector to determine the magnitude of the random numbers, and $\beta_{i,j}$ represents how attractive firefly i is to firefly j.

$$\beta_{i,j} = \beta_0 e^{-\gamma r_{i,j}^2} \qquad (4.10)$$

The variable β_0 represents how attractive fireflies are when $r_{i,j} = 0$, which indicates that the two are in the same position. Since $r_{i,j}$ represents the Euclidean distance between firefly i and j, their attractiveness varies depending on the distance between them.

Algorithm 2 Firefly algorithm

Initialize a population of fireflies $\vec{x}_i$ $(i = 1, 2, \cdots, n)$ ▷ Minimizing objective
function $f(\vec{x})$, $\vec{x} = (x_1, \cdots, x_d)^T$.
Define light absorption coefficient γ
$t = 1$ ▷ Generation count.
while $t < MaxGeneration$ and the stop criterion is not satisfied **do**
    for $i = 1$ to n **do** ▷ for all n fireflies
        for $j = 1$ to n **do** ▷ for all n fireflies
            Light intensity I_i, I_j at $\vec{x}_i, \vec{x}_j$ is determined by f
            if $I_i > I_j$ **then**
                Move firefly i towards j in all d dimensions
            end if
            Attractiveness varies with distance r via $e^{-\gamma r}$
            Evaluate new solutions and update light intensity
        end for
    end for
    Rank the fireflies and find the current best
    $t = t + 1$
end while
Postprocess results and visualization

The most glowing firefly moves around at random, according to the following formula:

$$\vec{x}_k(t+1) = \vec{x}_k(t) + \vec{\alpha}\left(rand(0,1) - \frac{1}{2}\right) \tag{4.11}$$

The reason for this is that the entire population converges to the locally best solution in an initial allocation.

As the distance becomes greater, the attractiveness becomes weaker. Therefore, under the firefly algorithms, fireflies form groups with each other at a distance instead of gathering at one spot.

The firefly algorithms are suitable for optimization problems on multimodality and are considered to yield better results compared to those obtained using PSO. It has another extension that separates fireflies into two groups and limits the effect on those in the same group. This enables global solutions and local solutions to be searched simultaneously.

4.4 Cuckoo Search

The cuckoo search (CS) [151] is a meta–heuristic based on brood parasitic behavior. Brood parasitism is an animal behavior in which an animal depends on a member of another species (or induces this behavior) to sit on its eggs. Some species of cuckoos (Fig. 4.19) are generally known to exhibit this behavior. They leave their eggs in the nests of other species of birds such as the great reed

Figure 4.19: Cuculus poliocephalus. The lesser cuckoo from a Japanese stamp.

warblers, Siberian meadow buntings, bullheaded shrikes, azure-winged magpies etc.[4] Before leaving, they demonstrate an interesting behavior referred to as egg mimicry: they take out one egg of a host bird (foster parent) already in the nest and lay an egg that mimics the other eggs in the nest, thus keeping the numbers balanced.[5] This is because a host bird discards an egg when it determines that the laid egg is not its own.

A cuckoo chick has a remarkably large and bright bill; therefore, it is excessively fed by its foster parent. This is referred to as "supernormal stimulus." Furthermore, there is an exposed skin region at the back of the wings with the same color as its bill. When the foster parent carries foods, the chick spreads its wings to make the parent aware of the region. The foster parent mistakes it for its own chicks. Thus, the parent believes that it has more chicks to feed than it actually has and carries more food to the nest. It is considered to be an evolutional strategy for cuckoos to be fed corresponding to their size because a grown cuckoo is many times larger than the host.

The CS models the cuckoos' brood parasitic behavior based on three rules as described below:

- A cuckoo lays one egg at a time and leaves it in a randomly selected nest.

- The highest quality egg (difficult to be noticed by the host bird) is carried over to the next generation.

- The number of nests is fixed, and a parasitized egg is noticed by a host bird with a certain probability. In this case, the host bird either discards the egg or rebuilds the nest.

Algorithm 3 shows the CS algorithm. Based on this algorithm, a cuckoo lays a new egg in a randomly selected nest, according to Lévy flight. This flight presents

---

[4]Parasitized species are almost always fixed for each female cuckoo.

[5]Furthermore, a cuckoo chick having just been hatched expels all the eggs of its host. For this reason, a cuckoo chick has a pit in its back to place its host's egg, clambers up inside the nest and throws the egg out of the nest. This behavior was discovered by Edward Jenner, famous for smallpox vaccination.

Algorithm 3 Cuckoo search

Initialize a population of n host nests   ▷ Minimizing objective function
$f(\vec{x})$, $\vec{x} = (x_1, \cdots, x_d)^T$.
Produce one egg x_i^0 in each host $i = 1, \cdots, n$
$t = 1$ ▷ Generation count.
while $t < MaxGeneration$ and the stop criterion is not satisfied **do**
    Choose a nest i randomly
    Produce a new egg $\vec{x}_i^t$ by performing Lèvy flights   ▷ Brood parasite of the
cuckoo.
    Choose a nest j randomly and let its egg be $\vec{x}_j^{t-1}$
    if $f(\vec{x}_j^{t-1}) > f(\vec{x}_i^t)$ **then**   ▷ The new egg is better.
        Replace j's egg by the new egg, i.e., $\vec{x}_i^t$
    end if
    Sort the nests according to their eggs' performance
    A fraction (p_a) of the worse nests are abandoned and new ones are built by
performing Lèvy flights
    $t = t + 1$
end while
Postprocess results and visualization

---

mostly a short distance random walk with no regularity. However, it sometimes exhibits a long-distance movement. This movement has been identified in several animals and insects. It is considered to be able to represent stochastic fluctuations observed in various natural and physical phenomena such as flight patterns, feeding behaviors etc.

Specifically, Lèvy distribution is represented by the following probability density function (see Fig. 4.20):

$$f(x; \mu, \sigma) = \begin{cases} \sqrt{\frac{\sigma}{2\pi}} \exp\left[-\frac{\sigma}{2(x-\mu)}\right] (x-\mu)^{-3/2} & (\mu < x), \\ 0 & (\text{otherwise}), \end{cases} \quad (4.12)$$

where μ represents a positional parameter, and σ represents a scale parameter. Based on this distribution, Lèvy flight mostly presents a short distance movement, while it also presents a random walk for a long distance movement with a certain probability. For optimization, it facilitates an effective search compared to using random walk (Gaussian flight) according to a regular distribution [151].

Let us consider an objective function represented as $f(\vec{x})$ for $\vec{x} = (x_1, \cdots, x_d)^T$. A cuckoo then creates a new solution candidate for the nest i given by the following equation:

$$\vec{x}_i^{t+1} = \vec{x}_i^t + \alpha \otimes \text{Lèvy}(\lambda), \quad (4.13)$$

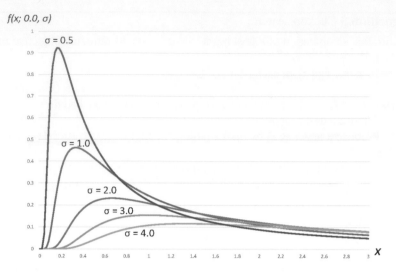

Figure 4.20: Lévy distribution.

where $\alpha(> 0)$ is related to the scale of the problem. In most cases, $\alpha = 1$. The operation $\otimes$ represents multiplication of each element by α. Lévy(λ) represents a random number vector whereby each element follows a Lévy distribution, and this is accomplished as follows:

$$\text{Lévy}(\lambda) \sim rand(0,1) = t^{-\lambda} \quad 1 < \lambda \leq 3, \tag{4.14}$$

where $rand(0,1)$ is a uniform random number between 0 and 1. This formula is essentially a random walk with the distribution achieved by powered steps with a heavy tail. Therefore, it includes infinite averages and infinite standard deviation. An exponential distribution with exponents from -1 to -3 is normally used for a long-distance movement of Lévy flight.

p_a represents a parameter referred to as the switching probability, and its fraction of the worse nests are abandoned from the nest by a host bird and new ones are built by performing Lèvy flights. This probability strikes a balance between exploration and exploitation.

CS is considered to be robust, compared with PSO and ACO [26].

4.5 Cat Swarm Optimization (CSO)

Cat swarm optimization (CSO) [25] is an optimization method based on a cat's behavior. Cats remain calm most of the time, however, they are interested in their surroundings and are prudent. The length of time spent chasing preys is extremely short to save energy, compared with that of their resting time.

CSO has two main modes:

- **seeking mode**: Represents the resting time (observing the surroundings while taking a rest). Cats make a decision to move when they sense preys and danger.

- **chasing mode**: Represents the time spent chasing preys. After finding a prey, they determine the chasing speed and destination. Thereafter they start moving.

With CSO, multiple cats are generated in a searching space and each of them becomes a solution candidate. These cats are divided into two groups: seeking mode and chasing mode. The ratio of these modes is a mixing ratio (*MR*: the number of cats in chasing mode / that in seeking mode). Cats spend most of their time in a calm state to observe the surroundings, therefore, *MR* is normally set small.

Seeking mode has four parameters as below:

- *SMP*: Indicates how many cats in seeking mode are considered. It is used to define the memory size of the cats.

- *SRD*: Indicates how much each parameter changes. It is the width of the mutation in a selected dimension. If changed, the difference between the old and new values should be within the range of *SDR*.

- *CDC*: Indicates how many of the parameters are changed. It defines the number of elements to change.

- *SPC*: Indicates whether a cat is a candidate for moving or not, i.e., whether the current location of a cat is a candidate for the destination.

Under the condition that *M* represents the number of dimensions in the searching space, the process involved in the seeking mode toward the k-th cat_k is as follows:

Step1 Set j as follows:

$$j = \begin{cases} SMP - 1 & \text{if } SPC \text{ is } TRUE \\ SMP & \text{otherwise} \end{cases} \tag{4.15}$$

Step2 Copy the current position of the k-th cat_k for j times.

Step3 For each copy created, replace the positions based on the following equation:

$$x_{k,d} = (1 \pm SRD \times rand(0,1)) \times x_{k,d}. \tag{4.16}$$

With the condition $d \in \{1, 2, \cdots, M\}$, the number of elements to be changed (different numbers of d) is selected within the upper limit of the *CDC*.

Step4 Calculate the adaptability (fitness) of the entire candidacy points (FS_i) under the condition $1 \leq i \leq j$.

Step5 Calculate the selective probability P_i of each candidacy point (cat_i) using the following equation:

$$P_i = \frac{|FS_i - FS_b|}{FS_{max} - FS_{min}}, \quad 1 \leq i \leq j, \tag{4.17}$$

where FS_i represents a functional value (adaptability, i.e., fitness value) of cat_i. FS_{max} and FS_{min} are the maximum and minimum value of the function, respectively. If an objective function is used for searching for the minimum, then $FS_b = FS_{max}$, if it is for the maximum, then $FS_b = FS_{min}$.

Step6 Based on roulette selection (see 47 page) with the selection probability P_i, select the destination among the current candidate positions at random, and replace the positions of cat_k.

When in tracing mode, each cat moves at its own speed. This mode is represented by the following three steps:

Step1 Update the velocity ($v_{k,d}$) for each dimension d by following the formula;

$$v_{k,d} = v_{k,d} + rand(0,1) \times c_1 \times (x_{best,d} - x_{k,d}). \tag{4.18}$$

With the condition $d \in \{1, 2, \cdots, M\}$, $x_{best,d}$ represents the position of a cat with the best adaptability. c_1 is a user-defined scaling parameter.

Step2 Check whether the velocity exceeds the maximum. If so, update the maximum speed.

Step3 Update the position of each cat, according to the following equation:

$$x_{k,d} = x_{k,d} + v_{k,d} \tag{4.19}$$

4.6 Swarms for Knapsack Problems

Let us solve the knapsack problem P07 outlined in Section 3.5. First, we use a cuckoo search (CS). For this purpose, the number of selections is set to be the number of abandoned nests. The results are shown in Table 4.5. The amount of computation in CS was less than 1/10 in comparison with that of GAs, but a similar precision was attained (see Table 3.3). The solution was more rapidly obtained with a decreasing number of nests. Decreasing the number of nests resulted in the quick solution but also had a chance of convergence to a local solution. As demonstrated in this example, CS can run a few times faster than GA because of the characteristics of the Lévy flight.

Algorithm 4 Cat swarm optimization

Initialize a population of cats cat_i $(i = 1, 2, \cdots, n)$ with random positions $\vec{x}_i$ in M-dimensional space ▷ n: the number of cats.

Randomly assign each cat a velocity in range of the maximum velocity value (i.e., $\vec{v}_i; i = 1, 2, \cdots, n$).

while the stop criterion is not satisfied **do**

    According to *MR*, assign each cat a flag of the seeking or tracing mode

    Calculate the fitness function values for all cats and sort them

    X_g = the best cat ▷ find the cat with the best solution.

    for $i = 1$ to n **do**

        if cat_i's mode is in seeking mode **then**

            Start seeking mode

        else

            Start tracing mode

        end if

    end for

end while

Postprocess results and visualization

Table 4.5: Solving knapsack problems by cuckoo search (different types of evolution).

#. of nests	#. of abandoned nest #. of selection	#. of generations		
		50	100	200
100	10	88.39	39.34	24.42
	25	35.59	24.17	16.79
	50	22.40	14.90	9.32
500	50	81.40	48.86	33.59
	125	38.57	26.88	19.73
	250	22.26	16.82	13.18

The only quantity that the user must adjust in CS is the number of abandoned nests. Therefore, the number of parameters is smaller than that of particle swarm optimization (PSO) or other metaheuristic searches. CS is also considered more robust than PSO or ant colony optimization (ACO) [103].

Next, let us try FA for solving the knapsack problems. Each individual in this search is a binary sequence with a length of 15 (i.e., number of items = 15). As in GAs, the item is included (not included) in the knapsack if the corresponding element is 1(0).

Algorithm 5 shows a firefly search for this knapsack problem [153]. We only describe the section where two fireflies move according to attractiveness. x_{ik} is information on the k-th item of firefly i. $f(x_i)$ is the value of the i-th firefly (total

---

Algorithm 5 Movement by firefly search (Knapsack problem).

---

if $f(x_i) < f(x_j)$ **then**   ▷ i is worse than j.
    Derive the distance r_{ij} between two fireflies.
    Derive the attractiveness β_{ij} from i to j.
    for $k = 1$ to #.of items **do**   ▷ Update i-th firefly according to j-th firefly.
        if $x_{ik} = x_{jk}$ **then**   ▷ x_{ik} is information of k-th item for i-th firefly.
            $x_{ik} := x_{jk}$ ▷ Update 0/1 value for k-th item.
        else
            Generate a uniform random r between 0.0 and 1.0.
            if $r < \beta(r_{ij})$ **then**
                $x_{ik} := x_{jk}$ ▷ Change 0/1 value for k-th item.
            else
                $x_{ik} := x_{ik}$ ▷ Do not change 0/1 value for k-th item.
            end if
        end if
    end for
end if

---

value of items in the knapsack) and corresponds to the fitness in a GA (becomes 0 when the weight exceeds the limit).

The attractiveness β_{ij} of firefly j to firefly i is given as follows:

$$\beta_{ij} = \beta_0 e^{-\gamma r_{ij}^2}, \tag{4.20}$$

where r_{ij} is the humming distance, i.e., the number of bits that are different (number of columns where one is 0 and the other is 1) between the two binary sequences. For example, the humming distance between 0101 and 0011 is 2 because the second and third columns are different.

Table 4.6 shows the results of the searches using this algorithm. The firefly population size was 500, and the total number of generated firefly individuals was 25,000. The amount of computation was equivalent to a GA with population size 500 and the number of generations 50 (see Table 3.3). The table shows the error from the optimum solution that was ultimately observed (average of 100 runs). The table indicates that using appropriate values of γ and β_0 can search for the solution efficiently in firefly searches.

Firefly searches occur in various groups, and thus, are unlikely to be trapped in one local solution. Therefore, many local solutions might be found simultaneously; hence, firefly searches are applied in various fields.

4.7   Swarm for Pareto-optimization

Let us try to realize multi-objective optimization by means of PSO. The following implementation is based on the literature [103]. In multi-objective PSO, we

Table 4.6: Solving knapsack problems by firefly search (different types of fireflies).

β_0	γ				
	0.004	0.006	0.008	0.01	0.012
0.1	4.790	3.850	5.090	4.940	5.280
0.2	2.810	3.210	3.140	3.040	3.650
0.4	1.410	1.600	2.030	1.480	1.840
0.8	1.150	0.590	0.430	0.740	0.630
1.0	4.040	2.300	2.150	1.400	1.500
1.2	6.970	5.280	3.970	2.980	2.610

need to decide how to choose the globally best solution ($\vec{p}_g$ in eq. (4.6)). One way is to use the best solution so that the following σ values are close:

$$\sigma = \frac{f_1^2 - f_2^2}{f_1^2 + f_2^2}, \tag{4.21}$$

where we assume the optimization $(f_1(x), f_2(x)) = (f_1, f_2)$ of the two-objective functions ($f_1 - f_2$ space). In this case, the slope of the line connecting (f_1, f_2) and the origin corresponds to σ. More precisely, σ states the angle between the line $y = \frac{f_2}{f_1}x$ and x-axis. Note that $-1 \leq \sigma \leq 1$. When f_1 (f_2) approaches 0, the value of σ will get close to -1 ($+1$).

In addition to the current population, a set called "archive" is prepared, and the best solution is stored in the archive at each time step. For each particle, the particle in the archive that minimizes the Euclidean distance between σ values is set as the global best of that particle. In other words, the best solution is stored in the archive according to the value of σ. When the particle is moved, it refers to the best value with the σ value closest to its own.

In order to adjust for the difference in scale between the objective functions, the following modification has been employed. Let K_1 and K_2 be the maximum values of the first and second objective functions, respectively. We calculate the σ value as follows:

$$\sigma = \frac{(K_2 f_1)^2 - (K_1 f_2)^2}{(K_2 f_1)^2 + (K_1 f_2)^2}, \tag{4.22}$$

where K_1 and K_2 values are updated at each time step.

The details of multi-objective PSO are shown in Algorithm 6. The Update function is used to update the archive at each time step so that there are only "good" particles in the archive. Here, the "goodness" of a particle means how close it is to the Pareto solution, and the archive is updated so that only particles that outperform other particles remain. R_T is a random number in $[0, 1]$. It is used to probabilistically add a small value to the current position of a particle.

Next, let us try to build multi-objective optimization using FA algorithm based on literature [153].

Algorithm 6 Multi-objective PSO

Initialize population P_c of N particles x_i ($i = 1, \cdots, N$) ▷ Objective functions:
$f_1(x), \cdots, f_m(x)$
Set archive A_t as empty set
$t = 0$
while $t < T_{max}$ **do**
    for $i = 1$ to N **do**
        $x_t^i = \text{CheckConstraints}(x_t^i)$ ▷ Revise the position of the particle x_i that
violates the constraints.
    end for
    $A_{t+1} = \text{Update}(P_t, A_t)$
    for $i = 1$ to N **do**
        $p_t^g = \text{FindGlobalBest}(A_{t+1}, x_t^i)$
        $v_{t+1}^i = w v_t^i + c_1 R_1 (p^i - x_t^i) + c_2 R_2 (p_t^g - x_t^i)$
        $x_{t+1}^i = x_t^i + v_{t+1}^i$
        if $p^i \succ x_{t+1}^i$ **then**
            $p^i = x_{t+1}^i$
        end if
        $x_{t+1}^i = x_{t+1}^i + R_T x_{t+1}^i$ ▷ with random probability
    end for
    $t = t + 1$
end while

To do this, we run the following process for all combinations of flies i and j:

1. If i is dominated by j, then move i toward j.

2. If i is not dominated by any of them, move the fly with the best value of the randomly weighted objective functions.

The first corresponds to eq. (4.9). In the second part, the Pareto front is searched extensively by seeking the best value of the objective functions with random weighting generated. In more detail, it is updated as shown in the following equation:

$$x_{t+1}^i = x_t^{g^*} + \alpha \varepsilon_t^i,$$
$$g^* = \arg \min \phi(x),$$
$$\phi(x) = \sum_{k=1}^{N} w_k f_k(x),$$
$$\sum_{k=1}^{N} w_k = 1,$$

Table 4.7: Multi-objective functions.

	definition	range	pareto-front
Function1	$f_1 = x^2$ $f_2 = (x-2)^2$	$x \in [-10, 10]$	$f_2 = (\sqrt{f_1} - 2)^2$ $0 \leq f_1 \leq 4$
Function2	$f_1 = x_1$ $f_2 = g \times h$ $g = 1 + 10 \sum_{i=2}^{10} \dfrac{x_i}{9}$ $h = 1 - \left(\dfrac{f_1}{g}\right)^{0.25}$ $\quad - \dfrac{f_1}{g} \sin(10\pi f_1)$	$x_i \in [0, 1]$ $i = 1, \cdots, 10$	$f_2 = 1 - (f_1)^{0.25}$ $\quad - f_1 \sin(10\pi f_1)$

where N is the number of objective functions and $\alpha \varepsilon_t^i$ is a random perturbation term. Individuals that are not dominated by any other individual are attracted to the individual with the smallest random weighted sum. This weighted sum is obtained through w_k, i.e., a random coefficient scaled so that the sum is 1. Note that w_k is generated anew every time step.

Let us optimize the multi-objective function in Table 4.7. An example of optimizing the same function with VEGA is given in appendix A.1.

The results of multi-objective optimization with PSO and FA are shown below. Note that the same algorithm was run multiple times from different initial values. For all the Pareto candidates obtained from multiple runs, we check again whether they are Pareto solutions or not. If not, they are deleted. The final result is the total of all the remaining candidates.

Figure 4.21 shows the estimated and true Pareto fronts for Function1. For both algorithms, the maximum number of iterations is 50, the number of runs of the algorithm is 10, and the number of particles or fireflies is set to be 50. In both cases, we successfully obtain many Pareto solutions along the true Pareto front. At both ends of the Pareto front, fewer solutions are estimated, but this may be due to the limitation of the number by the σ value.

Figure 4.22 shows the results for Function2. For both algorithms, the maximum number of iterations is 100, the number of runs of the algorithm is 50, and the number of particles or fireflies is set to be 100. It can be seen that PSO captures the true Pareto front only in the part where f_1 is small, while FA captures it in a wide range.

In general, when using PSO, the particle swarm converged too quickly and the broad Pareto front could not be obtained. On the other hand, using FA, the convergence is relatively slow and the particles move finely in each iteration, so more Pareto fronts can be obtained.

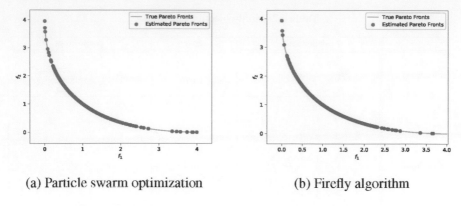

(a) Particle swarm optimization   (b) Firefly algorithm

Figure 4.21: Multi-objective optimization by swarms (Function1).

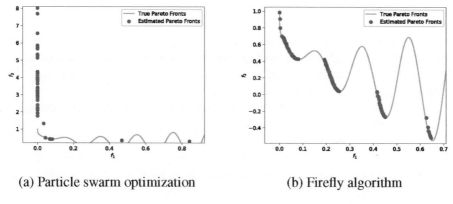

(a) Particle swarm optimization   (b) Firefly algorithm

Figure 4.22: Multi-objective optimization by swarms (Function2).

However, these are basic implementations and can be further improved. Therefore, each algorithm may perform differently in other functions.

Chapter 5

Deep Learning and Evolution

The artist El Greco had a reputation for painting his figures especially long and thin. It has been suggested that the reason for this is that he had a defect in his vision, which made everything appear stretched in the vertical direction. Do you think that is a plausible theory? (Richard Dawkins [31]).

5.1 CNN and Feature Extraction

When applied to image processing or text recognition, conventional neural networks tend to produce poor results in case of being translated, rotated, or distorted relative to the original training data. This is because these neural networks are trained using only raw data and ignore the topological features of the input data.

Convolutional neural networks (CNNs) were proposed to address this weakness. CNNs are based on the insight from neurobiology that the visual cortex includes neurons, the LGN-V1-V2-V4-IT layers (the ventral stream), that are both locationally and directionally selective. CNNs also hold promise as models of object recognition in the visual cortex. This approach involves modeling vision in terms of local receptive fields, simple cells, and complex cells. CNNs have their origins in the neocognitron approach proposed by Kunihiko Fukushima [42]. Another early model is LeNet [89].

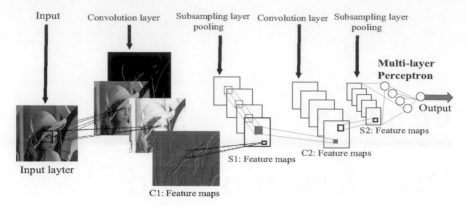

Figure 5.1: Example of a convolutional neural network (CNN).

CNNs are a type of multilayer feedforward neural network that can extract topological features from images, with training performed via backpropagation. The networks are designed so as to be able to recognize visual patterns directly from pixel images without hardly any pre-processing. This also allows handling patterns that can vary widely, such as handwritten text.

Figure 5.1 shows the configuration of a CNN, consisting of recursive C and S layers, as described below:

- C layers: Convolution layers to extract features.

- S layers: Pooling layers to achieve topological invariance with respect to shifts and distortions.

Each layer combines patterns from the preceding layer by integrating or smoothing them. Typically, a CNN can compress a large image into a small number of features that are robust to local deformation.

The C layers detect the same feature of an input image at different locations. This means that all of the neurons relating to a certain feature share the same weights (but with different biases). In this way, the preceding neuron responds to the same feature at different locations in the input. Then, if a certain neuron in a feature map fires, this is like matching a template (a pattern for extracting a feature). This is where convolution takes place (see Fig. 5.2). Convolution is a binary operation that calculates a sliding weighted sum of two functions, putting one function over another and summing the overlap. In two-dimensional image processing, this corresponds to multiplying the pixel values in the original image by a weighting matrix (known variously as a filter, mask, or kernel) and summing to obtain the results. This enables, for example, the original image to be softened or sharpened. Convolution is typically applied to a given pixel and its surrounding values, using a small filter matrix, often 3×3 pixels in size. This processing can be performed extremely quickly because pixels can be processed

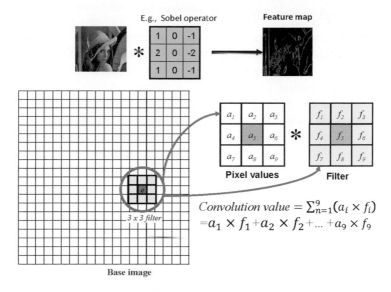

Figure 5.2: Example of convolution.

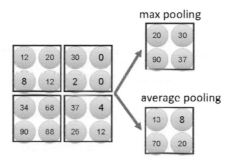

Figure 5.3: Example of a pooling layer.

in parallel. The C layer writes the results of the convolutions. This means that multiple feature maps can be generated by preparing a variety of filters.

The S layer reduces the spatial sensitivity of the feature map (Fig. 5.3). This makes it possible to achieve robustness against a certain degree of shifts and distortions. The goal is to group features with similar meanings. Weight sharing is applied at this layer as well, and this makes it possible to reduce the effects of noise. The S layer performs data compression and smoothing. In other words, this achieves robustness so that the output to the C layer is the same even when there are variations in the input to the S layer, such as small shifts. Normally this processing finds the average or maximum value of a pattern without any overlaps. This layer of processing is known as the pooling layer because it pools the output from the S layer neurons and outputs it to the C layer.

These two layers are normally created manually rather than trained. Thereafter, supervised learning is performed using training data [89]. This means that there is a requirement for a certain degree of regularity and continuity in the input data. Real world images have these kinds of features, and so statistical features can be expected to persist.

Let us take another look at the CNN processing shown in Fig. 5.1. The input image is convolved using three trainable filters and biases to generate four feature maps in the C1 layer. Each group of four pixels in the feature map is weighted and added to the bias values to generate four feature maps in the S1 layer via a sigmoid function. Filters are once again applied to these to generate the C2 level. S2 is generated in the same way as S1, and finally these pixel values are passed as input to a normal neural network.

Sparse coding, i.e., a numerical model of processing biological visual information, is related to the CNN mechanism. Sparse coding uses a small set of basis vectors chosen such that the given images can be expressed as linear combinations of these basis vectors. In other words, sparse coding extracts a small amount of information essential for forming a concept from the large amount of information that has been input to the neural network. As CNNs are given hidden layers of increasing depth, they express concepts with higher dimensionality, moving from the points in an image to lines, from lines to outlines, from outlines to parts, and from parts to the whole image.

Some researchers have attempted to train CNNs to extract high-level features, such as cats or human faces, from large volumes of images [88]. The network used in [88] had nine layers, consisting of three subnetworks, each with three layers and a pooling function. Ten million images were input, and the network was trained using an autoencoder [63]. As a result, the network succeeded in recognizing a wide range of objects, such as faces and cats. This recognition device also had a certain degree of robustness against variations such as rotation, scaling, or translation. Moreover, neurons have been formed that seem to respond specifically to high-level features, such as faces. The average features of many faces (a large amount of training data) are captured well. This can be thought of as the internal representation of the neural network obtained by face training.

This network is assumed to have about ten million parameters that need to be trained. In contrast, the neurons and synapses in the human visual cortex have a million times as many parameters as this. This fact should give a sense of the practicality of the model. However, it took 1000 cluster machines (with 16,000 cores) three days to train the network. This is an extraordinary amount of calculations.

The following methods were used to reduce overfitting, which might otherwise be a problem. These are called regularization.

■ Data augmentation: Increasing the number of training items by randomly cutting a relatively small image from the original image and then shifting or horizontally reflecting it to form the mirror image. Images where the RGB intensities have been changed slightly are also created.[1]

■ Drop out: The output from nodes in hidden layers are set to 0 at random (with a probability of 0.5). Zeroed nodes do not contribute to the output of downstream nodes, and so do not participate in backpropagation. In this way, training is performed with a different architecture every time input is presented.

■ Reduce weights: Large weights tend to cause overlearning. Thus, a penalty is imposed to prevent them from becoming too large. L2 norm normalization (the penalty is the sum of the squares of the weights, see 146 page) is often used.

Srivastava proposed dropout as a method for preventing the overtraining of neural networks [131]. In dropouts, by deactivating all elements of input in each layer at a certain probability during neural network learning, partial structures of the large networks are extracted, and targeted for learning. Let us consider a neural network that calculates the output $y \in \mathbb{R}^n$ with the activation function f, bias $b \in \mathbb{R}^n$, weight $W \in \mathbb{R}^{n \times m}$, and input $x \in \mathbb{R}^m$ as described below:

$$y = f(Wx + b). \tag{5.1}$$

When applying a dropout at this time, we use the following equation:

$$y = f(W(x \odot z) + b), \tag{5.2}$$

where $z \in \mathbb{R}^m$ is the dropout mask, and each element is a vertical vector that is either 0 or 1 at a set probability. By using a partial structure that is dropped out at the time of network evaluation, overtraining can be reduced.

It is assumed that applying dropouts to a forward propagation-type neural network will yield good results. On one hand, there were many cases of bad results when simply applying dropouts to recurrent neural networks that have feedback coupling. Gal and Ghahramani proposed a method of applying dropouts to recurrent neural networks by theoretically analyzing dropouts [44]. In this method, moderately good results were reported when using the same dropout mask across the board when inputting a series of data.

In dropouts, the input of all layers of the neural network was focused on de-activating some parts. On the other hand, focusing on the connection (weight) of neural networks while deactivating some parts is known as a drop connect [145]. By applying a drop connect to the neural network in eq. (5.1), it comes to resemble the following equation:

$$y = f((W \odot Z)x + b), \tag{5.3}$$

---

[1] Principal component analysis of the RGB values in the data set is performed and then random changes are made, centered on these axes, thereby preserving the essential features of the original natural images.

where $\mathbf{Z} \in \mathbb{R}^{n \times m}$ is a matrix where each element of the dropout max will be either 0 or 1 at a certain probability. Drop connects have generalized dropouts, and in many cases, yield better results than dropouts.

Merity et al. has applied drop connects to LSTM feedback connectors to prevent overtraining of LSTM [97]. Drop connects are said to have enabled fast LSTM learning while preventing overtraining.

5.2 Autoencoders

The extraction of internal representation in neural networks has been largely studied. Since the compression rate is not that high in relation to the encoder issue, it was not paid much attention in practical terms. However, recently, it has attracted attention as a pre-learning method for networks with many layers. This method is called an autoencoder. Additionally, a method called a stacked autoencoder, where data is compressed and learning is recursively repeated in multi-layered hierarchical networks, has been proposed and applied to various issues like image processing.

The performance of an autoencoder can be evaluated using the reconfiguration error calculated as the difference between the original and encoded-decoded data.

An example of an autoencoder is shown in Fig. 5.4 [63]. This is a 625-2,000-1,000-500-30 autoencoder (see (c) of the figure). There are 625 nodes in the input layer, 2,000 nodes in the next hidden layer, and 1,000, 500, and 30 nodes below that. After that, decoding (extraction) works in the opposite direction from the hidden layers of 500 nodes, 1,000 nodes, 2,000 nodes and performs learning to output the same data as the input. There are the same number of nodes in the output layer as the input layer, i.e., 625.

In autoencoder learning, feature extractors per layer are learned based on the per-layer pre-learning of RBM[2] (see Fig. 5.4(a)). First the synaptic weights W^1 between the 2,000-node hidden layer and the visible layer (input layer) are learned by means of backpropagation or Boltzmann machine learning algorithms. Additionally, this hidden layer is falsely considered to be the visible layer, and the synaptic weight W^2 with the 1,000-node hidden layer is learned. The synaptic weights W^3 and W^4 are also learned in a similar manner. Here, the encoder learning ends. Next, the obtained weights are extracted and the decoder is formed. For that, the (transposition of) weights that are learned in Fig. 5.4(b) is used in principle. After that, backpropagation is used and the weights are fine-tuned to output the same images as the input images (Fig. 5.4(c)).

Figure 5.5(a) shows the result of using the 784-1,000-500-250-30 autoencoder trained to recognize handwritten digits. After training with 60,000 digits

---

[2] Restricted Boltzmann Machine. A two-layer network consisting of a visible layer and a hidden layer, connected only between the visible and invisible layers (no connection between visible layers and between invisible layers).

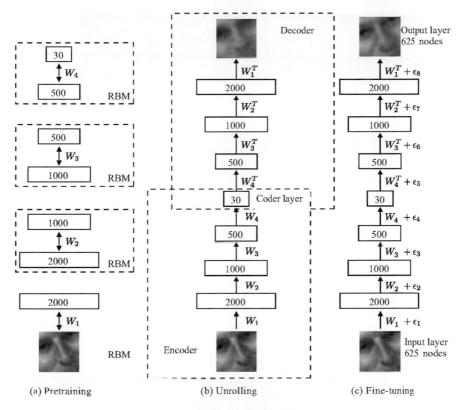

(a) Pretraining   (b) Unrolling   (c) Fine-tuning

Figure 5.4: Autoencoder [63].

from the MNIST dataset[3], the autoencoder was able to successfully recognize 10,000 digits from the test set with an error rate of 1.2%. In contrast, the error rate was 1.6% and 1.4% when applying a network trained using backpropagation and SVM, respectively, showing improvement upon previous methods. Visualizing the obtained internal representation as a two-dimensional layer resulted in Fig. 5.6. It can be noticed from the figure that the digits are plotted in separate places, and a reconstructed representation is obtained to some extent.

Figure 5.5(b) shows the results of recognizing face images[4] using the 625-2,000-1,000-500-30 autoencoder.

Originally, autoencoders were considered to be a method of compressing information and were used as a bottleneck, i.e., $d_h < d_x$, where d_h is the number of nodes in the hidden layer (coded layer), d_x is the number of nodes in the input layer. However, with the success of RBM, it was preferred to handle over-complete cases (i.e., $d_h > d_x$). Recently, the normalization method has also seen

---

[3]http://yann.lecun.com/exdb/mnist/index.html
[4]Olivetti face data, https://cs.nyu.edu/~roweis/data.html

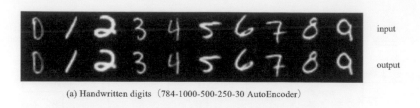

(a) Handwritten digits （784-1000-500-250-30 AutoEncoder）

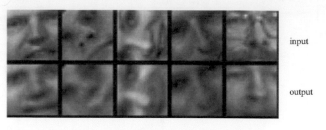

(b) Face images （625-2000-1000-500-30 AutoEncoder）

Figure 5.5: Results using autoencoder [63].

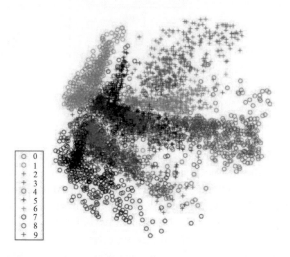

Figure 5.6: Internal representation using autoencoder [63].

frequent use. By introducing restrictions, the aim is to obtain rough (set) representations from input. As a result, there will likely be a lower level of freedom in the representations, resulting in representations with strong noise [18]. Additionally, a method of obtaining more versatile results through the application of random noise, and by performing pre-learning on input data during learning, has been proposed. This is called a noise removal autoencoder.

Variational AutoEncoder (VAE) [75, 32] is a generative model using neural networks. By capturing the latent representation of the data, it is possible to

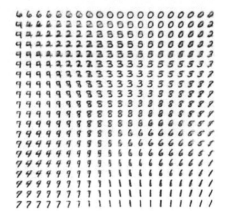

Figure 5.7: Handwritten digits generated by VAE [75].

generate new data that does not exist in the original data set (see Fig. 5.7). In variational autoencoders (VAEs), every latent variable z follows the standard normal distribution independently, while the conditional probability of the latent variable z for input x follows the multivariate normal distribution determined based on covariance matrix $\Sigma(x)$ and average vector $\mu(x)$. The purpose of training VAEs is to estimate the probability distribution $Pr(x \mid z)$ of x that is generated from z.

Figure 5.8 illustrates the VAE structures comprising an encoder representing the probability distribution $Pr(z \mid x)$ of a latent variable z given a generated input data x and a decoder representing the probability distribution $Pr(x \mid z)$ of data x given z.

The probability distribution of the latent variable z is generated by passing the encoder from the input x. Particularly, the average vector μ and covariance matrix Σ of the predicted multivariate normal distribution $\mathcal{N}(\mu, \Sigma)$ are output.

In the decoder, sampling is performed from the distribution $\mathcal{N}(\mu, \Sigma)$ generated by the encoder, which is then set as the input. The output data x' is trained to approach the values of the original data x. The loss function in VAE can be expressed as follows:

$$\mathbb{E}_{x \sim data}[\mathbb{E}_{z \sim Q}[\log Pr(x \mid z)] - KL(Q(z \mid x) \| Pr(z))],$$

where Q is similar to $Pr(z \mid x)$ generated by the encoder and KL denotes the Kullback–Leibler information quantity, which shows how close two probability distributions are. The first term denotes the error related to data reconfiguration, while the second term denotes the error related to the approximation of the pre-distribution of z. These are learned using backpropagation in the same way as in normal autoencoders.

By providing the decoder with a latent variable sampled from a standard multivariate normal distribution of the same dimension as input, new data can be

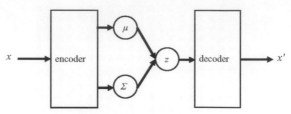

Figure 5.8: VAE structure.

generated from the learned VAE. This is the basic principle of VAE-EDA, which is explained in Section 6.2.

5.3 Let us Fool the Neural Network

5.3.1 Generative Adversary Networks: GAN

Deep learning as a generation model has yielded very interesting results in recent years. In particular, the GAN [48] proposed by Goodfellow et al. facilitates the generation of a much clearer image than the variational autoencoder, which had hitherto been known as the generation model. Thereafter, assorted variations, including the deep convolutional generative adversarial networks (DCGAN) [115] and variational autoencoder with GAN (VAEGAN) [86], have been proposed.

DCGAN is a generation model extended in a form that specializes the generative adversarial network (GAN) to image generation (see Fig. 5.9). In the GAN, the discriminator and generator learning machines are used to learn the shape of the distribution itself without being given the distribution of the training data set in advance, thereby developing the generator to generate data that are indistinguishable from the learning data set. A random number z sampled from a uniform distribution is input into the generator, and x is generated with this as a seed. The discriminator, a classifier that determines whether an input is derived from the learning data set or is generated by the generator, enables the generator to learn. In the DCGAN, the discriminator uses a normal CNN and the generator uses a reverse CNN starting from z.

More formally, GAN is described as follows. CNNs serve as the model for network architecture. The generator is expressed as $G(z; \theta_g)$, wherein the parameter is θ_g and the discriminator is represented as $D(x; \theta_d)$, where the parameter is θ_d. The generator returns image output x for the input of latent variable z, and the discriminator determines whether something is fake or real in response to image input x. At this time, if the object is determined to be close to real, a value near 1 is output, and if it is determined to be fake, a value near 0 is output. Latent variables are often generated using uniform or normal distribution. In response to generators and discriminators, loss is calculated with the loss function, and the weight is modified to minimize that value. The loss function is expressed with

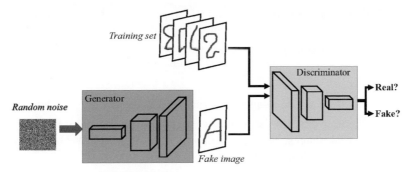

Figure 5.9: Generative adversary networks.

the following formula:

$$\min_{G} \max_{D} V(D, G) = \underset{x \sim p_{data}(x)}{\mathrm{E}}[\log D(x)] + \underset{x \sim p_z(z)}{\mathrm{E}}[\log(1 - D(G(z)))], \quad (5.4)$$

where z represents a random number and "data" represents the training data. Furthermore, $D(x)$ is the discriminator output and $G(x)$ is the generator output. p_{data} is the training data distribution, and p_z is the random numbers' distribution. E shows the expected value(s).

Let us consider the significance of this loss function. When a true image x is given to discriminator D, if it is correctly estimated as $D(x) = 1$, the first term on the right side is maximized. However, when the image $G(z)$ is given for D, and $D(G(z))$ is correctly estimated as 0, the second term on the right side is also maximized. This is the meaning of the objective function of D (maximization). Next, let us look at the generator G. The objective function of G is as follows:

$$\min_{G} V(D, G) - \underset{x \sim p_z(z)}{\mathrm{E}}[\log(1 - D(G(z)))]. \quad (5.5)$$

If G manages to cheat D, then $D(G(z)) = 1$, and the right side of eq. (5.5) is minimized. This signifies the min/max optimization of eq. (5.4).

DCGAN has the problem of mode collapse[5], in addition to the vanishing gradient problem, when the generator's performance can no longer improve despite the improvement of the discriminatory ability of the discriminator, which causes instability.

In the vanishing gradient problem, the loss approaches 0, without limit, because the discriminator's capability has improved, causing insufficient feedback for the neural network. Wasserstein GAN (WGAN) [3] was proposed to resolve this issue. In WGAN, the loss function is defined based on the Wasserstein distance between probability densities such that the feedback is effective even when

---

[5] A problem that leads to outputting only a few different results. This is due to the fact that the generator can only estimate a few maxima of the probability distribution of the data GAN should generate.

the discriminator (known as the "critic") is approaching the optimal value. The revised loss function is specifically defined as follows:

$$L = \mathop{\mathrm{E}}_{\tilde{x} \sim p_g} [D(\tilde{x})] - \mathop{\mathrm{E}}_{x \sim p_r} [D(x)], \tag{5.6}$$

where p_g denotes a set of images generated by the generator; p_r denotes a set of actual images; $\tilde{x}$ denotes the images generated from the latent variable z; and x denotes the real images. This loss function is minimized in WGAN. Note that log is not used in this loss function.

Additionally, the values output from the discriminator are restricted to range between 0 and 1, since the sigmoid function is passed at the end of the neural network in DCGAN but that sigmoid function does not exist in WGAN. Thus, the range of values output by the discriminator expands to all real numbers. Especially, since $D(x)$ does not signify discriminatory results in WGAN, it is called a critic instead of a discriminator.

Wu et al. [150] succeeded in generating 3D models with their voxel representation in the GAN part of DCGAN. The neural network used in this study includes five CNN layers, with a kernel size of $4 \times 4 \times 4$, a stride of 2, and the ReLU activation function[6].

5.3.2 Generating Fooling Images

DNNs can recognize images with high reliability, but DNNs can be easily deceived. For example, Zhang et al. [156] trained the CIFAR10 dataset[7] with randomly varying labels (class names) and pixel values. Specifically, they compared the following methods:

- true labels: Use the original unmodified dataset.

- random labels: Change all labels randomly.

- pixel shuffle: Pick pixel positions randomly and swap the order randomly. The same reordering is applied to all images in the training and test examples.

- random pixels: Apply a random pixel permutation to each image independently.

- Gaussian pixels: Generate pixel values randomly by a Gaussian distribution and replace the image. The mean and variance of the Gaussian distribution is determined from the original image.

---

[6]Rectified linear unit. It is defined as $f(x) = \max(0,x)$.
[7]https://www.cs.toronto.edu/~kriz/cifar.html.

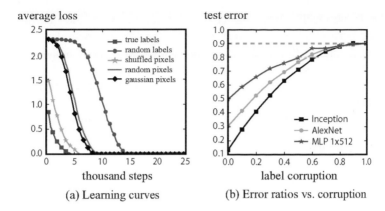

<figure>

average loss

test error

true labels
random labels
shuffled pixels
random pixels
gaussian pixels

thousand steps

Inception
AlexNet
MLP 1x512

label corruption

(a) Learning curves

(b) Error ratios vs. corruption

</figure>

Figure 5.10: Learning results for random labels and random pixels in CIFAR10 [156].

Figure 5.10 shows the learning results for each method. (a) shows the learning curve (showing the training loss at each training step) when using Inception V3[8]. Surprisingly, even with random labeling, the learning was accurate. Note that the random labels completely break the relationship between image and class. Even when shuffling pixels to break the structure of the image, or sampling from a Gaussian distribution, learning was a success.

With random labels, the label of the training example will change and become uncorrelated with the class. Thus, it is necessary to propagate a large prediction error, resulting in a long time to learn. However, since the labels themselves are fixed and consistent, they can be learned after all. Once learning starts, the learning converges to the correct answer quickly. In a sense, this can be regarded as overfitting. Generating a noise perturbation by pixel replacement or Gaussian distribution results in faster convergence than random labeling. This may be because random pixels are more separated and easier to learn than natural images (which were originally of the same class).

Figure 5.10(b) shows the test error after convergence. The deep learning models used here are Inception, AlexNet [84], and MLP (Multilayer Perceptron). The error in the training example is always zero so that the test error means the generalization error. Since the noise level becomes 1.0, the generalization error is approaching 90%[9].

In addition, the same results were obtained with the regularization method (see 136 page) for random labeling. This means that there is a limit to the effect of the regularization method on generalization. This raises important questions about the traditional statistical learning theory that explains generalization ability in deep learning. We look forward to further research in this area.

---

[8]Convolutional neural network trained with the ImageNet database [138].

[9]Note that CIFAR10 consists of 10 classes. Thus, the percentage of random answers will be 10% correct.

The above results show that changes in the pixels of the training example affect the performance of the test example. Fooling the neural network in this way and degrading the performance are called adversarial attacks. For example, Su et al. have successfully generated a single-pixel attack using differential evolution [136]. In the following, we will introduce their research on generating adversarial attacks using evolutionary computation.

Yamazaki et al. formulated image processing as the following problem [24]:

■ Traning data: $X_{training} = \{x_i, y_i\}$

■ Test data: $X_{test} = \{x_i, y_i\}$

■ x: Input image vector, y: Class, N_c: Number of classes($y \in \{1, 2, \cdots, N_c\}$)

Now consider adding noise to the image as follows. This is called a noise perturbation.

$$x_k^{noise} = x_k + \eta_k, \tag{5.7}$$

where the noise vector η should satisfy the following conditions:

$$\min_{y_i \neq y_j} \max_{y_i = y_j} \sum_{i,j} < \eta_i, \eta_j >, \tag{5.8}$$

$$| \eta_i |_{L_0} \leq N_p, \tag{5.9}$$

$$| \eta_i |_{L_\infty} \leq \varepsilon, \tag{5.10}$$

where $<,>$ is the inner product of vectors. The definition of the norm is as follows:

$$
\begin{aligned}
L_1 \text{ norm} \quad &: \quad |x_1| + |x_2| + \cdots + |x_n| \\
L_2 \text{ norm} \quad &: \quad \sqrt{x_1^2 + x_2^2 + \cdots + x_n^2} \\
L_\infty \text{ norm} \quad &: \quad \max\{|x_1|, |x_2|, \cdots, |x_n|\}
\end{aligned}
$$

Equation (5.9) indicates the maximum number of pixels to be replaced as noise, and eq. (5.10) defines the maximum number of values that can be given as noise.

The optimal solution to eq. (5.8) is a vector that increases the differences between different classes while decreasing the differences within the same class.

As a result, the optimal one is a vector that is identical for each class and orthogonal between the different classes. Therefore, in the following, we assume a noise vector described below:

$$x_k^{noise} = x_k + \eta^c \text{ where } y_k = c. \tag{5.11}$$

Now consider a neural network learned with training data destroyed by noise perturbation. Is it possible that the network has a high error rate on test images that are not destroyed?

To find such training data, CMA-ES (see Section 3.2) is used to evolve the noise generator.

The fitness of CMA-ES consists of the following two components:

■ low empirical risk: minimizing the false positive rate for the training sample ple

■ high goal risk: maximizing the generalization error (the false response rate to test data)

The goal of normal learning is to minimize the target risk. However, we only know the empirical risk in this case. Here, on the other hand, in addition to minimizing the empirical risk, we are trying to maximize the target risk, so that we can maximize the generalization gap[10]. For this purpose, we use the divergence score between probability distributions.

The genotype used in CMA-ES is a parameter of a high-dimensional Gaussian distribution. The image noise vector η is generated according to this distribution. However, for simplicity, we assume that the noise is the same for each class. The noise vector contains the position of the image and the change value of the pixel. In each generation of the evolutionary computation, the noise generation parameters (obtained as genotypes) are used to generate a corrupted image, which is used to train the CNN and calculate the fitness value. The deception rate is defined as follows:

$$100\% - \text{correct classification rate.} \qquad (5.12)$$

By using the training data evolved by CMA-ES, the adversary attack experiment has been conducted.

Figure 5.11 shows an example of noisy training data evolved at the 250th generations (for different ε and N_p values). Table 5.1 shows the classification accuracies for the test data. The more ε and N_p are increased, the worse the accuracy rate becomes. In other words, the accuracy decreases from 99% to 47% for the MNIST dataset, whereas the decrease is from 72% to 15% for the CIFAR10 dataset. We can see that $\varepsilon = 0$ and $N_p = 20$ resulted in the worst accuracy rate. Figure 5.12 plots the performance on the test data for each generation (averaged over three times for MNIST). In the early generations, the accuracy rate was 61%, but after 200 generations, the worst was 21% (see (a)). The generalization gap increases with the number of generations (see (b)). This noise is not easily perceptible by humans, as shown in Fig. 5.11. Complex datasets such as CIFAR100 and ImageNet [84] seem to be more gullible than simple MNIST data sets. This means that training images have specific spatial locations that are vulnerable to attack.

---

[10]In general, minimizing the training error does not necessarily result in minimizing the generalization error; the difference between the two errors is called "generalization gap."

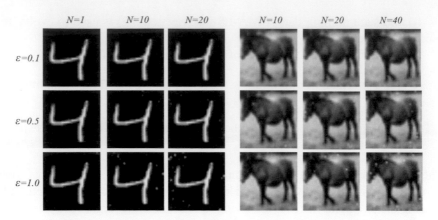

Figure 5.11: Evolved image examples (see eq. (5.9) for ε and eq. (5.10) for N_p) [24].

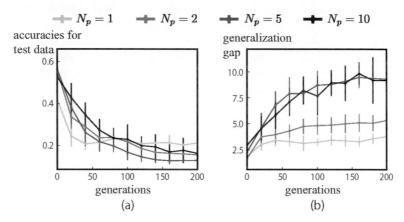

Figure 5.12: Test data performance for different N_p values (MNIST) [24].

Table 5.1: Comparison of accuracy rates.

	MNIST				CIFAR10		
ε	$N_p = 1$	$N_p = 2$	$N_p = 10$	$N_p = 20$	$N_p = 10$	$N_p = 20$	$N_p = 40$
0.01	99	99	99	99	72	70	71
0.05	99	98	82	91	71	57	40
0.1	82	87	70	47/5	33	31	27
0.5	54	73/8	64	66	19	21	15
1.0	58	66	55	52	15	17	16

In the following, we will take a different direction. We discuss the generation of images and sounds that fool the deep learning model.

As shown in Fig. 5.13, research conducted by Nguyen et al. [105] indicated that both the images of the actual objects (left) and patterns of the objects (right)

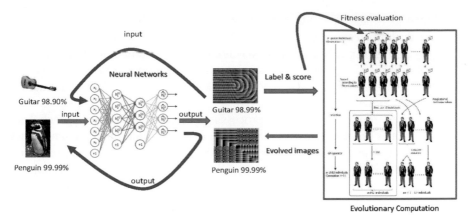

Figure 5.13: How to fool the deep learning model.

are recognized by DNN as being either a "guitar" or "penguin" with 99.9% confidence. In other words, although the images on the right are only a meaningless pattern for human beings, DNN recognizes them as meaningful objects.

The pattern on the right is a synthesized fooling image generated by GA, and the details of the generation process are as follows.

Step1 Express images as genotypes, and carry out crossover and mutations.
Step2 The new image is identified by the DNN model, and the reliability of the recognition result is used as the fitness value.
Step3 Select individuals (i.e., images) showing a high recognition level for all classes and use them for generating of the next generation.

An ordinary GA selects only solutions with high fitness in the target class in order to search for the optimal solution. For example, when the goal is to recognize an object as a "guitar," an image recognized to be a "guitar" and having high recognition reliability is selected. Meanwhile, when generating a fooling image, an image showing high reliability in all classes including the target class is selected, rather than an image with high recognition reliability in the target class. For example, when the aim is to generate a fooling image of a guitar, an image was selected that showed high reliability in all classes, including "guitar," "violin," and "biwa" at the same time, rather than an image showing high reliability as a "guitar."

In this study, the genotype of an image based on pixel unit or CPPN (see Section 5.9) was used. Evolutionary computation resulted in the successful generation of white noise and striped pattern fooling images, demonstrating the vulnerability of the DNN model.

Figure 5.14 shows synthesized images by means of evolutionary computation. To the human eye, the image appears to be a mere noise or pattern. However, CNN trained on ImageNet recognized it as some kind of object with a confidence level of over 99.6%. In other words, evolutionary computation can successfully generate fooling images of white noise and stripes. This shows the vulnerability of the DNN model.

In our research [154], a similar process is applied to the original speech data, and an attempt is made to synthesize speech that a computer can recognize, but humans cannot understand. In this experiment, false-positive speech has been synthesized using GA. It was experimentally shown that even for sounds that are heard only as white noise by a human, computers can recognize a meaningful word with high reliability.

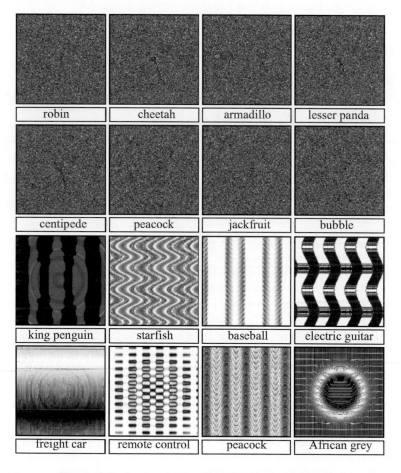

Figure 5.14: Images that fool deep learning models [105].

In the following experiments, we will use Julius[11]. Julius is an open source engine for the development of speech recognition systems and is capable of general-purpose large-vocabulary continuous speech recognition. GMM (Gaussian Mixture Model) and DNN based recognition models are provided as acoustic modeling for Japanese recognition.

In order to generate a deceptive voice that is as unrecognizable as possible to humans, the voice with the third highest recognition result (confidence level) is selected for the next generation.

In the experiment, the MFCC information[12] of speech is used as the genotype for evolutionary computation. Even though MFCCs are similar, some speech sounds are quite different to human hearing. Thus, by applying certain transformations to MFC, we can synthesize speech that has some confidence in speech recognition tools, but sounds like white noise to humans. In other words, the white noise tricks the speech recognition tool into misinterpreting it as meaningful sounds, letters, or text.

Figure 5.15 shows the evolutionary process of fooling speech recognized as the target word ("material"). The horizontal axis is the number of generations and the vertical axis is the confidence level. The left side in Fig. 5.15 corresponds to generation 0, i.e., the confidence level of the original speech. As the number of generations increases, the reliability of the word does not decrease.

Figures 5.16~5.18 show the first three dimensions of the MFCC for speech. The "origin," "20," and "50" are the MFCCs of the original voice and the fooling voice obtained in the 20th and 50th generation, respectively. It can be seen that the MFCC data of the fooling voice has finer vibrations than the original voice. Especially in the first dimension of the MFCC, the oscillations become more intense as the number of generations increases. On the other hand, looking at the data in the second dimension, we can see that the overall value of the fooling voice is approaching zero. In the third dimension, there is less change with generations. If we listen to the voices, we can see that they are indeed becoming more cluttered as the generations progress.

Unlike the human ear, the computer understands sound information based on features such as the ones shown here. Therefore, there are situations where the computer recognizes the sound, but the human can only hear it as noise. As more and more devices are operated by voice, they may be operated incorrectly without the human's knowledge, or they may become malware. It may also be possible to generate cryptic voice that humans cannot recognize by means of fooling voices.

---

[11] https://julius.osdn.jp/.

[12] The frequency spectrum of speech is converted to the Mel scale (a psychological measure of the pitch of a sound), which is called the Mel frequency spectrum. The inverse Fourier transform of the Mel frequency spectrum gives the distribution of the frequency features of speech. This is called Mel frequency cepstrum (MFC). MFCC (Mel-frequency cepstral coefficients) is a discrete sequence representation of the MFC.

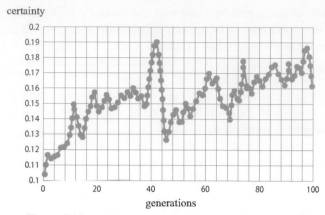

Figure 5.15: Evolutionary transitions in word confidence.

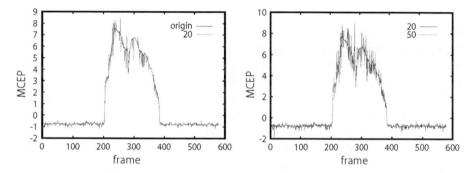

Figure 5.16: The first dimension of the MFCC in "material".

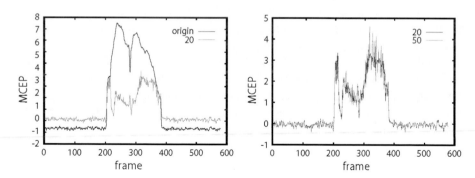

Figure 5.17: The second dimension of the MFCC in "material".

5.4   LSTM

A recurrent neural network (RNN) is a network that allows connections to itself and cyclical connections. Since RNNs can use an internal memory state, they are

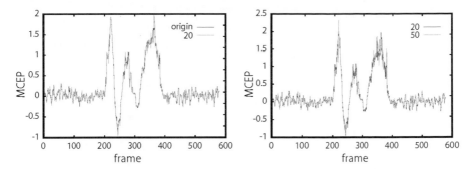

Figure 5.18: The third dimension of the MFCC in "material".

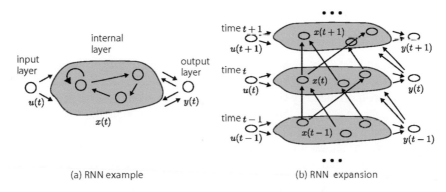

(a) RNN example

(b) RNN expansion

Figure 5.19: Recurrent neural network (RNN).

frequently used to handle temporal sequences of data. For example, the RNN in Fig. 5.19(a) allows interconnections in its hidden layers. Let the state vector of a hidden layer at time t be $x(t)$, and the state vectors of the input and output layers be $u(t)$ and $y(t)$, respectively. RNNs are often used for natural language processing and speech recognition, because they are suitable for predicting the next word based on past words and utterances. Some studies are also being conducted to address the problem of machine translation using autoencoders for word prediction [6].

Since RNN contains loops, backpropagation cannot be applied. Therefore, RNN is rolled out in the time direction to form a normal feedforward network. For example, Fig. 5.19(b) illustrates that the connection between hidden layers at time t in this case can be regarded as the connection between the hidden layer at time t and the hidden layer at time $t + 1$, making it possible to apply backpropagation. However, the network may become too large using this method, leading to unsuccessful learning due to expansion in the time direction. This is known as the error vanishing (exploding) problem, where backpropagation takes

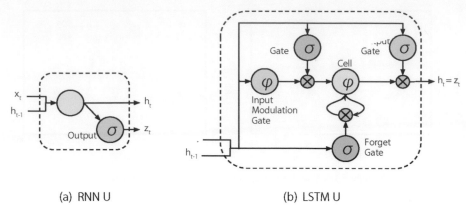

(a) RNN U

(b) LSTM U

Figure 5.20: Long short-term memory (LSTM).

a long path, and the error disappears or increases. Due to this problem, learning becomes difficult when time lags exceed 5–10 units.

Long short-term memory (LSTM) has been proposed to resolve this problem. LSTM has a forget gate regulating whether to forget or update the state of hidden layers up until a given time.

Figure 5.20(a) shows a typical RNN structure. Here the input x_t, output z_t, and hidden layers' state vector h_t at time t are defined as follows:

$$h_t = \sigma(W_{xh}x_t + W_{hh}h_{t-1} + b_h), \qquad (5.13)$$

$$z_t = \sigma(W_{hz}h_t + b_z), \qquad (5.14)$$

where σ denotes the sigmoid function $\sigma(x) = (1 + e^{-x})^{-1}$; h_t is the N-dimensional vector in relation to N hidden layer nodes; W_{xh} and W_{hz} denote the weights between the input and hidden layers and hidden and output layers, respectively; W_{hh} denotes the matrix of weights between hidden layer(s); and b_h and b_z denote the bias values of the hidden and output layer node(s), respectively. When initializing RNN such that $h_0 = 0$, and given the input column $x_1, x_2, \cdots$, then $h_1, y_1, h_2, y_2, \cdots$ is calculated sequentially.

Let the numbers of dimensions of the input and output layers be m and n, respectively. Figure 5.20(b) shows the structure of LSTM [33], which includes the following elements:

■ $x_t \in \mathbb{R}^m$: input to the layer at time t,

■ $h_t \in \mathbb{R}^n$: hidden layer state vector of time t,

■ $i_t \in \mathbb{R}^n$: input gate of time t,

■ $f_t \in \mathbb{R}^n$: forget gate of time t,

■ $o_t \in \mathbb{R}^n$: output gate of time t,

- $z_t \in \mathbb{R}^n$: input adjustment gate of time t, i.e., input to memory cell,

- $c_t \in \mathbb{R}^n$: memory cell of time t.

Memory cell c_t is the sum of the information of the past memory cell c_{t-1}, which was adjusted in f_t, and z_t, which was adjusted with input i_t. Note that z_t is a function of the current input and past hidden layer state. It is expressed as follows in more detail:

$$i_t = \sigma(W_i x_t + R_i h_{t-1} + b_i), \tag{5.15}$$
$$f_t = \sigma(W_f x_t + R_f h_{t-1} + b_f), \tag{5.16}$$
$$o_t = \sigma(W_o x_t + R_o h_{t-1} + b_o), \tag{5.17}$$
$$z_t = \phi(W_z x_t + R_z h_{t-1} + b_c), \tag{5.18}$$
$$c_t = f_t \odot c_{t-1} + i_t \odot z_t, \tag{5.19}$$
$$h_t = o_t \odot \phi(c_t), \tag{5.20}$$

where ϕ denotes the hyperbolic tangent function $\phi(x) = \frac{e^x - e^{-x}}{e^x + e^{-x}} = 2\sigma(2x) - 1$, with the input value ranging between -1 and $+1$, and $\odot$ denotes the product per element[13]. The trainable parameters in an LSTM layer are the feedforward weights $W_z, W_i, W_f, W_o \in \mathbb{R}^{n \times m}$, the recurrent weights $R_z, R_i, R_f, R_o \in \mathbb{R}^{n \times n}$, and the biases $b_z, b_i, b_f, b_o \in \mathbb{R}^n$. They are trained using the method called truncated backpropagation through time, where the loop structure of LSTM is unrolled for a finite length of time, and backpropagation is applied just like normal feedforward neural networks.

LSTM's i_t and f_t control the learning process by choosing either to consider the current input or to forget the past information. Similarly, the output gate o_t learns how many memory cells to move to a hidden state. Hence, LSTM succeeds in long-term learning while reducing errors by applying a feedback structure[14]. Through this, the issue of error vanishing is resolved, and long-term time lags of about 1,000 units can be handled.

As a result, LSTM has been successfully applied to voice recognition and machine translation. Additionally, the technique of using long-term recurrent computational networks along with convolutional neural networks (CNN, see Section 5.1) has been proposed [33]. Through this method, variable-length image input can be handled by supplying CNN output to LSTM.

Furthermore, a method of expanding RNN via memory modules has recently been proposed. Within that, there is interesting research on neural Turing machine (NTM) [52]. This network has tape-shaped memory where RNN can both read and write. Thus, NTM is not just a simple memory device, but can execute

---

[13] Hadamard product (element-wise product), i.e., $(a_1, \cdots, a_n) \odot (b_1, \cdots, b_n) = (a_1 \times b_1, \cdots, a_n \times b_n)$.

[14] The original LSTM architecture [64] only included input and output gates; as a result, errors frequently increased explosively. The additional forget gate allows to address this problem by discarding unnecessary information.

tasks like copying, associative recall, and sorting that normally require symbolic reasoning.

Traditionally, the symbolist approach was used for Turing machines and machine translation. However, when looking at the success stories of RNN in terms of the aforementioned machine translation or NTM, the usefulness of neural networks and distributed representation is apparent. Thus, the use of non-linearity in large weight matrices and activation vectors, which are quick and intuitive, has been promoted in combination with logical inferences. The success of neural networks causes one to feel immense doubt toward the suitability of relying on symbols, such as in terms of whether to necessitate internal symbols that operate via inference rules, to understand a sentence.

Dropout [131] can be applied to LSTM layers to prevent overfitting [44]. When dropout is applied, some elements of the input of each layer is randomly deactivated with a certain probability (dropout rate $p \in (0,1)$) during training. The network is trained with some noise, and thus becomes more robust. It can also be considered as training substructures of the network and using the whole network as the ensemble of the trained substructures.

Calculation of an LSTM layer with dropout during training is done by using (5.21) and (5.22) instead of (5.15)–(5.18), where $*$ can be i, f, or o. Here, $m_x \in \mathbb{R}^m$ and $m_h \in \mathbb{R}^n$ are dropout masks and each element of them is either 0 with a probability of p or $1/(1-p)$ with a probability of $(1-p)$. Dropout masks m_x and m_h are independent of time t, and the same masks are used for the entire sequence of input.

$$z_t = \phi\left(W_z\left(x_t \odot m_x\right) + R_z\left(h_{t-1} \odot m_h\right) + b_z\right) \tag{5.21}$$

$$*_t = \sigma\left(W_*\left(x_t \odot m_x\right) + R_*\left(h_{t-1} \odot m_h\right) + b_*\right) \tag{5.22}$$

Dropconnect [145] can also be applied to LSTM layers to prevent overfitting [97]. This method is a generalization of dropout, and it gave better results in many cases. While dropout focuses on the input of each layer and deactivates a part of it, dropconnect focuses on the connections (weights) of the network and deactivates a part of them randomly.

Calculation of an LSTM layer with dropconnect during training is done by using (5.23) and (5.24) instead of (5.15)–(5.18), where $*$ can be i, f, or o. Here, $M_*^W \in \mathbb{R}^{n \times m}$ and $M_*^R \in \mathbb{R}^{n \times n}$ are dropconnect masks and each element of them is either 0 with a probability of p (dropconnect rate) or $1/(1-p)$ with a probability of $(1-p)$. Dropconnect masks M_*^W and M_*^R are independent of time t, and the same masks are used for the entire sequence of input.

$$z_t = \phi\left(\left(W_z \odot M_z^W\right)x_t + \left(R_z \odot M_z^R\right)h_{t-1} + b_z\right) \tag{5.23}$$

$$*_t = \sigma\left(\left(W_* \odot M_*^W\right)x_t + \left(R_* \odot M_*^R\right)h_{t-1} + b_*\right) \tag{5.24}$$

5.5 What is Neural Darwinism?

Neural Darwinism is the concept of neuroevolution proposed by Gerald Edelman[15]. The basic idea is to "grow, and then prune" neurons (Fig. 5.21). In more detail the concept is summarized as follows [37]:

Neural Darwinism

■ Create too many neurons and then trim the unsed ones.

■ Basic policy is to use it or lose it.

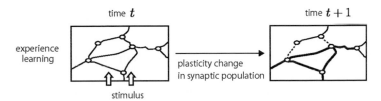

Figure 5.21: Neuro Darwinism.

The survival of neurons in this theory is similar to the survival of the fittest in evolutionary theory. In fact, it is known that there are more than 30~60% more brain cells in infants than in adults. Dynamic synaptic activity encodes patterns of neural activity until permanent connections are strengthened and stored as memories.

In Neural Darwinism, the process of learning is explained as a selection process that occurs within the nervous system. The theory emphasizes the ways in which stimuli and habits increase connections in specific areas of the brain. In other words, by practicing a task, the neural network used for that particular task is strengthened. The idea of "task specificity" in learning is important in Neural Darwinism. All skills are task-specific, and learning of skills is thought to be done specifically.

Based upon this idea of Neural Darwinism, neuroevolution is a framework that integrates learning and evolutionary computation of neural networks.

Many neural structures have been elucidated by the phenomenon in the developmental system based on Neural Darwinism. For example, in rodents, barrel structures[16] have been found that have the same patterns corresponding to whisker arrangement [127] (Fig. 5.22).

---

[15]Gerald Edelman (1929–2014): American physician and physical chemist. Awarded nobel prize in physiology or medicine in 1972.

[16]A columnar region in the cerebrum containing neurons of similar properties. In the sensory cortex of rodents, a column for each whisker is believed to exist.

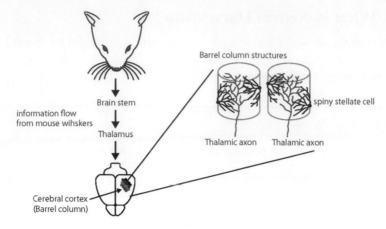

Figure 5.22: Neural structures corresponding to the whisker arrangement.

As we will see in Section 5.8, this is similar to the structure obtained in neuroevolution.

Edelman said that the human genome is too small to encode the entire structure of the brain. In other words, the amount of information in the genome is too insufficient to describe the connectivity of all the neurons. This means that it is not the structure of the brain that is encoded in the genes, but the process of brain development that is regulated and modeled by the gene network.

5.6 Neuroevolution

"Neuroevolution" is an active area of research in machine learning. This approach, also known as evolutionary artificial neural networks (EANNs) [155], integrates evolutionary methods with neural networks. The key feature of evolutionary neural networks is a genetic search for an optimal network. This saves the effort normally required to search for a neural network (such as constructing networks through trial and error).

Training via backpropagation, the method normally used to train neural networks, has been shown to often become stuck in only locally optimal solutions because it is based on the gradient descent method. To address this flaw, methods have been proposed that use evolutionary methods to learn which link weights to use. In other words, these methods express the link weights in a network as genotypes, and then use evolutionary computation to search for the best network. In this case, we derive the fitness value by the error in the output of the neural network (represented as a genotype, with lower errors representing better fitness). Methods for expressing link weights (genotypes) include binary strings and numeric vectors.

Note also that, when training a neural network, the network structure needs to be provided in advance. Neuroevolution, in contrast, can adaptively learn a network structure and size (number of nodes) appropriate to the task. Two different genotype representations have been proposed for driving the evolution of network structures.

Direct coding   Directly represents the link state of the network structure

Indirect coding   Encodes production rules for generating networks as genotypes

Direct coding is closer to biological models than direct coding is. For example, direct coding might represent a network consisting of N nodes $(n_1, n_2, \ldots n_N)$ as an $N \times N$ adjacency matrix, with each element taking a value of 0 or 1 such that a value of 1 for row i and column j indicates that there is a link from n_i to n_j and a value of 0 indicates that there is no such link.

For indirect coding methods, the focus of attention has been encoding for developmental systems. This approach uses observations from developmental biology as a basis to create abstract models of natural development in order to drive evolutionary computation algorithms. These models range from low-level cytochemistry through to high-level grammar-rewriting systems.

Once the genotype is determined, the following procedure is used to conduct training through evolutionary computations on network structures.

Step1   Find the phenotypes (the network structure of the EANNs) by decoding the genotypes for each individual.

Step2   Train each EANN. In this case, change the weights according to a predetermined training rule (such as backpropagation).

Step3   Derive the fitness value for each individual based on the training results. Normally, the squared error relative to the desired output is used for this.

Step4   Select candidate parents according to the fitness values, and then create the child generation by applying genetic operators to the selected parents.

Step5   Return to **Step1** if the termination condition has not been met.

Furthermore, although Hebb's rule is the training rule typically used for neural networks, parameters such as the learning rate and momentum during backpropagation are not easy to tune because they are task dependent. Accordingly, there is active research into evolutionary methods for learning appropriate parameters as well as into using evolutionary computation to search for more general training rules than Hebb's rule.

5.7 Let us Drive a Racing Car and Control a Helicopter

Let us experiment with neuroevolution with a simple example. In the following, we will use MindRender (see Appendix A.3 for details), a VR software for education.

MindRender is a programming learning app that lets you create and play with VR programs. There are labs for different themes, such as drones and racing cars. You can create your own program by completing the missions in each lab. You can experience the created programs with VR glasses.

(a)

(b)

(c)

Figure 5.23: Learning how to drive a racing car.

An example of a racing circuit is shown in Fig. 5.23(a). Mind Render allows you to create a Google Blockly[17] to drive a racing car. (b) shows an image of the VR experience from the driver's perspective. When you actually try it out, you will find that it is not easy to go around the track at high speed without crashing into a wall.

Proper driving control can be learned by defining sensor inputs and operational outputs for neuroevolution. The inputs are seven distance sensors $(0°, 45°, 70°, 90°, 110°, 135°,$ and $180°)$[18], a gyroscope (accelerometer) and a velocity sensor. Thus, the total number of sensors is nine.

---

[17]https://developers.google.com/blockly/guides/configure/web/themes.

[18]The right side of the vehicle is $0°$, and the front is $90°$. Red lines in Fig. 5.23(c) indicate sensor directions.

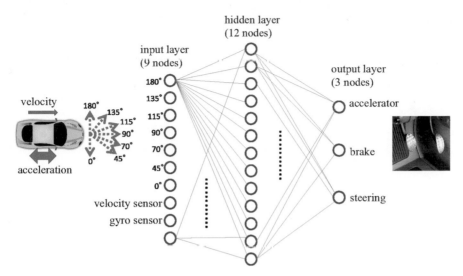

Figure 5.24: A neural network structure of a racing car.

The output is the gas pedal, brake, and steering[19] of the car.

The neural network we use (Fig. 5.24) is a fully coupled structure with three layers: input layer (9 nodes), hidden layer (12 nodes), and output layer (3 nodes). The weights between these layers are the genotypes to be evolved. The total number of the weights is $9 \times 12 + 12 \times 3 = 144$.

The fitness is the distance the car has run before hitting the wall. If the car runs around the course in Fig. 5.23(a), the fitness is about 700. The parameters for neuroevolution are as follows: the number of populations 100, the mutation rate 5%, and the crossover rate 100%.

Figure 5.25(a) shows the performance with neuroevolution. As you can see from the figure, it takes about 19 generations to complete a cycle. In this example, we did not optimize the parameter values and sensors to run the neuroevolution. If we choose appropriate sensors, parameters and network structure, we can improve the search performance[20].

Note that neuroevolution differs from normal neural network learning in the sense that it does not perform error backpropagation. Therefore, evolutionary search can be carried out as long as the fitness (i.e., selection pressure) is defined. In a control problem such as a racing car, it is not easy to define the error that should be propagated at each time step. On the other hand, neuroevolution has the advantage of being able to define the fitness based on a measure of achievement

---

[19]The output value takes values from -1 to $+1$, with the left direction being negative and the right direction being positive. The higher the value, the steeper the steering.

[20]The AI version of Mind Render is also available. In addition to neuroevolution, it is possible to experiment with evolutionary computation, reinforcement learning, and game AI. The readers are encouraged to try it for themselves. See Appendix A.3 for details.

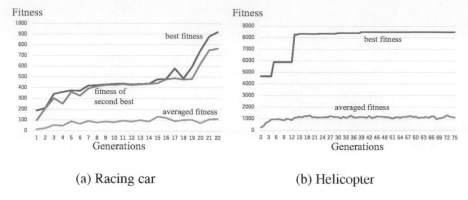

(a) Racing car   (b) Helicopter

Figure 5.25: Performance with neuroevolution.

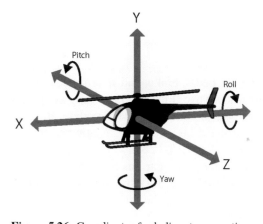

Figure 5.26: Coordinates for helicopter operation.

(e.g., distance driven). Also, although Q-learning has been successful for simple courses, it fails in cornering on a complex course such as shown in Fig. 5.23(a). This is due to the difficulty of defining states in Q-learning.

Next, let us try to fly the helicopter to its destination. Controlling a helicopter is not an easy task for a beginner. In the following explanations, we will set Y-axis (the axis from the floor through the propeller) and Z axis (the axis from which the helicopter originates and points forward) in the helicopter's local coordinate system as shown in Fig. 5.26.

The network input of neuroevolution consists of the following seven items:

- Vector to target position (3 dimensions)

- Velocity vector (3 dimensions)

- Angular velocity of the helicopter around the Y-axis (1 dimension)

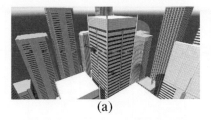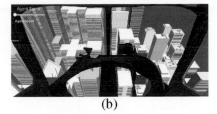

(a) (b)

Figure 5.27: Helicopter piloting.

The network outputs the following five items:

■ Lateral and forward/backward tilt

■ Torque around the Y-axis (the axis that runs from the floor of the helicopter through the propeller)

■ Engine power

The network structure consists of two hidden layers (8 nodes).

The fitness is calculated in the following way. Give a random target point and keep the helicopter moving for a limited time. Once the target point is reached, randomly give the next target point. During that sequence, the fitness is derived according to the following items:

■ Angular difference between the helicopter's direction and the target direction (shift in direction of travel)

■ Distance to the target position at each time step

■ Number of times the helicopter has reached the target points

Figure 5.25(b) shows how neuroevolution works. In a typical trial, we were able to reach the destination 8 out of 13 times. However, unlike driving a racing car, the helicopter requires a complex control in 3-D space, so performance is not always stable. Therefore, further improvements to handle more realistic data will be necessary.

5.8   NEAT and HyperNEAT

A typical example of neuroevolution is NeuroEvolution of Augmenting Topologies (NEAT) [133], a method for efficiently optimizing the structure and parameters of neural networks. NEAT has demonstrated performance superior to that of conventional methods in a large number of problems. The NEAT method makes it possible to evolve variable network structures by gradually increasing the complexity of a low number of small networks with each successive generation.

Figure 5.28 shows how NEAT produces network phenotypes from genotypes. A genotype consists of two parts.

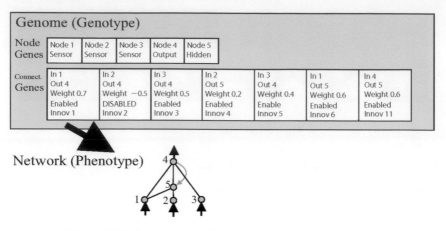

Figure 5.28: A genotype to phenotype mapping example [133].

- Node information: lists of input nodes, hidden nodes, and output nodes

- Link information: a list of the arcs linking pairs of nodes

Link information contains descriptions of the nodes forming the beginning and end points of an arc, link weightings, flags indicating whether an arc is enabled or disabled, and ID numbers. For example, in Fig. 5.28 there are three input nodes, one hidden node and one output node. Note also that although seven arcs are described in the link information, the second arc is disabled and therefore not expressed in the phenotype (the corresponding arc does not exist in the network).

NEAT includes two types of spontaneous mutations (see Fig. 5.28).

- Node additions

- Arc additions

In Fig. 5.28, the arrays describe the link information within genes. The numbers at the top of each gene are ID numbers. New genes are allocated ID numbers in such a way that the sequence of ID numbers is strictly increasing. In the top example in Fig. 5.29, an arc has been added. Here the new gene (arc) has been assigned the next available ID number (in this case, 7). In the bottom example, the arc to be removed is first disabled, and then two new arc genes (with IDs 8 and 9) are added. A new node is added between these two arcs, and the node information is recorded as a new gene (the node descriptions have been omitted from the figure).

When genes are crossed, children inherit their parents' genes and retain the same ID numbers. In other words, the ID numbers do not change. In this way, the representation makes it possible to track the history (ancestry) of each gene.

Figure 5.30 shows how genetic crossover works with NEAT. Parent 1 and Parent 2 have different shapes, but by looking at the commonality between the

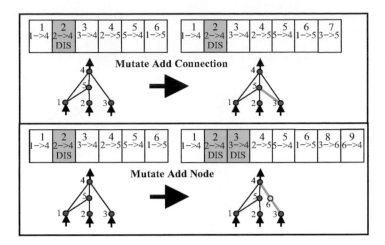

Figure 5.29: The two types of structural mutation in NEAT [133].

gene ID numbers we can tell which genes match. Matching genes are inherited at random. In contrast, disjoint genes (the non-matching genes in the middle section) and excess genes (the non-matching genes at the end) are inherited from the parent with better fitness. In the figure, both parents are assumed to have the same fitness, and so genes are inherited randomly in both cases. Disabled (resp., enabled) genes may become enabled (disabled) in the future.

The efficacy of NEAT has been verified through application to a wide variety of fields. For example, modular NEAT has demonstrated better results than conventional methods in learning to play the Ms. Pac-Man video game (Fig. 4.6) [124]. This NEAT expresses multiple modules simultaneously. Each module learns different policies, and decisions as to which policy to use at any given time are also evolved through evolutionary processes. Inputs take the form of feature values, such as the positions of the player and the ghosts. In games such as Pac-Man, where rewards and penalties are delayed so that conditions need to be judged from a long-term perspective, traditional reinforcement learning does not perform adequately. Modular NEAT succeeds in scoring points by means of "luring modules" and appropriately selecting which one to use according to the situation.

5.9 CPPN and Pattern Generation

NEAT has been extended via a coding method known as composition pattern-producing network (CPPN) to create hyperNEAT.

CPPN is a model for developmental systems that can express complex recursive patterns by using cartesian coordinates. Fig. 5.32 shows a schematic of the behavior in the two-dimensional case. In Fig. 5.32(a), the genotype is a function

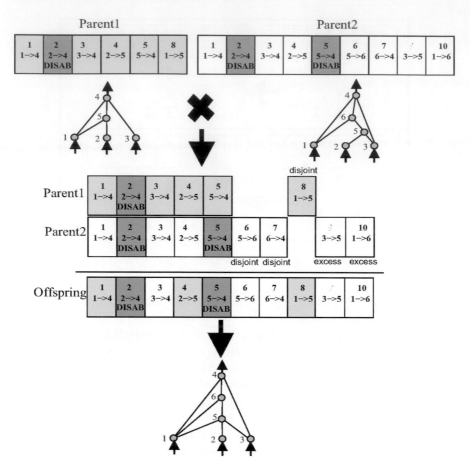

Figure 5.30: Matching up genes for different network topologies using ID numbers [133].

f and the corresponding phenotype is a spatial pattern generated by passing two-dimensional coordinates (x, y) as inputs to f and then using the resulting value at the (x, y) coordinate position as the output. To express this function f, CPPN uses encoding via a network formed by composing various functions. Figure 5.32(b) shows a two-dimensional CPPN in which the input is the coordinate (x, y) and the output is the value of the phenotype obtained at that coordinate. Just as for neural networks, weights are defined for each link, and the output from a given node is multiplied by the link weight before becoming the input value for the next node.

CPPN can use primitive functions (such as Gaussian and sine functions) to express complex regularities and symmetries, as shown in Fig. 5.33. Note that this figure was arrived at via interactive evolutionary computations (IEC) [134]. The primitive functions used here model particular phenomena in developmental systems. For example, the Gaussian function models left–right symmetry, while

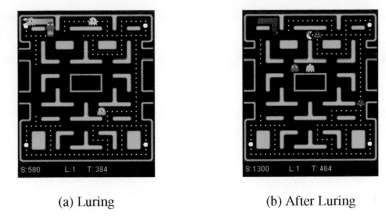

(a) Luring   (b) After Luring

Figure 5.31: Behavior with a luring module [124].

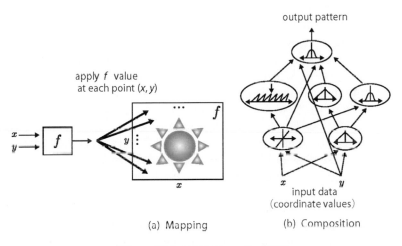

(a) Mapping   (b) Composition

Figure 5.32: CPPN Encoding [134].

periodic functions (such as the sine function) model differentiation into body segments.

The resulting phenotypes (Fig. 5.33) are geometrically important features observed in the natural world. For example, the figure in (a) can be viewed as a model for bilateral symmetry in vertebrates, while the imperfect symmetry and recursion in (b) can be thought of as models for right-handedness and receptive fields in the cortex, respectively. The recursion accompanied by transformation in (c) can be thought of as a model for the cortical column or columnar region (see Fig. 5.22).

Note the structural similarity between CPPN and neural networks. This means that NEAT can also be applied to optimizing the structure and parameters of CPPN. This method is known as hyperNEAT [135].

   (a) Symmetry   (b) Imperfect symmetry   (c) Repetition with variation

Figure 5.33: CPPN-generated regularities [134].

The basic idea of hyperNEAT can be summarized as the following two points:

1. Use CPPN to express the links and weights of a neural network.

2. Use NEAT to optimize CPPN.

The spatial patterns produced by CPPN can be thought of as linking patterns for a neural network. For example, if a four-dimensional CPPN outputs w in response to the input (x_1, y_1, x_2, y_2), then this can be interpreted as meaning that the link weight between a node at coordinates (x_1, y_1) and another node at coordinates (x_2, y_2) is w. When the absolute value of w is below a certain value, this is taken to indicate that there is no link between the nodes (a weight indistinguishable from 0). Note that the output values for CPPN are scaled appropriately. Consider, for example, nodes placed on a 5×5 lattice, with a normal two-dimensional coordinate system with the origin located at the center of the lattice. Given these node positions, the link weights between pairs of nodes are found by passing their coordinates to the CPPN (Fig. 5.34). Recall the regular and symmetrical spatial patterns produced by CPPN. These kinds of patterns generate regular linkage patterns for the neural network. For example, CPPN can easily express the link relationships shown in Fig. 5.35, such as symmetry, incomplete symmetry, recursion, and recursion accompanied by transformation.

Moreover, the input and output layers of a neural network can be set to arbitrary locations. This enables more geometrical relationships to be used. For example, Fig. 5.36 shows input layers whereby a robot's input sensors (I) and output modules (O) are placed either in a circle or in parallel.

By precisely arranging neurons in this way, geometrical regularity can be achieved using CPPN encoding. Biological neural networks have many such functions. The neurons in the visual cortex are arranged in the same topological two-dimensional pattern as the light receptors in the retina, an arrangement that is believed to acquire locality through regular connections to adjacent neurons based on simple recursion. In a certain group of fish, various pyramidal cells are known to be arranged in regular arrays along the curved surface of the retina. For example, a pattern of four different pyramidal cells can be observed in the retina of zebrafish, each with different peaks in light sensitivity, corresponding to the wavelengths for blue, red, green and ultraviolet light.

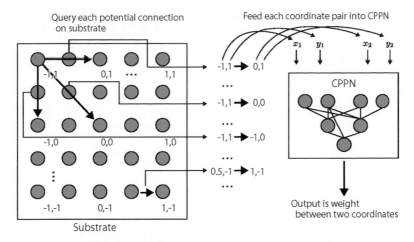

Figure 5.34: Hypercube-based geometric connectivity pattern interpretation [135].

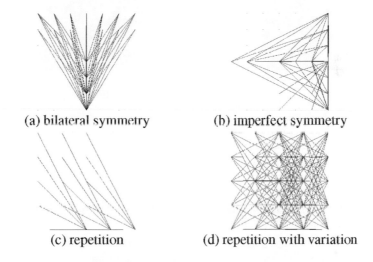

(a) bilateral symmetry (b) imperfect symmetry

(c) repetition (d) repetition with variation

Figure 5.35: CPPN output images [135].

We believe that CPPN has the same kind of capacity for pattern composition. In fact, geometrically valid information provides a domain-specific bias in evolutionary processes that often surpass simple optimization methods.

HyperNEAT has been applied to Atari games [58]. It has also been applied to video games such as super Mario, and there is great interest in its efficacy.

In recent years, DeepNEAT has been proposed, which is a most immediate extension of NEAT to deep learning [99].

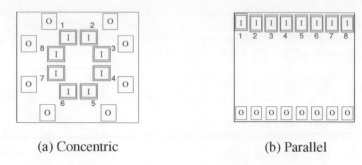

(a) Concentric   (b) Parallel

Figure 5.36: Placing inputs and outputs [135].

(a) self portrait   (b) The Knight with His Hand on His Breast

Figure 5.37: El Greco paintings.

5.10   El Greco Test

Now consider the question quoted at the beginning[114] (see Fig. 5.37). This is a question invented by Peter Medawar[21] for an oral entrance examination at the department of zoology of Oxford university [31].

When passed through a neural network of the visual perception of El Greco[22], is there a feature transformation of stretching in the vertical direction?

In fact, this theory is wrong, because a painter with such a cognitive network will see his painting as more stretched when he looks at it. Then what about the feature transformation for shortening (vertical shortening)?

Think about it in the same way.

---

[21] Peter Brian Medawar (1915–1987): British biologist, known for his work on the immune system against transplanted tissue. He was awarded the 1960 Nobel Prize in Physiology or Medicine for this work.

[22] El Greco (1541–1614): Painter of Greek origin, active in Spain.

Chapter 6

Deep Swarms and Evolution

Go to the ant, you lazy person; observe its ways and grow wise. The ant has no commander, officer, or ruler. Even so, it gets its food in summer; gathers its provisions at harvest. (The Old Testament Proverbs 6: 6 11).

6.1 ACO for Construction of Evolutionary Trees

6.1.1 Phylogenetic Tree Derivation

Phylogeny is a discipline that estimates the history of evolution from the trait data of organisms by means of a phylogenetic tree (or evolutionary tree), which shows the phylogenetic relationship between organisms. The estimated phylogenetic tree is not merely a foundation for classification but is also used to verify various hypotheses regarding the evolution process, providing phylogenetic hypotheses that are as accurate as possible given the available information on traits. For example, Fig. 6.1 is a phylogenetic tree of strange organisms from the Cambrian period. This is based on fossils found in Burgess shale in the Canadian Rockies (Fig. 6.2).

Many fossils of interesting organisms have been recovered, such as the Opabinia, which has five eyes and an organ similar to an elephant's trunk, and the Anomalocaris, a shrimp-like large predatory animal. These were initially considered ancestors of animals living today and early evolutionary forms of arthro-

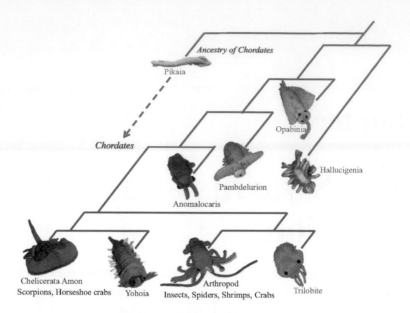

Figure 6.1: A phylogenetic tree of strange organisms from the Cambrian period.

pods. However, further research led Stephen Gould to argue that these animals do not fit in current taxa and are different types of organisms[1]. He claimed that these forms are not found in animals today because they could not adapt to changes in the environment; they were lost in the proving grounds of evolution. Stuart Kauffman proposed "general biology" as a more advanced version of artificial life theory, and proposed the hypothesis that life has created a search space (i.e., fitness landscape) in which its own search methods work well [71]. The validity of this hypothesis is currently unknown and is the subject of much debate, but it will be interesting and important to re-examine evolutionary theory and biology from this perspective. Is it really possible to think about and study life in a way that we cannot even imagine, and what is life in the first place? For example, most organisms, including humans, have two eyes. What is life? Is it worthwhile to consider organisms with eyes that cannot be assumed from existing members?

Although phylogenetic trees were originally estimated based on the "shape" of existing organisms and fossils, there were ambiguities in the analysis. The phylogenetic tree of the Cambrian organisms shown in Fig. 6.1 is still under debate. With the advent of genome analysis, molecular data, such as amino acids, are rapidly becoming a common information source for phylogenetic estimation (Fig. 6.3). The field of "molecular phylogenetics" has been established; amino

---

[1]The book "Wonderful life" by Stephen Jay Gould is a must-read for those interested in evolution. This book describes strange animals, and anecdotes leading to their discoveries, that lived in prehistoric times, approximately 525 million to 505 million years ago (the latter years of the early Cambrian period, Paleozoic era).

Figure 6.2: Burgess shale and Mount Stephen (Yoho National Park, Canada). Many Cambrian organisms were found, most notably, fossils of trilobites and Anomalocaris. The finger is pointing to a trilobite fossil.

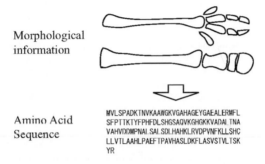

Morphological information

Amino Acid Sequence

MVLSPADKTNVKAAWGKVGAHAGEYGAEALERMFL
SFPTTKTYFPHFDLSHGSAQVKGHGKKVADAL TNA
VAHVDDMPNAL SAL SDL HAHKLRVDPVNFKLLSHC
LLVTLAAHLPAEFTPAVHASLDKFLASVSTVLTSK
YR

Figure 6.3: From morphological information to molecular sequence information.

acid sequence data from organisms are used to estimate the evolution process that leads to the sequence set. This requires the establishment of an evolution model and analysis of a vast number of amino acid sequences; thus, coordination with mathematical information science is inevitable.

Molecular phylogenetic tree derivation is used from medical standpoints in addition to a tool for biological evolution research. One example is a study on the phylogenetic relationship of repeated sequences in the human genome [78]. The repeated sequences are related to schizophrenia and are considered to be caused by the inclusion of a retrovirus in the human genome. The process of the spread of repeated sequences in the human genome was estimated by deriving a phylogenetic tree.

Input data for phylogenetic tree generation are DNA or amino acid sequences of genes common to organisms in the targeted scope[2]. However, the lengths of the sequences are different because of deletions and insertions during evolution;

---

[2]Genes that are separated by speciation among genes, which are derived from the same ancestor (orthologous genes).

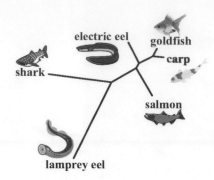

Figure 6.4: An example of phylogenetic tree.

thus, gaps must be inserted using multiple alignment techniques[3] to obtain good correspondence relationships. An example of amino acid sequences after multiple alignments are shown below.

```
goldfish       G-----SGPVKKHGKTIMGAVGDAVSKIDD---LVGALSALSELHAFKLRIDPANFKILA
carp           G-----SGPVKKHGKVIMGAVGDAVSKIDD---LVGGLAALSELHAFKLRVDPANFKILA
electric eel   G-----SAAVKKHGKTIMGGIAEAVGHIDD---LTGGLASLSELHAFKLRVDPANFKILA
salmon         G-----SAPVKKHGGVIMGAIGNAVGLMDD---LVGGMSGLSDLHAFKLRVDPGNFKILS
shark          A-----APSIKAHGAKVVTALAKACDHLDD---LKTHLHKLATFHGSELKVDPANFQYLS
lamprey eel    ADDLKQSSDVRWHAERIINAVNDAVKSMDDTEKMSMKLKELSIKHAQSFYVDRQYFKVLA
```

Phylogenetic trees can be expressed using binary trees. Figure 6.4 shows a molecular phylogenetic tree generated using the above amino acid sequences. The leaf nodes of the binary tree correspond to aligned sequences (i.e., sequences of proteins or DNAs) and are existing organisms (evolutionary objects). The tree structure represents the familial relationships or the evolutionary history of the objects. The lengths of the edges correspond to how similar or far the sequences are.

Analysis of sequence substitutions alone cannot confirm the direction of substitution, resulting in an unrooted phylogenetic tree (there is no ultimate ancestor of all sequences). However, adding organisms that are very different in the course of evolution allows estimation of the root. The lamprey, which is a primitive vertebrate, is one such organism in Fig. 6.4.

The branching pattern of a phylogenetic tree is called the "topology" of the tree. Let the number of leaves be denoted as n, which is the number of organism sequences to be analyzed. Then, the number of branches in the phylogenetic tree is $2n-3$; thus, adding another organism sequence increases the number of topology patterns by $(2n-3)$-fold. As a consequence, the number of phylogenetic trees with n leaves is $3 \times 5 \times 7 \cdots \times (2n-5) = \Pi_{i=3}^{n}(2i-5)$. For example, there are approximately two million unrooted phylogenetic tree patterns for $n = 10$.

---

[3]See [41] for details.

Therefore, the estimation of phylogenetic trees is a very difficult problem with high computational costs.

Several methods have been proposed to estimate an appropriate phylogenetic tree from multiple aligned sequences. Examples are distance matrix, maximum parsimony, and maximum likelihood methods. Figure 6.4 was estimated using the neighbor-joining method [104], which is one variant of the distance matrix method. For details on these algorithms for phylogenetic tree estimation, the reader can refer to the bioinformatics textbook. The maximum likelihood method is explained in the next section.

The maximum parsimony principle is important in phylogenetic inference and has been implicitly assumed in evolutionary theory. It can be considered an example of Occam's razor[4] in scientific debate. The maximum parsimony principle is the idea that, in explaining similarities between species, it is more economical to assume the existence of a common ancestor from which a common trait was inherited than to assume that the same trait arose twice, independently. However, there are criticisms of this principle. For example, it has been pointed out that although the maximum parsimony principle is true for an infinitely long time, there are situations where the maximum parsimony is not necessarily the most likely (see [130] for more details on this discussion).

Let us make a phylogenetic tree. A number of tools for creating phylogenetic trees are available from the WWW[5]. For example, Fig. 6.5 shows a phylogenetic tree obtained from the amino acid sequences of the chain of hemoglobin. The transition of vertebrates from fish to mammals in this phylogenetic tree is the same as the morphological classification.

6.1.2 Estimation using the Maximum Likelihood Method

The maximum likelihood method presumes that mutations are neutral in the sequence. The probability of phylogenetic tree candidates is obtained under this assumption, and the topology with the highest probability is chosen. This method is known to be robust compared to other methods, such as the distance matrix and maximum parsimony methods. Drawbacks are the large cost of likelihood calculations and the necessity of searching over the vast phylogenetic tree space.

To derive the probability of a phylogenetic tree, the probability $P(x|y,t)$ that a sequence y evolves into sequence x by tracking a branch with length t must be obtained. Assume that each locus of the input sequence is independent and there is no insertion or deletion. Because each locus is independent, the transition probability of the entire sequence can be derived by obtaining the probability of a locus in a sequence and then multiplying them. If all bases transition at the

---

[4] The principle that one should not assume more than is necessary to explain a matter. The 14th century philosopher and theologian William of Ockham used it frequently in his arguments.

[5] https://www.megasoftware.net/, http://www.atgc-montpellier.fr/phyml/, http://doua.prabi.fr/software/seaview.

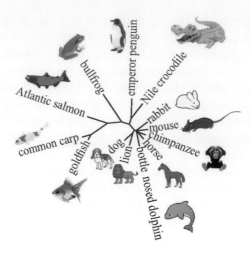

Figure 6.5: Phylogenetic tree inferred from Hemoglobin–α chain.

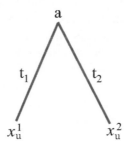

Figure 6.6: A simple phylogenetic tree.

same frequency ε, the probability that base a transitions into base b is given as follows[6]:

$$P(b|a,t) = \begin{cases} \frac{1}{4}(1+3e^{-4\varepsilon t}) & \text{when } a = b, \\ \frac{1}{4}(1-e^{-4\varepsilon t}) & \text{when } a \neq b. \end{cases} \tag{6.1}$$

Let the topology of a phylogenetic tree be denoted as T, and the branch length as t in the following discussion. First, we evaluate the likelihood of a phylogenetic tree when there are two input sequences. Consider the topology and branch length of the phylogenetic tree as given in Fig. 6.6. The input sequences are denoted as x^1 and x^2, and one locus of the sequence u is assumed.

The probability that base a is chosen to be replaced by x^1 and x^2 is as follows:

$$P(x_u^1, x_u^2, a | T, t_1, t_2) = q_a P(x_u^1|a,t_1)P(x_u^2|a,t_2),$$

---

[6]Bases are major components of DNA or proteins. See 37 page.

where q_a is the occurrence of base a. In general, the bases that may be allocated to a are not known; thus, the substitution matrix to x^1 and x^2 is the sum over all possible a, i.e.,

$$P(x_u^1, x_u^2 | T, t_1, t_2) = \sum_a q_a P(x_u^1 | a, t_1) P(x_u^2 | a, t_2).$$

Therefore, the overall likelihood given the total length of the sequence (N) is given as follows:

$$P(x^1, x^2 | T, t_1, t_2) = \prod_{u=1}^{N} P(x_u^1, x_u^2 | T, t_1, t_2).$$

Similarly, the likelihood of a sequence with arbitrary length can be obtained by considering all possible base allocations as an ancestor. An algorithm to obtain this probability is the post-order traversal that starts from the leaves and traverses the phylogenetic tree.

The phylogenetic tree with maximum likelihood under a fixed topology can be calculated analytically if the transition probability of bases is given as a function of branch length t (see Fig. 6.6). Therefore, the issue is determining the topology of the phylogenetic tree. The topology of a phylogenetic tree increases as the factorial of the number of input sequences, as described in the previous section. The objective is to find a tree structure that minimizes the score function. The total length of the edges can signify the score for the evolutionary tree. In the maximum likelihood method, the shorter edge lengths indicate higher likeliness for the transition of ancestral sequence to present sequence. The construction of the optimal evolutionary tree is a very challenging and NP-complete problem. Even though the problem has been studied extensively, evolutionary tree construction still remains an open problem.

Traditional methods for searching a phylogenetic tree with the maximum likelihood include:

■ Sequential addition
  Sequences are chosen randomly and are added, one by one, to a phylogenetic tree. The phylogenetic tree candidate with maximum likelihood is retained, and the rest is removed at each step (see Fig. 6.7).

■ Star-shaped tree division
  Star-shaped phylogenetic trees, where sequences are connected only at one internal node, are configured. Candidate phylogenetic trees are derived by connecting two arbitrary sequences at one internal node, and a candidate with maximum likelihood is selected (see Fig. 6.8).

However, there are drawbacks to these methods. For example, in the case of the sequential addition, the final topology is dependent on the order in which the sequences are selected. Also, although the performance of the Star-shaped tree

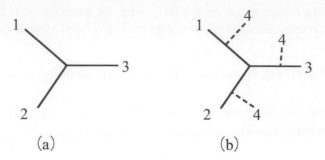

Figure 6.7: Sequential addition.

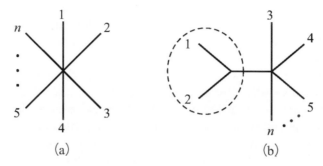

Figure 6.8: Star-shaped tree division.

division does not depend on the order of the sequences, it may fall into a local solution. Thus, some form of metaheuristics is necessary for the sake of effective tree search.

In the following sections, we describe ACO-based methodology of phylogenetic tree search (see [1] for details).

6.1.3   *How do Ants Search Trees?*

The total length of all edges in an evolutionary tree indicate the evaluation of the tree, since the shorter edge lengths indicate higher likeliness for the transition of ancestral sequence to present sequence in the maximum likelihood method. The total edge length of a tree can be obtained from circular tour length, $C(S)$, where S is a set of leaves, i.e., sequences of a protein or DNA.

Let us consider the example of DNA sequences and evolutionary tree structure shown in Fig. 6.9. The following equation gives the $C(S)$ value for that tree, which is the sum of the trail indicated by broken arrows:

$$C(S) = d_{0w} + d_{1u} + d_{2u} + d_{3v} + d_{4w} + d_{uv} + d_{vw}. \tag{6.2}$$

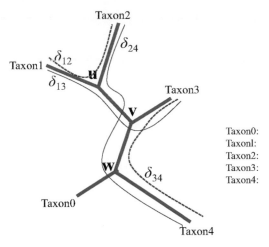

Figure 6.9: An evolutionary tree.

Here, d_{ij} is the edge length between i and j in the tree. For instance, d_{0w} is the edge length between Taxon0 and vertex w. Since the lengths of the edges represent the distances between the leaves, $C(S)$ can be calculated from distance matrix $[\delta_{ij}]$ as described below:

$$C(S) = (\delta_{01} + \delta_{12} + \delta_{23} + \delta_{34} + \delta_{40}) \times \frac{1}{2}. \tag{6.3}$$

A correct circular tour establishes the upper bound for the best score that can possibly be achieved by a given set of protein or DNA sequences. Both the bound and the circular tour can be derived without an explicit knowledge of the correct evolutionary tree. The circular tour length is equal for all isomorphic trees.

In our ACO-based method, $C(S)$ is used for scoring the tree, thus a distance matrix that shows the distance between every pair of sequences is required to calculate the score. Furthermore, our method can be used for any scoring function that correlates to the amount of changes along the branches of an evolutionary tree.

We represent the tree in suffix representation. An ant must visit N leaves once and the vertices $N-1$ times in between the cities while making a round trip. The vertices are not specified (as u, v, w), when the ants are making the rounds, and all vertices are indicated as $+$ in the representation, since the tree structure is indecisive until the rounds are completed. An evolutionary tree shown in Fig. 6.9 is represented as the following suffix representation:

$$T_{x0} T_{x1} T_{x2} + T_{x3} + + T_{x4} +, \tag{6.4}$$

where T_{xi} is an abbreviation for Taxon$i$. Figure 6.10 shows how to generate an evolutionary tree from a given suffix expression. To make a suffix expression to

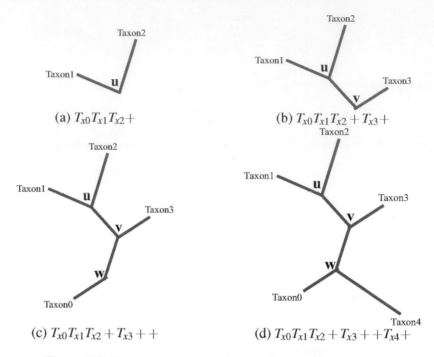

(a) $T_{x0}T_{x1}T_{x2}+$

(b) $T_{x0}T_{x1}T_{x2}+T_{x3}+$

(c) $T_{x0}T_{x1}T_{x2}+T_{x3}++$

(d) $T_{x0}T_{x1}T_{x2}+T_{x3}++T_{x4}+$

Figure 6.10: How to generate a tree structure from a suffix expression.

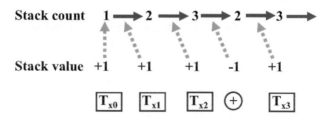

Figure 6.11: Stack count of the tree shown in Fig. 6.9.

actually form a tree, certain requirements have to be met. This constraint can be easily explained with the idea of the Stack count. We assign leaves, i.e., terminals, with the Stack value of $+1$ and assign non-terminal vertices with -1. The Stack count of a tree is the sum of the Stack value of all its vertices. If the suffix representation of the tree structure is valid, Stack count should be $+1$. Furthermore, any subtree of that tree would have $+1$ as its Stack count. Thus, while adding up the vertices of a valid representation in sequential order, Stack count should never subceed $+1$ (see Fig. 6.11).

While the ants are making a round trip, they hold the history of leaves it has visited, so as not to visit a leaf more than once. At any point during the trip,

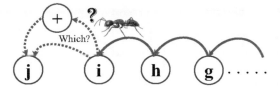

Figure 6.12: History of visited leaves and how to choose the next.

the Stack count for the visited leaves and non-terminal vertices cannot subceed +1. This Stack count constraint prohibits the ant from visiting the non-terminal vertices, until the Stack count has accumulated up to +2 or more.

The Stack count constrains the ant not to go to vertices at inappropriate timing. The following rule determines the probability that the ant will choose to go to the vertex, thus connecting the branches to form larger ones. For sequential order of leaves $S = \{T_{x0}, T_{x1}, T_{x2}, T_{x3}\}$, which appears in the order of the index, we define $\Delta(S)$ as follows:

$$\Delta(S) = \mid \delta_{01} + \delta_{23} - \delta_{02} - \delta_{13} \mid . \tag{6.5}$$

In the evolutionary tree, the edges indicate the distances between the leaves. If T_{x1} and T_{x2} are connected by a vertex, then $\Delta(S) = 0$. When inner two leave are not connected by a vertex, $\Delta(S) > 0$. For instance, $\Delta(S') = \mid \delta_{12} + \delta_{34} - \delta_{13} - \delta_{24} \mid = 2 \times d_{uv} > 0$ for $S' = \{T_{x1}, T_{x2}, T_{x3}, T_{x4}\}$.

When the ant, currently at leaf i, chooses j as the next visiting leaf, and has the latest history of visiting g, h (see Fig. 6.12), it calculates $\Delta(S)$ for $S = \{g, h, i, j\}$. If the $\Delta(S)$ is small, the ant is highly probable to go to the vertex $(+)$ before going to the next leaf j. The probability P is determined using the largest distance D in the distance matrix and an empirical parameter k as follows:

$$P = k\Delta(S)/2D \quad \text{where } 2D > \Delta(S). \tag{6.6}$$

When the history of the ant includes a vertex $(+)$, the calculation of $\Delta(S)$ is slightly modified. $\Delta(S)$ is calculated by representing the subtree with one of the consisting leaf. This enables the calculation of $\Delta(S)$ for all S. When a vertex connects a leaf (T_{x3}) and a subtree $St(T_{x1}, T_{x2})$, $\Delta(S)$ is equal to 0 for $S = \{T_{x0}, St, T_{x3}, T_{x4}\}$ because $\Delta(S) = \mid \delta_{01} + \delta_{34} - \delta_{03} - \delta_{14} \mid = 0$.

Note that a leaf can be a form of a subtree. The revised algorithm for deciding whether to go to a vertex, would be as follows: An ant at a vertex in the current subtree I, which has chosen j as the next leaf to visit, and whose two previously visited subtree, G and H, will go to a vertex $(+)$ before going to j by the probability of $P = k\Delta(S)/2D$ when $2D > \Delta(S)$ for $S = \{G, H, I, j\}$. The visited vertex can be identified by the partial sum of the Stack count (see Fig. 6.13).

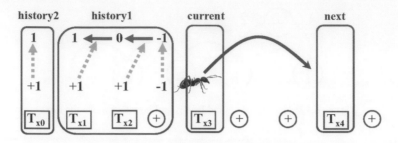

Figure 6.13: Partial sum of the Stack count.

6.1.4 ACO Simulation Results

Several experiments have been conducted to show the effectiveness of ACO-based method. The simulation is done as follows: Based on a specified evolutionary tree structure, random sequences of nucleotides are generated. We used Seq-Gen, a sequence generator software[7]. It simulates the evolution of nucleotide sequences along a phylogeny, using common models of the substitution process. Thus, we know the correct tree for the set of sequences in each simulation. Then, distance matrix between all the sequences is computed by PHYLIP program [93, 116]. It computes a distance measure for DNA sequences, using maximum likelihood estimates based on the Dayhoff PAM matrix. The input of sequence and distance matrix were also fed to FITCH and Neighbor algorithm of the PHYLIP programs for comparison.

The simulation was executed under different evolutionary tree parameter settings, which include maximum distance in the matrix, sequence length, and number of leaves. The structure for 8-leaf tree simulation is shown in Fig. 6.14. The ACO parameters are as follows: $\rho = 0.1$, $K = 0.2$, $\alpha = 1.2$, $N = 16$ and $M = 1000$.

The simulation result is summarized in Table 6.1. The ant algorithm gave good results in general. FITCH program gave the best result when the largest distance D was small, and otherwise the ant algorithm gave the best. We can conclude that this ant algorithms is useful and produces good results compatible to popularly used tree construction algorithms.

We have also tested the method on an example protein family of the Cytochrome P450 CYP050A. As shown in Table 6.2, the sequences of 15 species were taken from Cytochrome P450 Database[8]. The sequence lengths differ from 414 to 561, as indicated in the table. The multiple sequence alignment is obtained by ClustalW software [140]. The distance matrix is calculated by protdist of PHYLIP programs. Again, the comparison is made to FITCH and Neighbor programs, and also tree drawing algorithms of ClustalW. All the algorithms

---

[7]http://tree.bio.ed.ac.uk/software/seqgen/.
[8]http://cpd.ibmh.msk.su/.

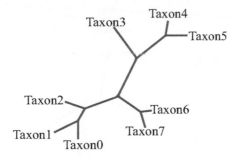

Figure 6.14: 8-leaf target tree.

Table 6.1: 8-leaf simulation result.

D	FITCH	Neighbor	Ant
−3	85%	78%	82%
3–6	60%	33%	78%
6–	35%	12%	64%

Table 6.2: 15 species and lengths of their CYP sequences.

arabidopsis thaliana	489
penicillium italicum	515
candida albicans	528
rat	503
candida glabrata	533
baker yeast	530
tomato	485
schizosaccharomyces pombe	495
human	509
wheat	453
issatchenkia orientalis	414
smut fungus	561
mycobacterium tuberculosis	451
grape powdery mildew fungus	524
rice	427

agreed on the tree topology, shown in Fig. 6.15. This result represents a very feasible structure, and our ACO-based method gave the best score of 4023.8.

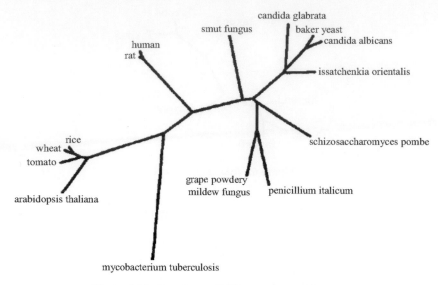

Figure 6.15: Cytochrome P450 tree obtained by ACO.

6.2 Evolutionary Optimization Extended by Deep Learning

VAE-EDA (see Algorithm 7) is an optimization method that uses VAE as an estimation of distribution algorithm (EDA, see Section 3.8) model. By using a neural network as the model for EDA, we can capture the dependencies between variables in the problem more flexibly. It is also expected to work particularly well for problems that have latent representations.

Garciarena et al. [45] have proposed two structures of VAEs that would be more compatible with EDAs: E-VAE (Extended Variational Auto-Encoder) and CE-VAE (Conditioned Extended Variational Auto-Encoder).

Algorithm 7 VAE-EDA

$t \leftarrow 0$
Randomly initialize the initial set P_0.
Initialize VAE M.
while $t < MaxGeneration$ **do**
Select the individuals with high fitness values from P_t and generate the candidate set Q_t.
Use Q_t to learn VAE M.
Produce the next set P_{t+1} by generating individuals from M.
$\quad t \leftarrow t + 1$
end while

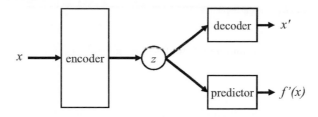

Figure 6.16: Structure of E-VAE.

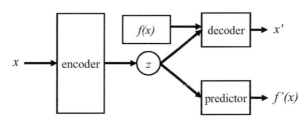

Figure 6.17: Structure of CE–VAE.

The EDA using E-VAE is called E-VAE-EDA (Fig. 6.16). In addition to the two networks of encoders and decoders that have normal VAE, a new network has been introduced to predict evaluation values. In this predictor network, the input is the same as the decoder input z, while the output is the predicted value $f'(x)$ of the evaluation value $f(x)$ for a solution x.

The mean squared error between the true evaluation value $f(x)$ and the estimated evaluation value $f'(x)$ from the predictor network is regarded as the error, which is added to the original VAE loss function. With this, the new network is trained simultaneously as the other two networks (encoder and decoder). The error of the new network can be expected to function as regularization when learning the latent representation z. Furthermore, it can substitute the evaluation function since the evaluation value solution $f(x)$ can be predicted from the latent representation z. When there is a large computational cost for the evaluation function, the calculation time can be reduced using this predictor network in place of the original evaluation function.

The conditioned, extended VAE (CE-VAE) is another VAE model (Fig. 6.17). Its basic structure is the same as that of the aforementioned E-VAE, except that the true evaluation value $f(x)$ for a solution x is added to the decoder input. A better solution can be generated by providing a clearly high evaluation value when sampling new solutions from the decoder.

Bhattacharjee et al. [12] proposed a population queue VAE-EDA (VAE-EDA-Q), which is a further extension of EDA with VAE. This algorithm learns VAEs from solutions sampled at previous generations instead of the current elite solu-

---

Algorithm 8 VAE-EDA-Q

$t \leftarrow 0$

Randomly generate n individuals and add them to the population queue *Queue*. ▷ $n =$ Queue size.

Initialize VAE M.

while $t < MaxGeneration$ **do**

Select the individuals with high fitness values from *Queue* and generate the candidate set Q_t.

Use Q_t to learn VAE M.

Produce the next set P_{t+1} by generating individuals from M.

Add individuals in P_{t+1} to *Queue*.

Remove individuals from *Queue* until the number becomes equal to n.

   $t \leftarrow t + 1$

end while

---

tions. This is expected to preserve the diversity in the set of solutions and suppress premature convergence. The flow of VAE-EDA-Q is shown in Algorithm 8.

We have evaluated the performance of VAE-EDA. The following methods have been used for comparison:

- $UMDA_c$

- VAE-EDA

- E-VAE-EDA

- CE-VAE-EDA

- VAE-EDA-Q

$UMDA_c$ (Univariate Marginal Distribution Algorithm for continuous domains) is a type of EDA, in which the mean and variance values are replaced with those of the top sampled individuals [47].

The used parameters in the experiments were set as follows:

- Population size: 500

- Maximum generation: 200

- Elite ratio: 30%

- Dimensions of latent variables: 3

- Intermediate layers: 20 dimensions

- Number of epochs during learning in each generation: 10

For CE-VAE, the fitness value for the decoder input shall range between 95% and 105% of the best value at the previous generation. The size of the population queue in VAE-EDA-Q corresponds to the number of individuals for 10 generations, i.e., 5,000.

We evaluated the performance of VAE-EDA using single-objective real-valued optimization benchmarks proposed in CEC2013 [92]. The used constants and functions are as follows:

- o: A constant that shifts the position of the optimal solution.

- D: Dimension of the problem. $D = 10$ in all problems.

- Search range: $[-100, 100]^D$

- Global optimal solution: 0 for all functions.

- M_1, M_2: Rotation matrix.

- Λ^α: D-dimensional diagonal matrix. i-th diagonal component is $\alpha^{\frac{i-1}{2(D-1)}}$.

- T_{asy}^β, T_{osz}: The transformation that gives the oscillation.

We used the following ten functions from CEC2013 benchmarks:

1. Sphere function

$$f_1(x) = \sum_{i=1}^{D} z_i^2, \; z = x - o$$

2. Rotated high conditioned elliptic function

$$f_2(x) = \sum_{i=1}^{D} (10^6)^{\frac{i-1}{D-1}} z_i^2, \; z = T_{osz} \cdot M_1(x - o)$$

3. Rotated Discus function

$$f_3(x) = 10^6 z_1^2 + \sum_{i=2}^{D} z_i^2, \; z = T_{osz} \cdot M_1(x - o)$$

4. Different powers function

$$f_4(x) = \sqrt{\sum_{i=1}^{D} |z_i|^{2+4\frac{i-1}{D-1}}}, \; z = x - o$$

5. Rotated Rosenbrock function

$$f_5(x) = \sum_{i=1}^{D-1} \left\{ 100(z_i^2 - z_{i+1})^2 + (z_i - 1)^2 \right\}, \; z = M_1 \frac{2.048(x - o)}{100} + 1$$

6. Rotated Weierstrass function

$$f_6(x) = \sum_{i=1}^{D}\left\{\sum_{k=0}^{kmax} a^k \cos(2\pi b^k(z_i + 0.5))\right\} - D\sum_{k=0}^{kmax} a^k \cos(\pi b^k)$$

$$a = 0.5,\ b = 3, kmax = 20,\ z = \Lambda^{10} M_2 T_{asy}^{0.5} M_1 \frac{0.5(x-o)}{100}$$

7. Rotated Griewank function

$$f_7(x) = \sum_{i=1}^{D}\frac{z_i^2}{4000} - \prod_{i=1}^{D}\cos(\frac{z_i}{\sqrt{i}}) + 1,\ z = \Lambda^{100} M_1 \frac{600(x-o)}{100}$$

8. Rastrigin function

$$f_8(x) = \sum_{i=1}^{D}\left\{z_i^2 - 10\cos(2\pi z_i) + 10\right\},\ z = \Lambda^{10} T_{asy}^{0.2} T_{osz} \frac{5.12(x-o)}{100}$$

9. Non-continuous fotated Rastrigin function

$$f_9(x) = \sum_{i=1}^{D}\left\{z_i^2 - 10\cos(2\pi z_i) + 10\right\}$$

$$\hat{x} = M_1 \frac{5.12(x-o)}{100},\ y_i = \begin{cases} \hat{x}_i & (\text{if } |\hat{x}_i| \le 0.5) \\ \text{round}(2\hat{x}_i)/2 & (\text{otherwise}) \end{cases}$$

$$z = M_1 \Lambda^{10} M_2 T_{asy}^{0.2}(T_{osz}(y))$$

10. Lunacek bi-Rastrigin function

$$f_{10}(x) = \min\left[\sum_{i=1}^{D}(\hat{x}_i - \mu_0)^2, dD + s\sum_{i=1}^{D}(\hat{x}_i - \mu_1)^2 + 10\left\{D - \sum_{i=1}^{D}\cos(2\pi\hat{x}_i)\right\}\right]$$

$$\mu_0 = 2.5,\ \mu_1 = -\sqrt{\frac{\mu_0^2 - d}{s}},\ s = 1 - \frac{1}{2\sqrt{D+20} - 8.2},\ d = 1$$

$$y = \frac{10(x-o)}{100}),\ \hat{x}_i = 2sign(x_i)y_i + \mu_0$$

$$z = \Lambda^{100}(\hat{x} - \mu_0)$$

The approximate form of each function in two dimensions is shown in Figs. 6.18 to 6.33.

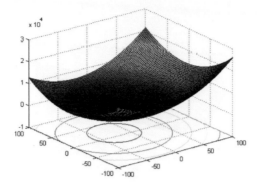

Figure 6.18: f_1: Sphere function [92].

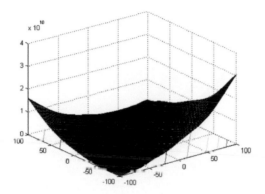

Figure 6.19: f_2: Rotated high conditioned elliptic function [92].

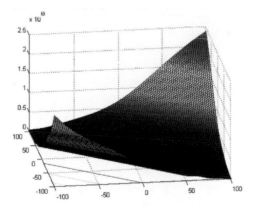

Figure 6.20: f_3: Rotated discus function [92].

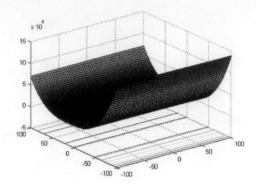

Figure 6.21: f_4: Different powers function [92].

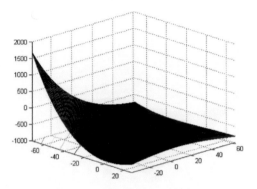

Figure 6.22: f_5: Rotated Rosenbrock function [92].

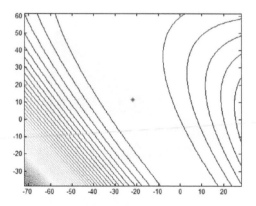

Figure 6.23: Contour graph of f_5 [92].

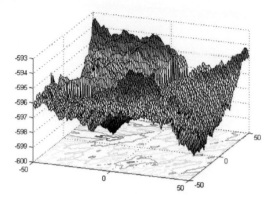

Figure 6.24: f_6: Rotated Weierstrass function [92].

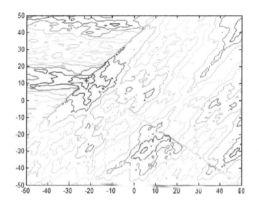

Figure 6.25: Contour graph of f_6 [92].

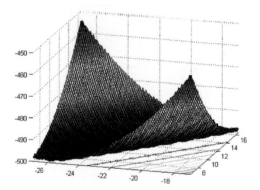

Figure 6.26: f_7: Rotated Griewank function [92].

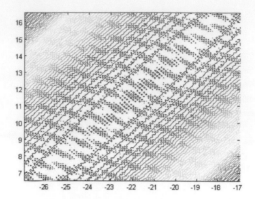

Figure 6.27: Contour graph of f_7 [92].

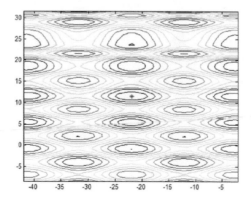

Figure 6.28: f_8: Rastrigin function [92].

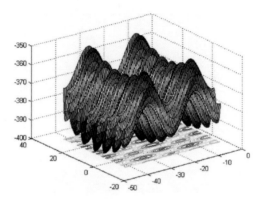

Figure 6.29: Contour graph of f_8 [92].

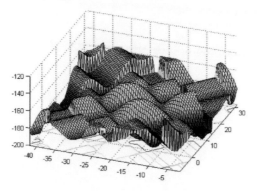

Figure 6.30: f_9: Non-continuous rotated Rastrigin function [92].

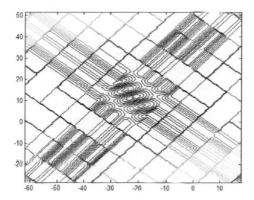

Figure 6.31: Contour graph of f_9 [92].

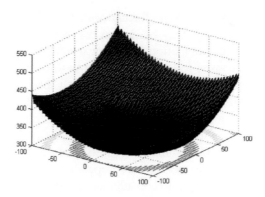

Figure 6.32: f_{10}: Lunacek bi-Rastrigin function [92].

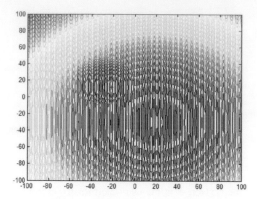

Figure 6.33: Contour graph of f_{10} [92].

Thirty runs were performed per method for each function, and the best (Best), worst (Worst), median (Median), mean (Mean), and standard deviation (SD) values obtained are shown in Table 6.3. The $UMDA_c$ results are taken from [47].

As can be seen from Table 6.3, the performance of the VAE-EDA algorithm was similar to that of $UMDA_c$ for all functions. Also, for most of the functions, VAE-EDA and E-VAE-EDA showed better performance than VAE-EDA-Q and CE-VAE-EDA. A detailed discussion is given below.

f_1, f_2, f_3, and f_4 are a unimodal function, continuous and differentiable at all points and have a relatively simple shape. However, the VAE-EDA algorithms did not necessarily proceed well in the search. This suggests that VAE-EDA may be running into premature convergence even on simple slopes, which are not flat areas in the search space where the evaluation value hardly changes, or small valleys near the local optimal solution.

In addition, except for f_3, the performance of VAE-EDA-Q was lower than that of other algorithms. This may be due to the fact that solutions with good performance remain in the population queue for several generations and thus the diversity of solutions chosen for the training set is lost. This may have caused the premature convergence on the slope of the search space mentioned above to occur at an earlier stage, resulting in a decrease in search efficiency.

f_2 and f_3 are functions with rotation. In these functions, compared with the results of f_1 and f_4 without rotation, VAE-EDA algorithm are inferior to $UMDA_c$, but have some good results. This result can be attributed to the fact that $UMDA_c$ is an EDA that does not assume dependency among variables, while VAE-EDA uses a neural network to consider such dependency.

f_5 to f_{10} are multimodal functions. For these functions, in addition to the premature convergence that occurs on the slope of the search space as described above, the initial convergence that occurs near the local optimal solution is supposed to have a negative impact on the search.

Table 6.3: Experimental results (VAE-EDAs v.s. UMDA$_c$).

function	method	Best	Worst	Median	Mean	SD
f_1	UMDA$_c$	0.00e+00	0.00e+00	0.00e+00	0.00e+00	0.00e+00
	VAE-EDA	7.84e+01	1.16e+03	4.93e+02	5.29e+02	3.01e+02
	E-VAE-EDA	5.27e+01	9.73e+02	3.98e+02	4.09e+02	2.07e+02
	CE-VAE-EDA	7.94e+02	3.32e+03	1.81e+03	1.82e+03	5.38e+02
	VAE-EDA-Q	2.79e+03	3.91e+03	3.41e+03	3.39e+03	2.69e+02
f_2	UMDA$_c$	1.30e+06	6.57e+06	4.96e+06	4.89e+06	9.95e+05
	VAE-EDA	8.04e+06	1.23e+07	9.85e+06	1.00e+07	1.17e+06
	E-VAE-EDA	8.40e+06	1.28e+07	1.06e+07	1.05e+07	1.03e+06
	CE-VAE-EDA	7.89e+06	1.33e+07	1.02e+07	1.03e+07	1.34e+06
	VAE-EDA-Q	1.54e+07	2.43e+07	1.83e+07	1.84e+07	1.94e+06
f_3	UMDA$_c$	8.32e+03	1.86e+04	1.28e+04	1.29e+04	2.43e+03
	VAE-EDA	1.40e+04	1.73e+04	1.58e+04	1.58e+04	8.74e+02
	E-VAE-EDA	1.30e+04	1.78e+04	1.58e+04	1.57e+04	1.24e+03
	CE-VAE-EDA	1.28e+04	2.02e+04	1.82e+04	1.81e+04	1.50e+03
	VAE-EDA-Q	1.32e+04	1.87e+04	1.77e+04	1.73e+04	1.26e+03
f_4	UMDA$_c$	0.00e+00	5.69e-01	0.00e+00	1.12e-02	7.97-02
	VAE-EDA	3.59e+02	9.52e+02	6.10e+02	5.94e+02	1.31e+02
	E-VAE-EDA	3.04e+02	1.07e+03	5.79e+02	6.27e+02	1.96e+02
	CE-VAE-EDA	6.47e+02	1.50e+03	1.08e+03	1.08e+03	1.91e+02
	VAE-EDA-Q	2.35e+02	2.82e+03	1.70e+03	1.71e+03	6.40e+02
f_5	UMDA$_c$	1.02e+01	6.27e+01	3.21e+01	3.21e+01	1.40e+01
	VAE-EDA	8.94e+01	2.41e+02	1.28e+02	1.33e+02	3.13e+01
	E-VAE-EDA	9.37e+01	1.88e+02	1.29e+02	1.32e+02	2.98e+01
	CE-VAE-EDA	1.38e+02	2.64e+02	2.00e+02	1.95e+02	3.35e+01
	VAE-EDA-Q	2.06e+02	4.24e+02	3.50e+02	3.42e+02	5.29e+01
f_6	UMDA$_c$	1.89e+00	4.48e+00	3.34e+00	3.35e+00	5.87e-01
	VAE-EDA	8.90e+00	1.24e+01	1.13e+01	1.12e+01	8.99e-01
	E-VAE-EDA	9.74e+00	1.26e+01	1.16e+01	1.14e+01	8.12e-01
	CE-VAE-EDA	8.85e+00	1.29e+01	1.11e+01	1.12e+01	9.50e-01
	VAE-EDA-Q	9.88e+00	1.22e+01	1.12e+01	1.10e+01	6.83e-01
f_7	UMDA$_c$	1.30e-01	4.92e+00	1.13e+00	1.55e+00	1.12e+00
	VAE-EDA	1.68e+02	3.16e+02	2.46e+02	2.54e+02	4.27e+01
	E-VAE-EDA	1.70e+02	3.60e+02	2.47e+02	2.54e+02	4.52e+01
	CE-VAE-EDA	2.33e+02	4.84e+02	3.44e+02	3.47e+02	5.83e+01
	VAE-EDA-Q	4.88e+02	6.88e+02	6.22e+02	6.15e+02	5.37e+01
f_8	UMDA$_c$	0.00e+00	0.00e+00	0.00e+00	0.00e+00	0.00e+00
	VAE-EDA	4.86e+01	9.26e+01	6.40e+01	6.51e+01	1.01e+01
	E-VAE-EDA	5.21e+01	9.76e+01	7.23e+01	7.22e+01	1.03e+01
	CE-VAE-EDA	6.26e+01	1.17e+02	8.02e+01	8.28e+01	1.29e+01
	VAE-EDA-Q	8.21e+01	1.20e+02	1.00e+02	1.00e+02	1.03e+01
f_9	UMDA$_c$	2.42e-04	6.09e+00	2.01e+00	2.27e+00	1.37e+00
	VAE-EDA	7.18e+01	1.11e+02	9.06e+01	8.95e+01	8.44e+00
	E-VAE-EDA	7.42e+01	1.11e+02	9.12e+01	9.07e+01	9.99e+00
	CE-VAE-EDA	9.04e+01	1.25e+02	1.09e+02	1.08e+02	8.29e+00
	VAE-EDA-Q	7.70e+01	1.09e+02	9.21e+01	9.22e+01	8.31e+00
f_{10}	UMDA$_c$	1.14e+01	1.92e+01	1.33e+01	1.36e+01	1.93e+00
	VAE-EDA	2.43e+01	4.62e+01	3.51e+01	3.60e+01	4.87e+00
	E-VAE-EDA	2.93e+01	5.46e+01	3.88e+01	3.95e+01	6.68e+00
	CE-VAE-EDA	2.87e+01	5.78e+01	3.51e+01	3.79e+01	8.00e+00
	VAE-EDA-Q	3.09e+01	5.90e+01	4.58e+01	4.52e+01	9.62e+00

Algorithm 9 adaVEDA

$t \leftarrow 0$
$v \leftarrow 1$ ▷ Set the variance to be used for sampling from the VAE.
Randomly initialize the initial set P_0.
$best_0 \leftarrow$ best fitness value in P_0
Initialize VAE M.
while $t < MaxGeneration$ **do**
Select the individuals with high fitness values from P_t and generate the candidate set Q_t.
Use Q_t to learn VAE M.
Produce the next set P_{t+1} by generating individuals from M.
     $best_{t+1} \leftarrow$ best fitness value in P_{t+1}
     if $best_{t+1} > best_t$ **then**
         $v \leftarrow \min(cv, v_{max})$
     else
         $v \leftarrow \max(v/c, v_{min})$
     end if
     $t \leftarrow t + 1$
end while

We have proposed a new algorithm adaVEDA (adaptive VAE-EDA) that would solve the problems of the existing VAE-EDA. The existing VAE-EDA often gets stuck in a local optimal solution in the middle of the search. This may be due to the problem of premature convergence like in genetic algorithms, where the diversity of solutions is lost as the search progresses, and only similar solutions are generated. In adaVEDA, when the search is no longer progressing, a change is made to generate more diverse solutions than usual.

Normally, a VAE generates new solutions by inputting values sampled from a standard multivariate normal distribution of the same dimension as the latent variable z.

When adaVEDA fails to improve the solution, it multiplies the variance of the normal distribution used for sampling by c ($c > 1$). By doing so, we try to escape from the local optimal solution and force the diversity of solutions to increase. Also, in order to maintain the ability to improve the solution, we multiply the variance of the normal distribution by $1/c$ when the solution is improved. This controls the value of the variance between v_{min} and v_{max}.

As a method to control the variance in EDA, Adaptive Variance Scaling (AVS) [43] was proposed. AVS basically decreases the variance only when the solution is not improved. On the other hand, adaVEDA not only increases but also decreases the variance according to the above criteria. This is because it considers the case when the solution is not improved with lack of diversity, and aims to recover the diversity by increasing the variance.

We have compared the best-performing VAE with our proposed method adaVEDA. The parameters used in the experiments were as follows:

- Population size: 500

- Maximum generatoin: 400

- Elite ratio: 30%

- Dimensions of latent variables: 3

- Intermediate layers: 20 dimensions

- Number of epochs during learning in each generation: 10

For adaVEDA, we chose the following parameters:

- Magnification of variance $c = 1.1$

- Minimum variance $v_{min} = 1$

- Maximum variance $v_{max} = 10$

Thirty runs were performed per method for each function, and the best (Best), worst (Worst), median (Median), mean (Mean), and standard deviation (SD) values obtained are shown in Table 6.4. For each method, two results are given: one at 200 generations (10,000 function evaluations) and the other at 400 generations (20,000 function evaluations). For the sake of statistical comparison, Welch's t-test was performed at the significance level, and if there was a significant difference, the background of the superior method was grayed out.

The maximum, average, and minimum values for each generation are plotted in Figs. 6.34 to 6.43, where the vertical axis is the evaluation value and the horizontal axis is the number of generations. The vertical axis is logarithmic except for f_6.

As can be seen from Table 6.4, adaVEDA performed better than the original VAE-EDA in many functions. A detailed discussion is given below.

In the results for the unimodal function of $f_1 - f_4$ in Figs. 6.34 to 6.37, VAE-EDA did not improve the solution from 200 to 400 generations, and the search was not stable. On the other hand, in adaVEDA, the solution was improved even after 200 generations except for f_1. This indicates that the premature convergence on the slope of the search space, which was pointed out above, has been eliminated in adaVEDA.

Different behaviors were observed in the multimodal functions of $f_5, f_6, \cdots, f_{10}$. In these functions, our proposed method performed better than the simple VAE-EDA, but only two functions, f_5 and f_7, showed some improvement from 200 to 400 generations. This may be due to the fact that for functions

Table 6.4: Experimental results (VAE-EDA v.s. adaVEDA).

func.	method	gen.	Best	Worst	Median	Mean	SD
f_1	VAE-EDA	200	5.51e-03	9.68e-01	8.53e-02	1.39e-01	1.84e-01
	VAE-EDA	400	5.51e-03	9.68e-01	8.53e-02	1.39e-01	1.84e-01
	adaVEDA	200	7.81e-04	3.15e-01	6.33e-03	2.45e-02	5.87e-02
	adaVEDA	400	6.25e-04	1.51e-02	3.89e-03	4.97e-03	3.70e-03
f_2	VAE-EDA	200	2.76e+06	4.12e+06	3.31e+06	3.33e+06	3.45e+05
	VAE-EDA	400	2.71e+06	4.11e+06	3.26e+06	3.30e+06	3.59e+05
	adaVEDA	200	1.51e+06	3.49e+06	2.88e+06	2.76e+06	4.27e+05
	adaVEDA	400	1.20e+06	3.00e+06	2.42e+06	2.30e+06	3.89e+05
f_3	VAE-EDA	200	9.03e+03	1.41e+04	1.30e+04	1.28e+04	1.04e+03
	VAE-EDA	400	9.03e+03	1.39e+04	1.29e+04	1.27e+04	1.01e+03
	adaVEDA	200	8.15e+03	1.34e+04	1.15e+04	1.14e+04	1.32e+03
	adaVEDA	400	7.81e+03	1.28e+04	1.12e+04	1.07e+04	1.34e+03
f_4	VAE-EDA	200	4.26e+01	1.92e+02	9.40e+01	1.00e+02	3.26e+01
	VAE-EDA	400	4.26e+01	1.92e+02	9.28e+01	9.96e+01	3.26e+01
	adaVEDA	200	4.42e+01	1.73e+02	7.96e+01	8.52e+01	2.85e+01
	adaVEDA	400	3.44e+01	1.33e+02	6.50e+01	6.99e+01	2.29e+01
f_5	VAE-EDA	200	5.81e+00	7.40e+01	1.68e+01	2.95e+01	2.51e+01
	VAE-EDA	400	5.81e+00	7.40e+01	1.68e+01	2.94e+01	2.51e+01
	adaVEDA	200	5.42e+00	7.47e+01	1.34e+01	2.60e+01	2.25e+01
	adaVEDA	400	3.65e+00	7.37e+01	1.04e+01	2.29e+01	2.16e+01
f_6	VAE-EDA	200	6.29e+00	1.29e+01	9.29e+00	9.67e+00	1.61e+00
	VAE-EDA	400	6.29e+00	1.29e+01	9.29e+00	9.67e+00	1.60e+00
	adaVEDA	200	4.63e+00	1.14e+01	9.19e+00	9.13e+00	1.76e+00
	adaVEDA	400	4.63e+00	1.13e+01	9.09e+00	9.07e+00	1.75e+00
f_7	VAE-EDA	200	9.34e-01	2.18e+01	6.78e+00	7.60e+00	4.98e+00
	VAE-EDA	400	9.34e-01	2.16e+01	6.78e+00	7.59e+00	4.96e+00
	adaVEDA	200	1.43e+00	1.34e+01	5.26e+00	6.61e+00	3.67e+00
	adaVEDA	400	7.39e-01	1.01e+01	3.96e+00	4.68e+00	2.62e+00
f_8	VAE-EDA	200	1.05e+01	4.74e+01	2.58e+01	2.67e+01	9.09e+00
	VAE-EDA	400	1.05e+01	4.74e+01	2.58e+01	2.67e+01	9.09e+00
	adaVEDA	200	1.10e+01	4.48e+01	2.24e+01	2.39e+01	8.81e+00
	adaVEDA	400	1.09e+01	4.48e+01	2.24e+01	2.38e+01	8.80e+00
f_9	VAE-EDA	200	1.53e+01	6.62e+01	4.94e+01	4.72e+01	1.28e+01
	VAE-EDA	400	1.53e+01	6.62e+01	4.94e+01	4.72e+01	1.27e+01
	adaVEDA	200	1.61e+01	5.69e+01	4.22e+01	4.18e+01	1.12e+01
	adaVEDA	400	1.61e+01	5.60e+01	4.15e+01	4.04e+01	1.05e+01
f_{10}	VAE-EDA	200	1.79e+01	3.72e+01	2.75e+01	2.76e+01	4.20e+00
	VAE-EDA	400	1.79e+01	3.72e+01	2.75e+01	2.75e+01	4.13e+00
	adaVEDA	200	1.39e+01	3.56e+01	1.96e+01	2.06e+01	4.66e+00
	adaVEDA	400	1.39e+01	3.47e+01	1.91e+01	2.03e+01	4.48e+00

with a search space shape like a large hollow around the locally optimal solution, it is not easy to escape from the local optima if the variance is increased.

One of our future tasks is to maintain the diversity of solutions in the early stage of the search. If we can maintain the diversity of solutions from the beginning of the search, we will be able to get better results for multimodal functions. Also, by reusing the obtained networks, we can realize more robust optimization

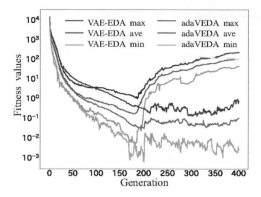

Figure 6.34: Results for f_1.

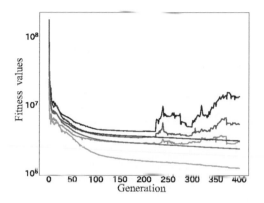

Figure 6.35: Results for f_2.

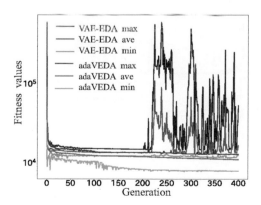

Figure 6.36: Results for f_3.

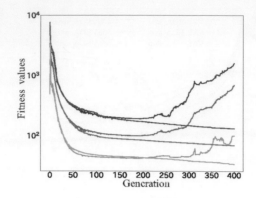

Figure 6.37: Results for f_4.

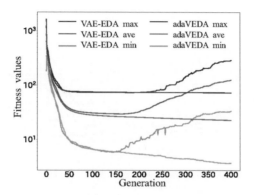

Figure 6.38: Results for f_5.

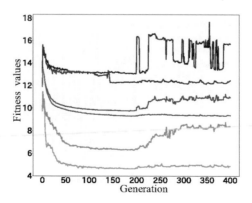

Figure 6.39: Results for f_6.

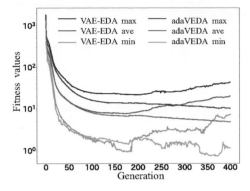

Figure 6.40: Results for f_7.

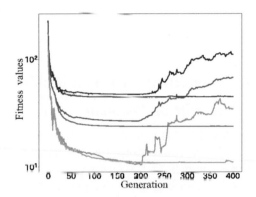

Figure 6.41: Results for f_8.

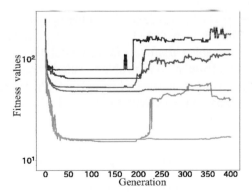

Figure 6.42: Results for f_9.

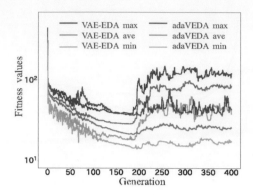

Figure 6.43: Results for f_{10}.

methods. For example, the application to other similar functions and dynamic optimization is an interesting research topic.

6.3 Preventing Overfitting of LSTMs using ACO

6.3.1 LSTM and Overfitting Problem

Long Short-Term Memory (LSTM) is a particular type of recurrent neural networks (RNN). It has feedback connections and can handle sequences of data. However, because of the complex and expressive structure of LSTM, it often suffers from a problem of overfitting; it is liable to overfit only the training data and gets low generalization performance.

Too complex a model architecture compared to the training samples or the nature of the prediction target is one of the causes of overfitting in neural networks. In other words, too many trainable parameters in the neural network would be a cause of overfitting. Thus, it is expected that overfitting can be suppressed by reducing the number of trainable parameters in the model. However, if the model is oversimplified, it suffers from another problem called underfitting, where the properties of the prediction target cannot be learned enough. Therefore, it is necessary to find the complexity and structure of the model that is neither excessive nor insufficient for prediction.

6.3.2 Optimizing the Structure of Neural Networks using ACO

The structure of a neural network affects its performance. Too simple a structure will fail to learn enough information from the training data and too complex one takes too much time to train and suffers from overfitting. The optimal structure depends on the dataset to be trained and manually determining the structure for each dataset is a hard task. Such an optimization problem can be solved using

ACO as a combinatorial problem, in which a structure with maximum complexity is set and its substructure is selected.

Salama and Abdelbar represented the structure of a feedforward neural network by a combination of connections between neurons and applied ACO in order to optimize the structure [121]. The graph for constructing a solution is composed of two paths for each connection between neurons in the neural network, indicating whether or not the connection should be included in the network. The neural network with the constructed structure is trained using backpropagation and the performance of the trained network is used for the evaluation value of the solution.

ElSaid et al. used ACO to optimize the internal structure of LSTMs [38]. The structure of LSTMs was represented in a simplified graph, and multiple ants traversed the graph to select a structure. It greatly reduced the number of trainable parameters and achieved better performance. However, this method requires repeating the heavy process of training LSTM many times, which makes the whole algorithm very time-consuming.

6.3.3   ACO for LSTMs (ACOL)

We have proposed a method for preventing overfitting of LSTMs by means of ant colony optimization, which we call *ACOL* (ACO for LSTMs, [77]). The basic strategy is to optimize the internal structure of LSTM using ACO, changing its structure while training using backpropagation. *ACOL* can reduce vast amount of computation time which was a problem with the traditional ACO-based methods. The additional procedures required for *ACOL*, ACO related ones such as constructing solutions and updating pheromone, take much shorter computation time compared to that of normal training of LSTM using backpropagation. Therefore, the increase in the computation time using *ACOL* is only subtle.

The initial structure of the LSTM model is described in Table 6.5. The model takes an n-dimensional sequence of length L as input and outputs a one-dimensional value as the prediction. Two layers of LSTM are stacked, and a fully connected layer for scaling up follows them. The second LSTM layer only carries the last output in the sequence to the succeeding fully connected layer. The output of each LSTM layer is computed using eqs. (5.18)–(5.20). The output of the fully connected layer is computed using $y = Wx + b$, where x is the input of the layer and y is the output.

The basic flow of *ACOL* is shown in Fig. 6.44. It is basically a repetition of four steps: (1) constructing a structure stochastically using the information of the pheromone; (2) training the LSTM model with the structure using backpropagation; (3) evaluating the structure; and (4) updating the pheromone. However, before beginning the iteration, some operations have to be done for initialization.

A graph representing the internal structure of LSTM has to be created first. It is shown in Fig. 6.45, which is the same as the one used in [38]. How it corre-

Table 6.5: Architecture of LSTM Model.

Layer	Output of the Layer
Input	$L \times n$
LSTM 1	$L \times n$
LSTM 2	1
Fully Connected	1

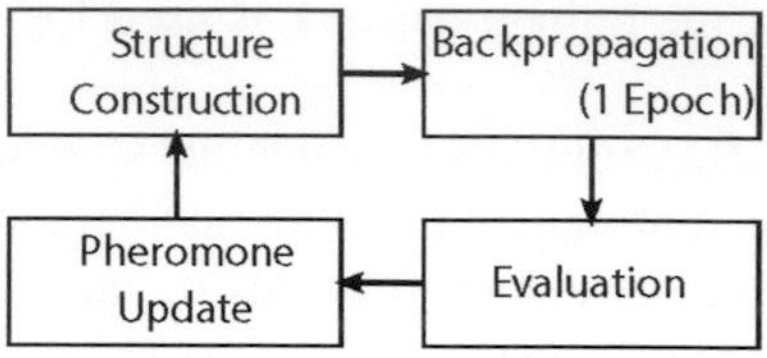

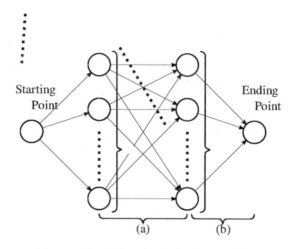

Figure 6.44: Basic flow of *ACOL*.

Figure 6.45: ACO graph for two-layer LSTM.

sponds to the structure of LSTM is explained in the next paragraph. The amount of pheromone deposited on each edge of the graph is set to an equal value to finish the initialization.

Each iteration begins with constructing a structure for LSTMs. It is done by multiple ants traversing the graph from left to right at one time. The part (a) of the graph corresponds to the weights of the first LSTM layer ($\boldsymbol{W}_*^1, \boldsymbol{R}_*^1 \in \mathbb{R}^{n \times n}$, where $*$ can be $\boldsymbol{z}, \boldsymbol{i}, \boldsymbol{f}$, or $\boldsymbol{o}$), and the part (b) corresponds to the feedforward weights of the second LSTM layer ($\boldsymbol{W}_*^2 \in \mathbb{R}^{1 \times n}$). n is the number of dimensions of the layer. The weights which one or more ants have passed will be used as a part of the structure (activated), and the weights which no ant has passed will be eliminated from the structure (deactivated). The activation/deactivation of weights can be straightforwardly expressed using the dropconnect masks. The element of the dropconnect masks M_*^{W1}, $M_*^{R1} \in \mathbb{R}^{n \times n}$ and $M_*^{W2} \in \mathbb{R}^{1 \times n}$ will be set to 1 (0), if it corresponds to an edge which some ants have (have not) passed. For example, when $n = 4$ and five ants have traversed the graph following the colored paths as in Fig. 6.46, the dropconnect masks representing the constructed structure will be given as eq. (6.7) and eq. (6.8). Note that the masks with the same dimensionality all share the same structure.

$$
M_*^{W1}, M_*^{R1} = \begin{bmatrix} 0 & 0 & 0 & 1 \\ 1 & 0 & 0 & 1 \\ 1 & 0 & 1 & 0 \\ 0 & 0 & 0 & 0 \end{bmatrix} \tag{6.7}
$$

$$
M_*^{W2} = \begin{bmatrix} 1 & 1 & 1 & 0 \end{bmatrix} \tag{6.8}
$$

When the ants move across the graph, they probabilistically choose one edge after another using eq. (4.1). However, because no efficient heuristics are available, α and β in eq. (4.1) is set to 1 and 0, respectively. In simple words, the ants choose the edges with a larger amount of pheromone with higher probabilities.

After constructing a structure for LSTMs, the second step of iteration is training the LSTM model with the constructed structure using backpropagation. The calculations of LSTMs are done using eqs. (5.19), (5.20), (5.23), (5.24), and the constructed dropconnect masks, such as eqs. (6.7) and (6.8). In our method, LSTMs are trained for one epoch, i.e., until all the training data are used once.

The third step is evaluating the structure. The constructed LSTM structure is evaluated using the validation data, which were set apart from the training data and never used for training. The evaluation value of the selected internal structure $V(S)$ will be the inverse of the prediction error on the validation data.

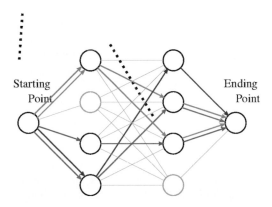

Figure 6.46: Example of ants traversing the graph.

Lastly, the pheromone information is updated based on the evaluation of the structure $V(S)$. The amount of pheromone increase on each edge is calculated using the following equation:

$$\Delta \tau_{ij} = Q \cdot V(S) \cdot N_{ij}, \tag{6.9}$$

where N_{ij} is the number of ants which have passed the edge (i, j), and Q is a positive constant. Then, the amount of pheromone is updated using eq. (4.4). After the update, the next iteration repeats itself to construct a structure until the maximum number of iterations (or epochs) is exceeded.

In the early stages of training, there is no significant difference in the amount of pheromone in the graph, and all weights are chosen with approximately equal probability. As the training proceeds, a large amount of pheromone are deposited on the paths that contributes to better performance, and it is expected to converge to the optimal structure in the end.

6.3.4   Experiments with *ACOL*

ACOL was applied to LSTM models for time-series prediction of real-world data to test its performance. It was compared with three models: the one without any methods to prevent overfitting (base model), the one with dropout, and the one with dropconnect. Three types of datasets were prepared for training: sensor data from burners in a coal-fired power plant, weather data, and stock price data. Each dataset was divided into three parts: training data, validation data, and test data. Training data were used for training LSTM models with backpropagation. Validation data were used for selecting hyperparameters and for early stopping. They were also used for the evaluation for ACO in *ACOL*. Test data were used to evaluate the generalization performance on unseen data.

The detailed information of datasets is as follows:

1. Burner

    This dataset consists of per-minute time-series data collected from burners in a coal-fired power plant, and there are 10 days of data from 12 burners. This dataset was originally used in [39] for time-series prediction, and it is available at the author's GitHub repository[9]. A part of the dataset is shown in Fig. 6.47. The data at a point in time consist of 12 parameters, such as coal supply, temperature, and air flow etc. All data were preliminarily normalized so that the range of values is 0 to 1.

    In this study, "Main Flame Intensity," one of the 12 parameters, was selected for the prediction target as it was in [39]. The data of 12 burners were split into three parts, and the data of 10, 1, and 1 burners were allocated to training, validation, and test data, respectively.

---

[9]https://github.com/travisdesell/exact/tree/main/datasets/2018_coal.

Sensor data from coal-fired power plants

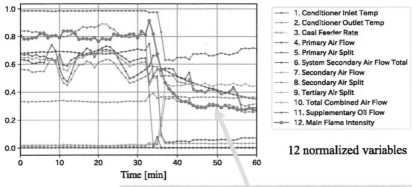

12 normalized variables

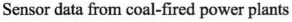

Predict 12. Main Flame Intensity in 10 minutes

Figure 6.47: A part of burner dataset.

2. Weather

This dataset consists of 15 parameters, such as date and time, temperature, atmospheric pressure, and humidity, recorded every 10 minutes at a weather station of the Max Planck Institute of Biogeochemistry in Germany (see Fig. 6.48). The original data are available at the institute's website[10]. In this study, the data of eight years from 2009 to 2016 were used. The data were preprocessed as described below, and the number of dimensions was 19 for the input data. One of the parameters, "temperature," was selected for the prediction target for this study. The 70%, 20%, and 10% of the data were allocated to training, validation, and test data, respectively, in order of oldest to newest.

3. Stock Price

This dataset consists of opening prices of the stocks that make up the Dow Jones Industrial Average (DJIA)[11]. The data of five years from 2016 to 2020 were used in this study. DOW[12] was excluded from the dataset because full five years of data were not available, and 29 components were in the dataset (see Fig. 6.49). The data were obtained from Yahoo!Finance[13]. The opening price of AAPL[14] of the next trading day was selected for the prediction target in this study. The 70%, 20%, and 10% of the data

---

[10]https://www.bgc-jena.mpg.de/wetter/weather_data.html.

[11]A stock market index that measures the stock performance of 30 large companies listed on stock exchanges in the United States.

[12]Dow Inc. stock quote.

[13]https://finance.yahoo.com/.

[14]Apple Inc. stock quote.

Meteorological data such as temperature, humidity, and pressure (normalized 19 variables)

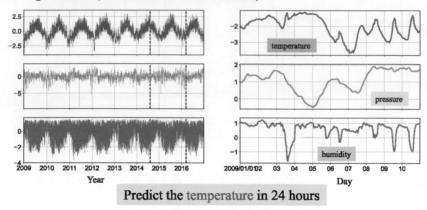

Predict the temperature in 24 hours

Figure 6.48: A part of weather dataset.

Opening prices of the 30 Dow Jones Industrial Average components (excluding DOW)   Normalized 29 variables

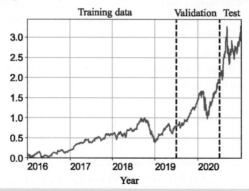

Predict the opening price of AAPL on the next business day

Figure 6.49: A part of stock price dataset.

were allocated to training, validation, and test data, respectively, in order of oldest to newest, and they were normalized using the training data.

All models are first trained for the same numbers of epochs, and then ideal early stopping [113] was applied for the sake of comparison. For the sake of model evaluation, we used the prediction error of the test data at the epoch where the error of the validation data is minimized. For the prediction error, the mean squared error (MSE) was used. Since training LSTM with backpropagation

Table 6.6: Hyperparameters for LSTM.

Dataset	Burner	Weather	Stock Price
Input dimension	12	19	29
Input length L	10	24	10
P time step ahead prediction	10	24	1
Training epoch	1000	5000	10000
Batch size	128	64	16
Learning rate	10^{-4}	10^{-5}	10^{-5}
Dropout rate	0.1	0.2	0.1
Dropconnect rate	0.1	0.1	0.2

Table 6.7: Hyperparameters for ACO.

Dataset	Burner	Weather	Stock Price
Number of ants	288	722	1682
Initial pheromone	1	1	1
Coefficient Q	6.9×10^{-6}	3.5×10^{-4}	2.4×10^{-4}
Evaporation rate ρ	0.05	0.05	0.05

and using ACO are both stochastic processes, each method was run for multiple times, and the average was used for the comparison. The numbers of runs were 20 for the burner dataset, and 10 for the other datasets.

Hyperparameters for LSTM are shown in Table 6.6. The number of input dimension to LSTM was equal to that of each dataset. The length L of the input data and the parameter P of how many time steps ahead to predict were determined in consideration of the periodicity of the datasets. LSTM training was done by backpropagation using Adam optimizer [76]. The learning rate was first tuned using an arbitrarily fixed batch size, and the batch size was adjusted afterward. This is because the results from [53] suggest that those two parameters could be adjusted independently. Applying dropout to the feedforward part of the first LSTM layer led to bad performance, and thus excluded. Dropconnect was applied to all weights in the two LSTM layers, and the same dropconnect rate was used for all parts. Tensorflow (version 2.3.0) was used for training and evaluation of LSTMs.

Hyperparameters for ACO used in *ACOL* are shown in Table 6.7. The number of ants traversing the graph in Fig. 6.45 at a time was set to be twice the number of edges in part (a) of the graph, i.e., if the input is n-dimensional, the number of ants is $2n^2$. The coefficient Q was set so that the increasing amount of pheromone on an edge would be about 1.0 when the prediction error of the model was about the target error and about half of the total number of ants passed through the edge. The target error used was the error for the validation data obtained during the hyperparameter tuning. The evaporation rate ρ was set so that the amount of pheromone would settle around 20.0 provided that the increasing amount of pheromone was about 1.0, which was the upper limit reported in [38].

6.3.5 Results of Ants

The learning curves for the burner dataset are shown in the top row of Fig. 6.50. They are averaged over 20 runs. From left to right, the transitions of prediction errors for training data, validation data, and test data are shown with the horizontal axis being the epoch. The prediction errors for the training data tended to decrease for all methods, but, except for *ACOL*, the prediction errors for the validation and test data started increasing in the middle, indicating that overfitting has occurred.

The learning curves for the weather dataset are shown in the center row of Fig. 6.50. They are averaged over 10 runs. The prediction errors for the training data tended to decrease for all methods. However, in case of the base model and dropout, the prediction errors for the validation and test data started increasing in the middle, indicating that overfitting has occurred. For dropconnect and *ACOL*, there was little increase in the prediction errors, indicating that overfitting was suppressed.

The learning curves for the stock price dataset are shown in the bottom row of Fig. 6.50. They are averaged over 10 runs. For all methods, there was little increase in the prediction errors, indicating that overfitting did not occur. However, the prediction errors stopped decreasing in the middle of the process for all methods except *ACOL*.

Figure 6.51 shows the boxplots of the prediction errors for the test data when early stopped (i.e., when the prediction errors for the validation data hit the minimum). From top to bottom, the prediction errors are shown on the burner, weather, and stock price datasets. Averages are indicated as cross marks (X), and outliers are plotted individually as white dots. Welch's *t*-test was used for the sake of statistical comparison, and the method name is underlined if it had significantly smaller prediction error than the base model at the 5% level. If it had significantly smaller error than any other methods at the 5% level, the method name is highlighted in **bold italic**. For the two datasets of burner and stock price, *ACOL* achieved significantly better performance than that of the base model, while the other methods had no significant improvement. For the weather dataset, dropout, dropconnect, and *ACOL* all performed better than the base model, but there was no method which significantly outperformed any other methods. When compared with the minimum values, *ACOL* achieved the best results on all datasets.

Figure 6.52 shows the ratios of weights selected in the constructed structures using *ACOL* with epochs. They are averaged over 20 runs for the burner dataset and over 10 runs for the other datasets. For all datasets, the ratios of weights decreased almost monotonically as the training proceeded. The average ratios at the early stopped epoch, when the prediction errors for the validation data hit the

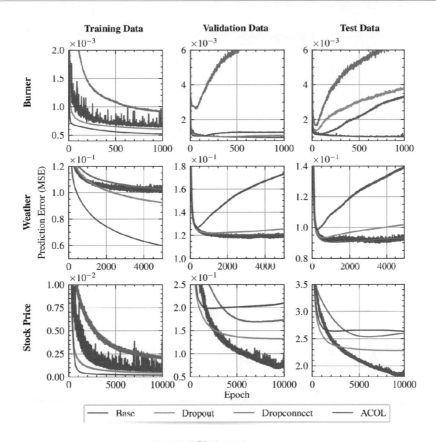

Figure 6.50: Learning curves.

minimum, were 67%, 39%, and 18%, respectively for the burner, weather, and stock price datasets.

As shown in Fig. 6.50 and Fig. 6.51, overfitting was prevented using *ACOL*, which resulted in better performance than other methods in case of the two datasets, i.e., burner and stock price. Even in the weather dataset, *ACOL* did not perform any worse. Therefore, we can say that *ACOL* is an effective method for preventing overfitting of LSTMs for time-series prediction.

Note that the ratios of weights used in the acquired structures by *ACOL* tended to decrease monotonically and did not converge to some fixed ratios (see Fig. 6.52). This is an expected result considering the characteristics of *ACOL*. When constructing a structure with *ACOL*, multiple ants traverse the graph in Fig. 6.45, choosing edges of more pheromones with higher probabilities. In many cases, *ACOL* resulted in an unstable equilibrium, in which two or more paths are selected, with the amount of pheromone deposited on those paths being exactly the same and the number of ants following the paths being exactly the same. Thus, *ACOL* is capable of omitting needless structures, but it cannot necessarily

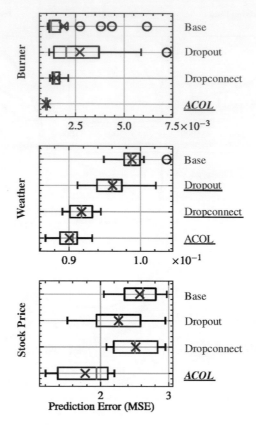

Figure 6.51: Boxplots of prediction errors.

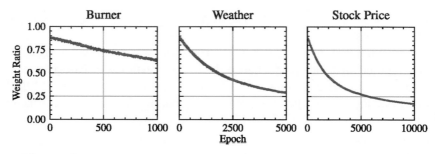

Figure 6.52: Ratios of weights selected in the constructed structures using *ACOL*.

keep the vital structures. A possible remedy for this would be to set an upper limit for the amount of pheromone. This strategy was chosen in [38] so as to make the above-mentioned equilibrium stable. Another remedy is to change the graph structure of LSTM to the ones used in [94] or [121], in which the graph consists of path pairs for each weight, indicating whether the weight should be included in the model. This would also enable the model to keep the necessary structures.

6.4   Deep Interactive Evolution

6.4.1   GAN and DeepIE

Some studies considered using GANs to combine deep learning with interactive evolutionary computation (IEC; see Section 3.10). This approach is called "deep interactive evolution."

For example, let us consider GAN as related to images. At this time, the images that are exported per the latent variable z value vary, but it is difficult to search for the latent variable space z when targeting a specific image. This is caused by the latent variable z being a vector that exceeds at least 10 dimensions (occasionally 20 dimensions). Moreover, the product traits that each dimension is acting upon are unclear. Therefore, the method of using evolutionary computation for searching for this latent variable space is being studied and is called "latent variable evolution." For example, CPPN2GAN [125] enables stage generation in games (i.e., Mario and Zelda) by combining CPPN and DCGAN. Additionally, deep master print [15] enables the generation of a master fingerprint (a fingerprint that matches any person's fingerprint and that can trick the fingerprint authentication system) by combining CMA-ES and GAN.

The deep interactive evolution framework [16] is shown in Fig. 6.53. The overall flow is given in Algorithm 10.

Deep interactive evolution uses general crossover, along with WGAN for GAN models. Figure 6.54 illustrates examples of sneakers and face images evolved using deep interactive evolution [16]. Target images are shown in the left column. Final images are the last selected image. Best images are the images

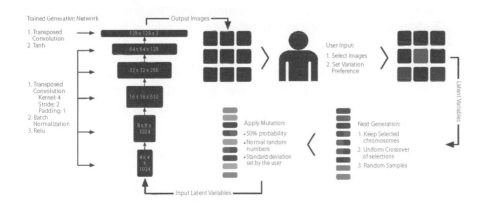

Figure 6.53: Overview of Deep Interactive Evolution (DeepIE) [16].

Algorithm 10 Deep Interactive Evolution

1: Create a generator by training a GAN.
2: Generate m latent variables z using the standard normal distribution. ▷
  Generation of initial population.
3: **while** the user's preferred images are not generated **do**
4:   Input latent variable z to the generator and obtain an image corresponding to
  z.
5:   Show the exported images to the user to select his/her preferred image(s). ▷
  The user can choose multiple preferred images.
6:   Perform genetic operations such as mutations and crossover. ▷
  The latent variables of the selected images are considered to be genes with high
  fitness values.
7:   The generated new genes are set as the latent variables at the next generation.
8: **end while**
9: Output the generated image from the obtained latent variable z.

---

that the user selected as best from a compilation of all their selections over the
entire evolutionary process.

6.4.2 DeepIE3D

DeepIE3D [147] uses deep interactive evolution and WGAN-GP [54] to generate
3D models. WGAN-GP employs a gradient penalty term related to the critic's
slope added to the WGAN loss function.

Interactive 3D modeling [95] is a framework of deep interactive evolution
developed to facilitate users' 3D modeling. The difference with the traditional
GAN structure is that, in addition to a generator, a phase called "projection" is
added. This is similar to the voxels structure of input x and provides the latent
variable $P(x)$ that generates a realistic product. Specifically, a projection model
$P(x)$ is designed to output latent variable z while keeping in mind the following
two points:

- Structure $G(z)$ generated from $z = P(x)$ should look similar to x. With
  this, edits matching the user's input are prioritized. For example, if the
  user selected an armchair when designing a chair, the model would prefer
  chairs with arms.

- Structure $G(z)$ should be feasible. This means that the generation of ex-
  port $x' = G(P(x))$ is prioritized so that it does not differ from the GAN
  training examples.

The structure generated via the user stacking voxels is used as the input for
interactive 3D modeling [95]. Instead of generating a structure from scratch, the

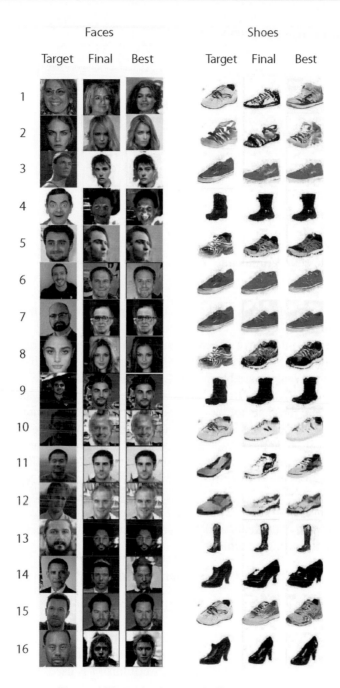

Figure 6.54: Evolved images by DeepIE [16].

Algorithm 11 Interactive 3D Modeling

1: Generate generator: $G(z)$.   ▷ GAN training.
2: Generate projector: $P(x)$.   ▷ Create projection.
3: Set $t := 1$.
4: The user generates the structure x_t by stacking voxels.
5: **while** the user's preferred image(s) is(are) not generated **do**
6:     Obtain x_{t+1} from x_t as follows:

$$z_{t+1} = P(x_t) \tag{6.10}$$
$$x_{t+1} = G(z_{t+1}) \tag{6.11}$$

7:     The user edits x_{t+1}.
8:     Set $t := t + 1$.
9: **end while**
10: Output the obtained structure.

---

main goal is to provide a rough skeleton and shape. The overall flow is described in Algorithm 11.

The focus in interactive 3D modeling is on the "realism" of the generated structure. Figure 6.55 shows a realistic structure z and nonrealistic structure z' generated in the latent variable space. Let us take a look at the diagram of the latent variable space in the figure. There is an area shown in red and another area in yellow. While the shape of the chair generated based on the latent variables in the red area is physically reasonable, the chair generated from the yellow area has legs that are cut off in the middle and a handrail that is broken off in the middle, resulting in a floating part. It is undesirable to generate physically unreasonable structures such as the ones in the yellow area when using GAN to design any structure.

By utilizing the training system of $P(x)$, the mapping to the latent variable space is restricted to the realistic domain z. Particularly, the projection is executed based on the following conditions [95]:

$$P(x) = \underset{z}{\text{argmin}}\ E(x, G(z)), \tag{6.12}$$
$$E(x, x') = \lambda_1 D(x, x') - \lambda_2 R(x'), \tag{6.13}$$

where $D(x_1, x_2)$ denotes the differences between two structures, x_1 and x_2. $R(x')$ is the evaluation function for the authenticity of the structure x' generated by the generator. The output value of the GAN discriminator is used for this evaluation function [95].

---

[15]Dataset of 3D models with manually verified categories and alignment annotations. See `https://shapenet.org/`.

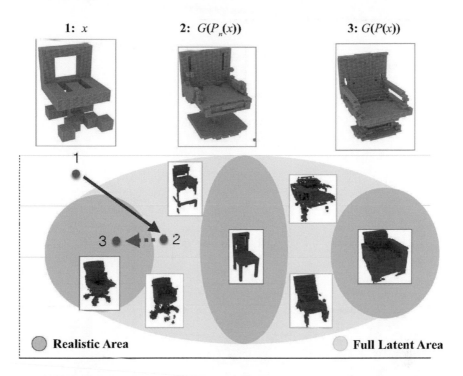

1: x **2:** $G(P_n(x))$ **3:** $G(P(x))$

Realistic Area   Full Latent Area

Figure 6.55: Depiction of how subcategories separate into realistic regions within the latent variable space of a generator [95].

Let us examine whether there is a relationship between the discriminator output value and the realism of the structure when setting the product of DeepIE3D as the input for the discriminator. The main parameters we used for DeepIE3D are shown in Table 6.8. The results of generated chairs are shown in Fig. 6.56. Each of the discriminator's output values is in Table 6.9 (the figure and table correspond to the same 3×3 individuals). As can be seen from the results, Individual #1's value is 0.7319, which is outstandingly large compared to the others. Individual #2 and Individual #4 have a value of a little more than 0.5. The other five individuals all have values slightly above 0.1. Let us recall that the closer to 1.0 the discriminator output values are, the more realistic. The closer to 0.0 they are, the more false they are determined to be; as a result, Individuals #1, #2, and #4 are determined to be more realistic. When observing the geometry of the exported structures, Individuals #1, #2, and #4 are chairs with a wide base and arms attached, while the other chairs have no arms and are narrow. However, from the point of view of realism, the Individual #1, #2, and #4 chairs all have legs that are cut off and appear unrealistic in some respects. The other five chairs do not have legs that are cut off for the most part and may actually be superbly realistic. Based on this, the discriminator does not determine the realism of chairs but

Table 6.8: Parameters for DeepIE3D.

Model	DCGAN [115]
Optimizer	ADAM [76]
#. of epochs	10,000
Batch size	64
#. of data	129
Dataset	shapenetcore v2[15]
Data format	voxel

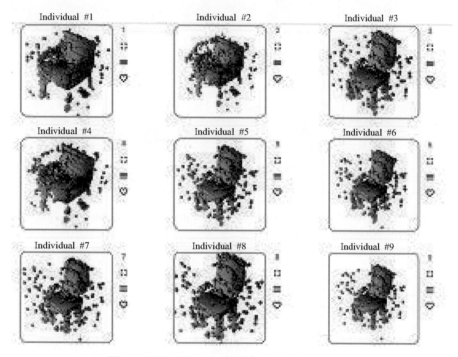

Figure 6.56: Example of generated chair structures.

Table 6.9: Results of applying the structures in Fig. 6.56 to a discriminator.

0.7319	0.5156	0.1328
0.5249	0.1296	0.1506
0.1192	0.1236	0.1268

shows whether it is similar to a chair with certain characteristics (here, a wide chair with arms).

6.4.3 Deep Interactive Evolution Based on Graph Kernel: DeepIE3DGK

In order to enable users to generate their preferred structures more efficiently, it is necessary to present solution candidates using evaluation value prediction. For this purpose, we have proposed a method called DeepIE3DGK (Deep Interactive Evolution based on Graph Kernel, [70]). The algorithm consists of two parts: (a) similarity comparison between 3D structures, and (b) genetic operation of IEC based on the comparison. The basic idea is based on Weisfeiler-Lehman graph kernel method [129].

To compare 3D structures, they have to be converted to graphs, after which the similarity between the graph structures are calculated. Each of the above steps is described in detail in Algorithm 12.

The first step in converting a 3D structure to a graph is clustering. This reduces the number of nodes in the graph and lowers the computational complexity of the Weisfeiler-Lehman method [129]. Additionally, it also allows us to extract global features without being affected by details. The K-means method is used as the clustering method. The number of clusters is proportional to the number of voxels in the original structure. This corresponds to the process of finding *num_clusters* in the Algorithm 12. Simonovsky et al. [128] proposed the voxel grid method, but this method is vulnerable to small shifts in coordinates and does not give good results. Therefore, we have chosen to use clustering.

After clustering by the K-means method, the data are converted to graphs. The data after clustering can be regarded as point cloud data. We will denote a point after clustering as $p \in P$, a node of the graph as $i \in V$, and an edge as $(i, j) \in E$. First of all, a point p is assigned to a node i, which corresponds to the **add_node** function in Algorithm 12. Here, the label of node i is based on the distance from the origin (x, y, z), which is set in advance. If we just label the real-valued distances as they are, we will have different labeling for voxels with slightly different positions (e.g., $[0, 0, 0]$ and $[0, 0, 1]$), which will cause us to lose

---

Algorithm 12 Convert Voxel Data to Graph.

Initialize : G ▷ Defaults: *std_num* $\leftarrow 5000, \varepsilon \leftarrow 1, k \leftarrow 0.5, center \leftarrow [0, 0, 0]$
num_clusters $\leftarrow$ sqrt(count(*Voxeldata*)/*std_num*)
$P \leftarrow K$-means(*Voxeldata*, *num_clusters*)
for $i < size(P)$ **do**
    G.**add_node**(*label* =**makelabel**($P[i]$, *center*, ε))
end for
for $i < size(P)$ **do**
    G.**connect**(i, P, k)
end for

---

robustness against subtle misalignments and irregularities. Therefore, we use the labeling method described below.

When the distance between a point (p_x, p_y, p_z) and the origin (x, y, z) is D, and the constant ε is given to designate the interval of discrete value of each label, derive the following labeling:

$$\text{label} = \frac{\varepsilon}{0.5} \lfloor \frac{0.5}{\varepsilon} D - 0.5 \rfloor. \tag{6.14}$$

This corresponds to the **makelabel** function in Algorithm 12.

Now that the nodes have been created and labeled, the next step is to create the edges. For connecting edges from a point x, we use the following rule.

(a) Calculate the distance from a point x for all $p \in P$ and sort them in ascending order.

(b) Connect the point p closest to x with an edge, and let D be the distance between p and x.

(c) For all the above sorted points, repeat the connecting process described below:

   ■ The point connected in (b) corresponds to the first point, i.e., the nearest point.

   ■ Suppose that the distance is D_j for a j-th reference point, and the constant is k.

   ■ The j-th point and x are connected by an edge if the following equation is satisfied, and the connecting process is terminated if not satisfied:

$$D_j < (1 + \frac{k}{j})D. \tag{6.15}$$

The edge knotting method described above disallows nodes that are not connected to any point and avoids creating too many edges. As a result, graph construction faithful to visual perception is possible. The processes (a) through (c) correspond to the function **connect** in Algorithm 12.

We compare the similarity of created graphs using the Weisfeiler-Lehman subtree kernel introduced above. We chose this method because of the high performance in terms of computational complexity. Since we need to calculate the similarity during the process of interactive evolutionary computation, the low computational complexity is an important factor in this research.

Here is an overview of the Weisfeiler-Lehman subtree kernel algorithm.

Step1 Suppose we have two graphs G and G' (see (b) in Fig. 6.57). The numbers indicate the labels of the nodes. At this point, for each node, the labels of the neighboring nodes are taken and a new label is created as [node label, [array of neighboring node labels]] (Fig. 6.57(c)). This is called a multiset label.

Step2 Sort the created multiset labels and assign a new label to each multiset label (see Fig. 6.57(d)). In other words, a unique new label is assigned to each combination of [node label, array of adjacent node labels]. The new label should be a label that has not yet been used. In the example of Fig. 6.57, the labels 4,6,8,10,12, and 14 are are not chosen as the new label because they have already been used at the beginning.

Step3 Apply the new label to the graph, referring to the correspondence between the multiset label created in **Step2** and the new label (see Fig. 6.57(e)).

Step4 Repeat h times the process from **Step1** to **Step3**.

Step5 For each graph, we create a vector that counts the number of times each node label appears, take the inner product and normalize it to get the similarity (see Fig. 6.57(f)).

Figure 6.57 shows the process of one iteration. Thus, the number of times are counted for the initial labels and the labels after the first re-labeling.

Finally we use the following normalization equation;

$$k_{normalized} = \frac{K(G,G')}{\sqrt{K(G,G)K(G',G')}}. \tag{6.16}$$

If the number of iterations is h, the number of graphs is N, the largest number of nodes in all graphs is n, and the largest number of edges is m, then the computational complexity is given as $O(Nhm + N^2 hn)$ (see [129]).

The flow of DeepIE3DGK is shown in Algorithm 13. In DeepIE3DGK, there are three changes from the original DeepIE3D: crossover method, reproduction method, and selection method. Moreover, DeepIE3DGK can choose undesirable structures (NG structures) in addition to good structures. NG structures are used for negative selection in the evolutionary process.

In DeepIE3D, only one gene is adopted as a child after uniform crossover for a set of latent variables (i.e., two latent variables z), whereas in DeepIE3DGK, the mirror image gene is also adopted as a child. This means that two children are born from two parent genes. The crossover of latent variables does not always result in a good mixture of substructures, which has been a problem in DeepIE3D. DeepIE3DGK aims to alleviate this problem by employing mirror images and generating a variety of structures as candidates.

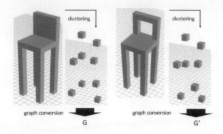

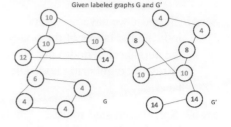

(a) Clustering and graph conversion.

(b) Graphs corresponding to the structures in (a). Labels are calculated by eq. (6.14). Edges are connected by eq. (6.15).

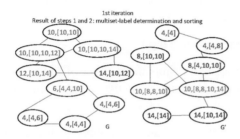

(c) A multiset label is given to each node.

(d) Assign a new label to a multiset label.

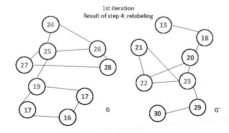

(e) Apply new labels.

(f) Calculate similarity K value.

Figure 6.57: A process of similarity comparison of 3D structures.

Algorithm 13 DeepIE3DG

$z \leftarrow$ interface.getPastZ()

function genCandidate($indices, s^2$)   ▷ s^2: mutation rate.
  $past_z \leftarrow z[indices[0]]$
  $cross_z \leftarrow$ Mutate(MirrorCrossOver($z[indices]$),s^2)
  $mutation_z \leftarrow$ Mutate($z[indices], s^2$)
  return $past_z + cross_z + mutation_z$
end function

$G_\theta \leftarrow$ trainGAN()
$indices \leftarrow$ interface.getSelectedImages()
$NGs \leftarrow$ interface.getNGImage()
$s^2 \leftarrow$ interface.getMutationParameter()
$candidate_z \leftarrow$ genCandidate($indices, s^2$)
$structures \leftarrow G_\theta(candidate_z) + G_\theta(z[indices]) + G_\theta(z[NGs])$
$graphs \leftarrow$ makeGraph($structures$)
$K \leftarrow$ WeisfeilerLehman($graphs, iteration$)
$new\_z \leftarrow$ select($candidate_z, K$)

Next, regarding the reproduction, the number of offspring is the same as the number of the next generation, and no selection is made in DeepIE3D. On the other hand, since the main focus is to narrow down the candidates using the similarity comparison of 3D structures, DeepIE3DGK generates a larger number of children. In addition, DeepIE3DGK keeps one of the individuals selected by the user in the previous generation to prevent the loss of the structure with the preferred characteristics. As for the crossover method, we use mirror image crossover as described above. The mutation method used is the same as DeepIE3D. If no structure has been selected in the previous generation, both DeepIE3D and DeepIE3DGK randomly generate candidate individuals.

Finally, the selection method is totally different from DeepIE3D. In DeepIE3DGK, the similarity between the user-selected structure and the candidate structures is calculated using the graph kernel method, and the system selects a few individuals with the highest fitness based on the similarity as the evaluation criterion.

In the case that only the NG was selected without any preferred structure, we compare the similarity between the next candidate structure and the NG individual. If the similarity with a certain NG individual is higher than the constant *border*, we eliminate such an individual from the list of candidates.

In order to prove the usefulness of the proposed method, we have made a set of experiments. First experiment is aimed at confirming the usefulness of the 3D structure comparison method. The detailed procedure is described as follows:

1. Determine a latent variable z_0 randomly.

2. Let $z(n) = z_0 + \mathcal{N}(0, nc)$ $(1 \le n \le 100)$. $\mathcal{N}(0, nc)$ refers to the normal distribution. c was set so that there would be some variation in the generated structures.

3. Generate $G(z_0)$ and a set of $G(z(n))$ by inputting z and z_0 into the generator.

4. Calculate the similarity K between $G(z(n))$ and $G(z_0)$ using the Weisfeiler-Lehman subtree kernel.

5. Set $\delta = \mathcal{N}(0, nc)$ and draw a scatter plot with $|\delta|$ on the horizontal axis and K on the vertical axis. This is to clarify the relationship between the latent variable distance and the product distance (i.e., similarity).

6. The structures corresponding to high, medium, and low similarities to the original structure are shown. This is to confirm that the proposed method intuitively judges similarity from a human perspective.

Experiments were conducted for two kinds of objects: chair and airplane. These objects were randomly generated with GAN. Examples of randomly generated structures $G_{\text{chair}}(z_0)$ and $G_{\text{plane}}(z_0)$, are as shown in Fig. 6.58. This latent variable z_0 was then used in the aforementioned process, yielding structures and similarity results as shown in Fig. 6.59.

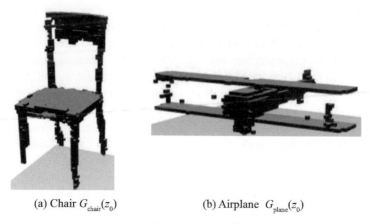

(a) Chair $G_{\text{chair}}(z_0)$ (b) Airplane $G_{\text{plane}}(z_0)$

Figure 6.58: Original structures.

Figure 6.59 (a) shows results for generating chairs. In this case we can see that for small $|\delta|$, most of the generated structures are similar to each other, with the similarity being almost constant between 0.7 and 0.8. On the other hand, the variance increases for large $|\delta|$, thus GAN seems to generate a diverse set of structures.

Figure 6.59 (b) shows results for generating planes. Results are similar to those of chairs. The variance is low for small $|\delta|$ and higher for big $|\delta|$. However, in case of generating plane structures we can observe higher overall variance, regardless of $|\delta|$. This means that it is easier to generate novel plane structures than to generate new chairs. Thus, we select designing chairs in the following experiment.

As we can see, GAN generates various structures, thus it may be difficult to select good features out of dissimilar structures. Using Weisfeiler-Lehman subtree kernel, we can calculate the similarity measure of the whole structure, allowing us to compare generated models. Furthermore, we can use this measure to calculate the similarity which can be used to guide the evolutionary process.

To confirm the superiority of DeepIE3DGK, we conducted a questionnaire-based experiment. We asked participants to actually work on IEC-based design, and evaluated the systems according to the data obtained in the process and questionnaires. In the experiment, volunteers were asked to use DeepIE3D and DeepIE3DGK, both of which use the same GUI as shown in Fig. 6.60. We asked the participants to generate two types of chairs: (i) office chair, which he/she would expect in the office; and (ii) artistic chair, which he/she would refer to as being "artistic". Volunteers participated in the experiment, with the following workflow:

1. We explained the operation of the system. Specifically, how to use the LIKE and NG buttons and how to set the mutation rate. We also mentioned that if no NG and LIKE buttons are chosen, the next generation will be randomly initialized.

2. We asked the participants to generate a chair that could be found in an office using either DeepIE3D or DeepIE3DGK.

3. We asked the participants to generate a chair that could be found in an office using the method not used above.

4. We asked the participants to generate an artistic chair using either the DeepIE3D or DeepIE3DGK.

5. We asked the participants to generate an artistic chair using the method not used above.

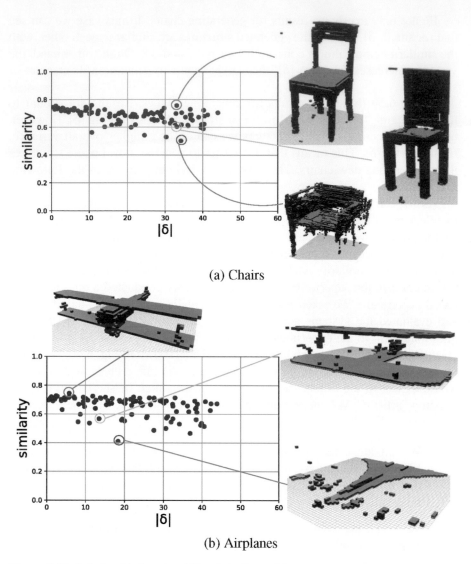

(a) Chairs

(b) Airplanes

Figure 6.59: Relationship between $|\delta|$ and similarity. The structures corresponding to high, medium, and low similarities are shown.

In order to avoid biased responses, the order of DeepIE3D and DeepIE3DGK was randomly switched. Additionally, to prevent the influence of the initial population on the results, we used exactly the same nine initial individuals in all experiments. The experiment was terminated when a satisfactory structure appeared or when the maximum number (=15) of generations has been reached. This condition was explained to the participants before the experiment. The results of the questionnaire are shown in Fig. 6.61. In the bar graph, a value close

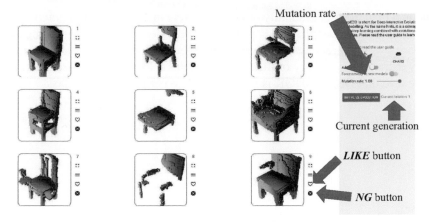

Figure 6.60: Overview of DeepIE3DGK.

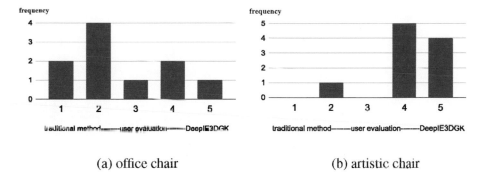

(a) office chair   (b) artistic chair

Figure 6.61: Which is better for designing a chair?

to 1(5) means that DeepIE3D (DeepIE3DGK) was rated high. The experiment took an average of 45 to 60 minutes per person. Ten male university students participated in the experiment. Their ages ranged from 20 to 30 years old.

Figure 6.61 plots the obtained results, which clearly show that DeepIE3DGK gave better performance in generating artistic chairs. Let us examine the responses of the questionnaire in detail. For the office chair, the average score for the question was 2.6, which does not indicate the superiority of DeepIE3DGK, whereas, in the task of artistic chair generation, the average score 4.2 clearly shows the superiority of DeepIE3DGK. This will be explained as follows. As a qualitative difference between the two tasks, designing an office chair can be described as a full-range search type task, in which the user searches for the structure he or she envisions in a vast latent variable space, because the image of the target structure is easily made concrete. On the other hand, the task of designing an artistic chair is more abstract, and is more of a periphery-searching task, in which the user gradually draws a concrete image through interaction with the system. Since DeepIE3DGK presents candidates that have a high degree of similarity to the structures selected in the previous generation, the system can easily output the periphery of the latent variables selected in the past. Therefore, we believe that DeepIE3DGK is superior for the peripheral search task.

Chapter 7

Emergence of Intelligence

> Evolution is cleverer than you are. (Orgel's second rule).

7.1 Genes of Culture – Memes

The island of Kojima lies 300 meters from the Ishinami coastline in Kushima City, about an hour and a half south of Miyazaki City in Japan. It is a small uninhabited island about 3.5 km in circumference, but it has become known worldwide for the potato-washing activities of its monkeys (Fig. 7.1). This began some years ago, when observers found that a female monkey later nicknamed *"Imo"* ("potato" in Japanese) developed the practice of taking sweet potatoes that had been left on the beach and dunking them in water, to clean off the sand before eating them–no doubt because she found the sand unappetizing. This in itself may seem simple happenstance and be nothing to write about. Of deeper interest was the fact that this activity promptly spread to nearly all of Potato's friends and relatives, other than some of the elder monkeys who never did indulge in this activity. It was later found that some of the monkeys developed the practice of dipping the potatoes in seawater even though they had no sand on them. This marked the birth of the "monkey gourmet" for salted sweet potatoes. According to other records, in 1963, a female monkey on this island discovered that she could separate cereal grains from the sand on the potatoes by throwing the potato into the water and then simply scooping up the grains together with the pulp when they floated to the top. Grain retrieval had previously been slow and tedious, and the water-floatation technique quickly spread to her friends and rela-

Figure 7.1: Japanese monkeys at Kojima island.

tives and ultimately to all the monkeys in the district. Today, the young monkeys learn it from their elders.

This kind of behavioral (cultural) transmission is now often referred to as "memetic transmission," a concept developed by Richard Dawkins. Biological genes are inherited only vertically, by blood line/relationship. Memes, in contrast, can be "inherited" horizontally, through interaction among the members of the population. Like genes, they may undergo mutation (as in the above salt flavoring) and crossover. The spread of fashions, "buzzwords" or vogue expressions, and false rumors in times of disaster can be explained in terms of memes. In part to distinguish the meme concept from the gene-centric paradigm, it was originally posited that the meme was available for humans as a means of cultural transmission. This was also applied to distinguish humans from other animals, as humans had the capability to inherit not only through biological genes but also through memes. However, it is clear that the mode of potato washing transmission by the monkeys of Kojima Island is memetic.

At present, about 100 monkeys inhabit the island. The Primate Research Institute of Kyoto University has compiled a registry of affiliations for every individual as part of their continuing research. The worldwide recognition of Japanese primatology stems from research on this island, led by Kenji Imanishi[1] and others at Kyoto University. The author has himself crossed to the island on a small ferryboat and landed there just as two researchers were beginning a roll call. The research effort on the island is quite well managed. The monkeys beg for food, but we were most impressed to see that they have no hostility toward humans. It is sometimes said one reason Japan rather than Europe or the U.S. has become the world leader in primatology is the traditional Japanese belief, grounded in Buddhism, that culture was a part of animal as well as human life, whereas the

---

[1] Kenji Imanishi (1946–): Japanese ecologist, cultural anthropologist, and mountaineer. He is known as the founder of primate research in Japan. Imanishi's theory of evolution, which was first developed based on extensive exploration and testing, is said to surpass the orthodox evolutionary theory. By looking structurally at actual organisms, such as mayflies, he vigorously explored the idea that segregation can be a catalyst for evolution, which is called "species societies."

basic tendency in the Western perspective may have been to attribute memes to humans alone.

The perspective of classical Eurocentrism that believes only humans have culture has been denied by subsequent studies. For instance, a group of chimpanzees living in the Western African forest placed nuts with hard shells on a stone base and used another stone as a hammer to break them. They have reportedly been teaching this method to their young through many generations. The fact that this group uses stones to crack nuts and another uses sticks for the same purpose is proof of this method being transmitted as social learning. It is also known that when a grown monkey is placed in another group, the monkey has difficulty learning. Moreover, each group of orcas has entirely different hunting methods and calling patterns [119].

Susan Blackmore mentioned that the mimicking ability of primates (e.g., humans) is the driving force behind memes [13]. A superior self-replicator must have the following three characteristics:

■ Loyalty

■ Prolificacy

■ Longevity

If these characteristics are present, competition between self-replicators, differences in terms of viability, and natural selection aiming toward gradual improvement will be inevitable. Particularly, memes began to evolve when the ability to mimic appeared in humans. As the study of genetics deals with the evolution of living things, memetics is considered to deal with cultural evolution described in Section 7.2.

The concept of memes is widely used in AI. For instance, the memetic algorithm (MA) is a well-known example of a search method for evolutionary computation that uses memes. This method can effectively expand the evolutionary processes and improve search efficiency. The MA concept is simple. It provides education to each generation of the evolutionarily obtained individual to make it more intelligent. In MA learning, "local search," where slightly altered individuals search the surrounding area, is often deployed. In each generation obtained in the evolutionary process, individuals "learn" and thereby become more "intelligent." Refer to [68] for more information on the details of MA and its practical application to financial engineering.

The mirror neuron was recently discovered in rhesus macaques. In this neuron, the following two spike patterns are observed (Fig. 7.2):

■ Spike patterns of the time when an individual is picking up a piece of fruit to eat,

■ Spike patterns at the time of observing a human perform the same action are extremely similar.

Firing patterns of neurons
when picking up and eating fruit

Neurons fired in the same way when
watching a human perform the same action.

Figure 7.2: Mirror neurons.

This discovery affirmed the hypothesis of the meme discussed above.

Few studies have been reported on a clear discovery of the mirror neuron in humans; however, the mirror neuron is considered necessary for living in a social environment because, in a society, it is necessary to collaborate with others, and understanding the feelings of others is required for this collaboration. The social brain hypothesis claims that the brain becomes larger to allow species to conduct a social life; consequently, advanced intelligence evolved. Indeed, a correlation has been found between the relative size of the cerebral neocortex and the size of a group. This means monkeys that form larger groups have a larger cerebral neocortex and more advanced intelligence.

In the case of humans, the section assumed to be the mirror neuron is considered to have a strong link to the brain region related to emotion (i.e., the amygdala and other cerebral limbic system regions) [59]. This is perhaps why humans feel the pain or joy of each other stronger than other primates.

Mirror neuron studies are not free from criticisms. They originated from the confusion of correlation with causality, which is generally related to brain science research that uses functional magnetic resonance imaging (fMRI) or electrophysiological methods. As a rule, fMRI can only obtain images that represent the bloodstream in the brain related to a specific mental activity as the degree of activation. This is called "nervous correlation." However, nervous correlation is merely the correlation between a mental activity and the nerve cells, and no causal relationship exists[2]. Therefore, it is difficult to prove the generation of concepts, such as empathy, through fMRI observations alone. In fact, no report has yet existed about people with damage on their ventral premotor area, which

---

[2] However, it might be possible to discover causality by intervening in the brain using a brain-machine interface (BMI).

is equivalent to the mirror neuron of monkeys, acting in a particularly colder manner. Moreover, the rhesus macaque, among which the mirror neuron has been discovered, is a species that cannot be regarded as virtuous at all. No signs of empathy have even been observed. Furthermore, recent neuroimaging studies have hardly found any connection between the brain region, where the mirror neuron has been discovered, and empathy [111]. Thus, some researchers doubt the relationship between the mirror neuron and collaborative/empathetic emotions.

7.2   Culture also Evolves

Charles Darwin cites the following three conditions for biological evolution:

■ Mutation: Individual difference

■ Struggle for life: Competition for survival, i.e., survival of the fittest

■ Succession: Inheritance

Evolution would not occur if one of the three was missing.

One school of thought believes that culture evolves in the same manner as a gene does [98]. Indeed, culture maintains the following three items, which correspond with the abovementioned three:

■ Cultural mutation: Mutation (unintended innovation) or directed mutation (correction of information by an individual through his/her cognitive bias)

■ Struggle for life: Cultural selection

■ Cultural succession: Transfer from the parents' generation or from others of the same generation

Cultural selection includes content bias (preference for essentially more attractive choice), model bias (preference for age, social position, similarity with oneself, etc.), and frequency dependence bias (preference based on frequency or conformity with others). Therefore, culture also evolves in a process called "cultural evolution." The cultural drift phenomenon equivalent to the genetic drift (see Section 3.6.2) was discovered in recent years. In this phenomenon, the evolutional change of cultural characteristics occurs without directionality (not based on content bias) when the group is not large. The way names are given to babies is considered to be an example of this phenomenon [98].

Let us consider language as the representative of culture. The evolution of language is similar to that of genes (DNA base) [118]. A frequently used word becomes shorter, and a repeatedly used word becomes abbreviated. Similarities can also be found between the evolution of biological and linguistic species. The flora and fauna species become less diverse as the latitude becomes higher.

(a) Outlook   (b) Local children and the author   (c) A class at the school

Figure 7.3: An elementary school in Papua New Guinea.

The closer a place is to the equator, the more diverse the species of that place becomes. In Alaska, only a few species exist in a large habitat. Similarly, the indigenous people of the State of Alaska only have a few spoken languages, while those in New Guinea have a few thousand spoken languages. There is even an example of one language and that from a neighboring valley being as different as English is from French. The author once visited the islands of New Guinea for work (Fig. 7.3) and witnessed the education situation at its schools. There, languages and life styles are significantly different, even among islands that are very close to each other. The fact that different translators and mediators are needed at each island affirmed this impression.

Moreover, studies on linguistic history have reported that a rapid change initially occurs when a new language diverges from an ancestral language. This corresponds with the punctuated equilibrium theory[3] in biological evolution.

The gene called FOXP2, which is found on Chromosome 7, is also known as the grammar gene [119]. This gene is indispensable for the fine motor control of the pharynx or the development of general grammar and speech abilities. Humans cannot form a grammatical sentence and speak a language when this gene is damaged. FOXP2 has also been discovered in some monkeys and mice; thus, having this gene alone does not result in speech. Interestingly, while this gene is not found in chimpanzees, it was discovered among the Neanderthals, leading some researchers to believe they spoke a language. How FOXP2 generates language is not well understood at this point. We do not know whether humans can speak because of FOXP2 or because the invention of speech somehow led to the FOXP2 mutation.

---

[3]A hypothesis advocated by Stephen Jay Gould (see 2 page) and Niles Eldredge. The idea that evolution occurs intensively in a short period of time when species diverge. Neutral gene recombination frequently takes place during long stagnation. Some kind of trigger, such as a change in the environment, causes a rapid evolution. "Stagnation is data" is a maxim by them.

More recently, studies applying the idea of development in biology to cultural evolution have been conducted and are categorized under cultural evolutionary embryology [98]. In an organism, the module-type development reduces the necessity to form a body from scratch. Similarly, cultural evolution is encouraged through the modular method. This prediction has been examined by the learning simulation of artifacts through a computer. According to that research, the technology of producing an arrowhead in the prehistoric time spreads through the fame bias[4] of the most successful hunter. Diversity steadily increases if one introduces a directed mutation here. Meanwhile, when there is a fame bias, the arrowhead design converges on the same design in an evolutionary phenomenon known as the convergent evolution[5]. This process can explain the diversity and the uniformity of the arrowhead designs found in many locations. Similarly, the fact that boomerangs from ancient Egypt and ancient Australia both had similar curved shapes can also be explained through the theory of cultural evolution [118].

7.3 How the Brain is Created: Darwin among the Machines

"Darwin among the Machines" is the title of the article published by Samuel Butler from England in 1863. In this paper, he indicated the possibility of machines evolving and excelling over humans. Recently, George D. Dyson discussed the accelerating blurring of the boundary between nature (brain) and technology (AI) with the background of the emergence of aggregated mechanical intelligence in a book with the same title [36].

The common debate regarding the brain, focuses on whether its character is determined by birth or upbringing. This is known as the "nature or nurture" debate. Let us apply this debate to AI research. "Nurture" corresponds with connectionist and deep learning, the mainstream of AI today. On the contrary, "nature" corresponds to evolutionary computation or complex system research based on emergent phenomena.

In deep learning, the brain is modeled as a general learning machine. However, a criticism exists on the theory of staged learning development known as "the learning paradox." This indicates the inability of the development process that accompanies learning models, such as a general machine, to anticipate the behavior of the higher order from that of the lower order. Modeling as general learning machine also leads to the idea that the parts processing empathy in vision or language are different between each person. However, many neuroscientific reports have affirmed the view that a specific section of the brain corresponds with a specific section of the mind.

---

[4] Tendency to prefer imitating the cultural characteristics of famous or successful people.
[5] Evolution of similar characteristics among different species independently from each other.

Matt Ridley calls the broader idea of evolution "the general theory of evolution" [118]. In contrast, Darwin's theory of evolution is called "the special theory of evolution" to distinguish it. As we have seen, the general theory of evolution explains many phenomena in society, currency, technology, language, culture, politics, and morality. These include path dependence[6], punctuated equilibrium, convergent evolution, coevolution, and origin with change (i.e., phylogenetic tree) etc. Naturally, however, there are some structures and organizations to which the theory of evolution does not apply. For example, governments, states, and other organizations that are forced to be changed from above or from the outside. These are constructed from the perspective of a god, king, or other superior.

Applying the perspective of the general theory of evolution to technology or culture gives an impression that progress is inevitable. In a sense, progress is believed to occur gradually and mercilessly and cannot be stopped [118]. Moore's law[7] and singularity[8] are examples of this view. Ray Kurzweil, who proposed the concept of singularity [83], discovered that Moore's law was valid, even before the existence of the silicon chip. If one extrapolates the ability of the computer in the early 20th century when a different technology was used, one could see that the straight line on the logarithmic scale followed Moore's law. From this discovery, he postulated that Moore's law would continue to be valid, even when we switch to a new technology. He also predicted that similar growth would occur, even when the limit of the chips is reached.

However, many researchers also hold negative opinions about the theory of singularity, including the evolutionary psychologist, Steven Pinker[9]. As discussed thus far, many phenomena and cultures do not evolve linearly (gradually); instead, evolution occurs through many stages, including punctuated equilibrium, exaptation, and convergence. When this is considered, the prediction that applies the gradual Moore's law is no longer convincing. Moreover, the fact that this prediction heavily relies on the hardware characteristics is a source of doubt. Needless to say, the main elements of AI and computer technology today are software and algorithms. Algorithmically, or in the sense of calculation efficiency, innovative algorithms are not necessarily discovered gradually as predicted by Moore's law[10]. The performance of deep learning relies on big data and hardware acceleration. Thus, there is an impression that the development of

---

[6]The decisions people and organizations make are constrained by the previous decisions they have made in the past. The famous examples are the Qwerty keyboard and VHS video. See [4] for the details.

[7]The number of transistors on a chip (accumulation rate of semiconductors) doubles every 18 months.

[8]Technological singularity. It predicts a radical change in social life caused by AI exceeding human ability. One theory predicts 2045 to be that year. An extreme view even predicts that humans will become unnecessary.

[9]See the footnote of page 3.

[10]Let us think what the equivalent of the straight line in Moore's law would be in the history of algorithms. Such examples could include the Euclidean algorithm, various sorting and retrieval methods, approximate optimization algorithm, backpropagation, the random algorithm, and Shor's prime factorization method.

software and algorithms is failing to keep up with the development of hardware and data accumulation.

When the author was in high school, the four-color theorem was proved. The four-color hypothesis predicted that no more than four colors are required to color the regions of the map on a plane, such that no two adjacent regions have the same color. This prediction was made in the mid-19th century. It had not been proven for more than 100 years, and no counterexample was obtained either. The published proof was made possible with the usage of a computer. One of the research themes of the university laboratory the author belonged to in the mid-1980s was the verification/examination of the validity of this proof. In the recent years, the Kepler conjecture, which had been unproven for more than 400 years, was also proven by using a computer. The Kepler conjecture involved piling equally sized oranges with the greatest density[11].

These methods of proving were criticized by many mathematicians because they were not the so-called "elegant proof." Despite such a critical background, the computer is undoubtedly a useful tool in proof examination or reduction of symbolic computation for contemporary mathematicians. Consequently, concerns have been raised regarding creative mathematical activities being taken over by computers and AI. This, however, has not yet happened. Why is that the case?

It is certainly true that more advanced parts of calculation, which are previously inconceivable, can be performed by computers and AI. As a result, mathematicians can divert extra free time to more intellectual and productive areas and progress to areas beyond those controlled by computers.

Recently, deep learning and machine learning have been expanding the applicable areas of AI. While this is a welcomed development, this might give the wrong impression that AI can solve everything. Unfortunately, the fact that it is not as simple and that is known as the NFL ("no free lunch") theorem [67]. This theorem mathematically proved that "there is no holy grail." Initially, it demonstrated that an optimization method that can be applied to every problem does not exist, but the same can be said about machine learning and AI. Particularly, "the no-free-lunch theorem" indicates that a universal learning machine does not exist. For instance, the performance of a classifier is heavily reliant on the characteristics of the data to be classified, and a classifier that shows the best performance at every problem does not exist.

Conversely, the claim of mathematical NFL can possibly save the future of many creative people, including mathematicians. Despite the rapid hardware progress and advanced information sharing through the internet and various so-

---

[11] The optimal method is the way oranges are piled at the storefront of a greengrocer. Even though it appears to be common sense, the most densely packed way could not be proven for 400 years.

cial media platforms, many problems remain as regards the realization of strong AI (true artificial intelligence, see [69]), and innovative challenges are expected to be made. Hardware and software (algorithm and mathematical research) will continue to coevolve. How will "Darwin among the machines" feel in such a future?

Appendix A

Software Packages

A.1 Introduction

We have made available software implementations of many of the evolutionary or swarm systems described in this book. We hope that this software will give the readers some hands-on experience with evolutionary systems, in addition to the theoretical knowledge provided by the previous chapters. We suggest that the readers explore the software while reading each chapter, trying new parameters and data sets. Doing this you will get a clearer understanding of the possibilities and limits of the presented systems.

In this appendix we give general instructions for the use of each available software package. The packages themselves can be downloaded from the Iba Laboratory's web page: http://www.iba.t.u-tokyo.ac.jp/english/.

Please follow the download instructions available in that webpage. Besides the software packages, the webpage also contains user manuals and bulletin boards. Please feel free to use those in case you need assistance using the software.

Please be aware that the software packages available in the above webpage are copyrighted to the authors. The programs may be altered, added to, or removed without notice. We accept no liability for any damages resulting from the use of the programs, or of the output generated by executing them. A more detailed license accompanies each software package.

A.2 Multi-objective Optimization by GA

To test and experiment with evolutionary multi-objective optimization (EMO; see Section 3.9), a Pareto GA simulator is available.

The program execution screen of the simulator is shown in Fig. A.1. Each red point is an individual, and the number of dominant individuals relative to that point (including itself) are shown nearby. For an individual on the Pareto front, the number is 1.

Let us use this simulator to minimize the value of two objectives (fitness functions) $f_1(x)$ and $f_2(x)$, using GA. The fitness functions can can be entered in the "Function 1" and "Function 2" boxes. After setting the GA parameters (for example, population size and generation number), click the "Start" button to begin the search. During execution, autozoom can be disengaged by clicking the graph and restored by clicking it again.

As an example, let us try using the following functions as the fitness functions:

$$
\begin{aligned}
f_1(x) &= x \\
f_2(x) &= 1 - x^\alpha.
\end{aligned}
$$

These functions will generate a concavity in the Pareto curve. In this problem, the Pareto front is convex when $\alpha = 0.5$ and non-convex when $\alpha = 2, 0$. Figures A.2 and A.3 show the results of execution with $\alpha = 0.5$ and $\alpha = 2, 0$, respectively. The former clearly results in a convex Pareto front, and the latter in a concave Pareto front.

Two test these two values for α, let us enter the corresponding functions directly into the function boxes. The fitness function for $\alpha = 0.5$ is written as

```
Function 1:  x
Function 2:  1-sqrt(x).
```

And the fitness function for $\alpha = 2.0$ is written as

```
Function 1:  x
Function 2:  1-x*x.
```

Let us now consider a more complex set of objective functions.

$$
\begin{aligned}
f_1(x) &= x \\
f_2(x) &= 1 - x^{0.25} - x \sin(10\pi x).
\end{aligned}
$$

This is regarded as a difficult problem, containing a discontinuous Pareto front. To describe these functions, enter the following in their respective boxes

```
Function 1:  x
Function 2:  1-pow(x,0.25)-x*sin(10*3.1415*x).
```

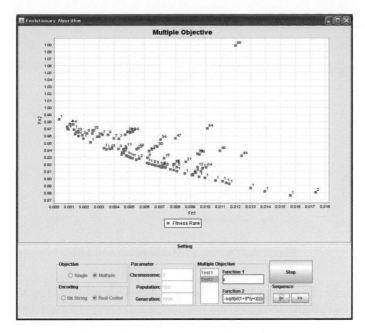

Figure A.1: Pareto optimization simulator.

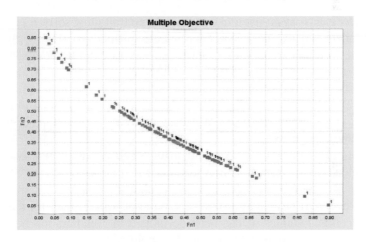

Figure A.2: A convex Pareto front ($\alpha = 0.5$).

After entering the functions, execute the simulation, and observe the complex Pareto front conformation (see Fig. A.2).

As shown in these examples, you can use transcendental as well as arithmetic functions to define the fitness functions on the simulator. Table A.1 list the functions that can be used. The input expression is a three-variable function, in x, y, and z. For each variable a range of possible values can be established as any two

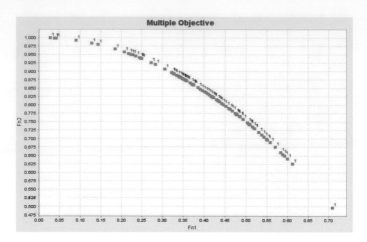

Figure A.3: A concave Pareto front ($\alpha = 2.0$).

positive numbers. On the simulator, the Pareto curve is displayed on a graph with $f_1(x)$ and $f_2(x)$ being shown on the horizontal and vertical axes, respectively.

A.3 MindRender and MindRender/AIDrill

MindRender is an easy-to-use and feature-rich programming software that allows both beginners and advanced learners to create full-fledged 3D programs while having fun. You can create a program by simply assembling command blocks just like Scratch, so it is easy to start off with. Also it is equipped with scientific elements such as 3D and physics engine of Unity environment, so it leads to think more in-depth. With a variety of character and background objects, and sound and visual effects included, it is easy to create various type of programs such as games and stories.

Mine Render supports iOS, Android, macOS and Windows. It is available for free download on the respective app stores (App Store, Google Play Store, Mac App Store, Microsoft Store) according to the platform you use.

MindRender/AI Drill is an extended version of MindRender for the purpose of AI educational studies. It has been developed in collaboration between the author's laboratory and Mobile Internet Technology, Co., Ltd.[1]. It is being used in the AI course of the Department of Technology at the author's university. Creating and experimenting by yourself (students) to understand theory in this way is called a structuralism approach and is widely adopted in many research fields such as artificial intelligence, artificial life, and robotics.

As the basic concepts of MindRender/AIDrill, several AI concepts, such as reinforcement learning, evolutionary computation, neural networks and game AI,

---

[1]http://www.mobileit.co.jp/.

Table A.1: List of available functions.

	Symbol	Description
Operators	$+\ -\ *\ /$	Four arithmetic operations
	$\wedge$	Power function
	$-$	Negation
	!	Factorial
Functions	abs(x)	Absolute function
	pi()	π(3.14159...)
	degrees(x)	Convert to angle
	round(x,0)	Rounding function
	fact(x)	Factorial function
	sqrt(x)	Square root function
	exp(x)	Exponential function
	log(x,y)	Logarithm function (base is y)
	sin(x)	Sine function
	cos(x)	Cosine Function
	tan(x)	Tangent function
	asin(x)	Arcsine function
	acos(x)	Arccosine function
	atan(x)	Arctangent function
	sinh(x)	Hyperbolic sine funcion
	cosh(x)	Hyperbolic cosine function
	tanh(x)	Hyperbolic tangent function
	rand()	Random number from 0 to 1
	Gauss(m,s)	Gaussian random number (mean=m, variance=s)
	Max(x,y)	A maximum value of x and y
	Min(x,y)	A minimum value of x and y
	if(bool,x,y)	Return x if bool is **true**, otherwise **false**

are provided. You will be able to learn various AI techniques by solving tasks with the following different methods:

- Evolutionary computation (Fig. A.3(a))

- Reinforcement learning (Fig. A.3(b))

- Neuroevolution (Fig. A.3(b))

- Neural networks

- Boid simulation ((Fig. A.3(c))

- Pheromone trail and ACO (Fig. A.3(d))

- Puzzle AI (Fig. A.3(e))

- Game AI (Fig. A.3(f))

The textbook of MindRender/AIDrill is available on Kindle and Apple Books.

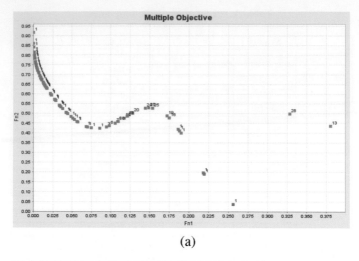

(a)

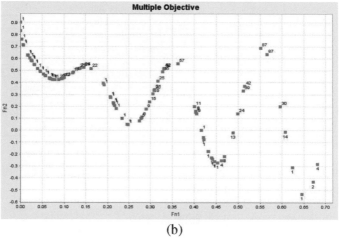

(b)

Figure A.4: Discountinuous Pareto fronts.

■ Kindle Edition

  ■ Mind Render/AIDrill vol.1
    https://www.amazon.com/dp/B08F7QR66X

  ■ Mind Render/AIDrill vol.2
    https://www.amazon.com/dp/B08F7VJKHM

■ Apple Books

  ■ Mind Render/AIDrill
    http://books.apple.com/us/book/id1526094955

(a) Evolution of bicycle shapes

(b) Automated driving of racing cars

(c) Boid simulation

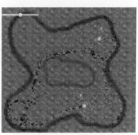

(d) Pheromone trail

(e) Puzzle AI for SOKOBAN problems

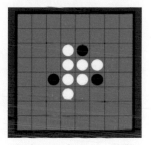

(f) Game AI for othello

Figure A.5: MindRender/AIDrill.

The source code is provided when you purchase the book and contact us at the support email address (support@mindrender.jp).

References

[1] Ando, S. and Iba, H. Ant algorithm for construction of evolutionary tree. In *Proc. of the 2002 Congress on Evolutionary Computation (CEC'02)*, pp. 1552–1557, 2002.

[2] Angeline, P.J. Subtree crossover causes bloat. In *Proc. of the Third Annual Genetic Programming Conference 1998*, (GP98), pp. 745–752, 1998.

[3] Arjovsky, M., Chintala, S. and Bottou, L. Wasserstein gan. arXiv:1701.07875, 2017.

[4] Arthur, W.B. *Increasing Returns and Path Dependence in the Economy.* UMPRE, 1994.

[5] Asoh, H. and Mühlenbein, H. On the mean convergence time of evolutionary algorithms without selection. In *Parallel Problem Solving from Nature 3*, Davidor, Y., Schwefel, H.-P. and Manner, R. (eds.). Lecture Notes in Computer Science, vol. 866, pp. 88–97, Springer, 1994.

[6] Bahdanau, D., Cho, K. and Bengio, Y. Neural machine translation by jointly learning to align and translate.' in *Proc. International Conference on Learning Representations*, http://arxiv.org/abs/1409.0473, 2015.

[7] Baldwin, J.M. A new factor in evolution. *American Naturalist*, 30: 441–451, 1896.

[8] Ball, P., *Flow: Nature's Patterns: A Tapestry in Three Parts*, Oxford University Press, 2011.

[9] Baluja, S. and Caraana, R. Removing the genetics from the standard genetic algorithm.' Carnegie Mellon University, Technical Report CMU-CS-95–141, 1995.

[10] Banzhaf, W., Nordin, P., Keller, R.E. and Francone, F.D. *Genetic Programming, An Introduction*, Morgan Kaufmann, 1998.

[11] Bentley, P.J., *Evolutionary Design by Computers*, Morgan Kaufmann, 1999.

[12] Bhattacharjee, S. and Gras, R. Estimation of distribution using population Queue based variational autoencoders. In *Proc. of 2019 IEEE Congress on Evolutionary Computation (CEC)*, pp. 1406–1414, 2019.

[13] Blackmore, S.J., *The Meme Machine*, Oxford Univ. Press, 1999.

[14] Bonet, J.S., Isbell, C.L. and Viola, P. MIMIC: finding optima by estimating probability densities. In *Proc. of the 9th International Conference on Neural Information Processing Systems (NIPS'96)*, pp. 424–430, MIT Press, 1996.

[15] Bontrager, P., Roy, A., Togelius, J., Memon, N. and Ross, A. DeepMasterPrints: Generating MasterPrints for dictionary attacks via latent variable evolution. In *Proc. of 2018 IEEE 9th International Conference on Biometrics Theory, Applications and Systems (BTAS)*, 2018.

[16] Bontrager, P., Lin, W., Togelius, J. and Risi, S. Deep interactive evolution. In *Proc. European Conference on the Applications of Evolutionary, Computation (EvoApplications)*, pp. 267–282, 2018.

[17] Barwise, J. and Perry, J. *Situations and Attitudes*, MIT Press, 1984.

[18] Bengio, Y., Courville, A. and Vincent, P. Representation Learning: A Review and New Perspectives. arXiv:1206.5538, 2014.

[19] Brackman, A.C. A delicate arrangement: The strange case of Charles Darwin and Alfred Russel Wallace. Times Books, 1980.

[20] Braitenberg, V. *Vehicles: Experiments in Synthetic Psychology*, Bradford Books, 1986.

[21] Brooks, R.A. A robust layered control system for a mobile robot. *IEEE Journal of Robotics and Automation*, RA-2, April, pp. 14–23, 1986.

[22] Brooks, R.A. Autonomous mobile robot. In *AI in the 1980s and Beyond*, Grimson, W.E.L. (ed.). MIT Press, 1987.

[23] Brooks, R. Intelligence without representation. *Artificial Intelligence*, 47(1-3): 139–159, 1991.

[24] Chaudhury, S. and Yamasaki, T. Adversarial attack during learning. In *Proc. of the 22nd Meeting on Image Recognition and Understanding (MIRU)*, OS2A-3,

[25] Chu, S.-C., Tsai, P.-W. and Pan, J.-S. Cat swarm optimization.' In *Proc. Pacific Rim International Conference on Artificial Intelligence (PRICAI 2006)*, pp. 854-858, 2006.

[26] Civicioglu, P. and Besdok, E. A conceptual comparison of the Cuckoo-search, particle swarm optimization, differential evolution and artificial bee colony algorithms. *Artificial Intelligence Review*, 39(4): 315–346, 2013.

[27] Clerc, M. and Kennedy, J. The Particle Swarm: Explosion, Stability, and Convergence in a Multimentional Complex Space. *IEEE Tr. Evolutionary Computation*, 6(1): 58–73, 2002.

[28] Crow, J.F. *Genetics Notes: An Introduction to Genetics*, 8th Edition, Benjamin Cummings, 1986.

[29] Dawkins, R. *The Selfish Gene*, Oxford University Press, 1976.

[30] Dawkins, R. *The Blind Watchmaker*, W.W. Norton, New York, 1986.

[31] Dawkins, R. *Brief Candle in the Dark: My Life in Science*, Black Swan, 2016.

[32] Doersch, C. Tutorial on variational autoencoders. arXiv:1606.05908, 2016.

[33] Donahue, J., Hendricks, L., Guadarrama, S., Rohrbach, M., Venugopalan, S., Saenko, K. and Darrell, T. Long-term recurrent convolutional networks for visual recognition and description. arXiv:1411.4389, November 2014.

[34] Dorigo, M. and Gambardella, L.M. Ant colonies for the traveling salesman problem. Tech. Rep. IRIDIA/97-12, Universite Libre de Bruxelles, Belgium, 1997.

[35] Dreyfus, H.L. *What Computers Can't Do: The Limits of Artificial Intelligence*, HarperCollins; Revised, Subsequent, 1978.

[36] Dyson, G.B. *Darwin Among the Machines: The Evolution of Global Intelligence*, Basic Books, 2012.

[37] Edelman, G. *Neural Darwinism: The Theory of Neuronal Group Selection*, Oxford University Press, 1989.

[38] ElSaid, A., Jamiy, F.E., Higgins, J., Wild, B. and Desell, T. Using ant colony optimization to optimize long short-term memory recurrent neural networks. In *Proc. of the Genetic and Evolutionary Computation Conference (GECCO2018)*, pp. 13–20, 2018.

[39] ElSaid, A., Benson, S., Patwardhan, S., Stadem, D. and Desell, T. Evolving recurrent neural networks for time series data prediction of coal plant parameters. In *Proc. of International Conference on the Applications of Evolutionary Computation (Part of EvoStar)*, pp. 488–503, 2019.

[40] Eshleman, L.J. and Schaffer, J.D. Real-coded genetic algorithms and interval-schemata.' *Foundations of Genetic Algorithms*, 2: 187–202, 1993.

[41] Fogel, G.B. and Corne, D.W. *Evolutionary Computation in Bioinformatics*, The Morgan Kaufmann Series in Artificial Intelligence, Morgan Kaufmann, 2002.

[42] Fukushima, K. Neocognitron: A self organizing neural network model for a mechanism of pattern recognition unaffected by shift in position. *Biol. Cybern.*, 36(4): 193–202, 1980.

[43] Grahl, J., Bosman, P. and Rothlauf, F. The correlation-triggered adaptive variance scaling IDEA. In *GECCO06: Proceedings of the 8th annual conference on Genetic and evolutionary computation*, pp. 397–404, 2006.

[44] Gal, Y. and Ghahramani, Z. A theoretically grounded application of dropout in recurrent neural networks. In *Advances in Neural Information Processing Systems*, pp. 1019–1027, 2016.

[45] Garciarena, U., Santana, R. and Mendiburu, A. Expanding variational autoencoders for learning and exploiting latent representations in search distributions. In *GECCO18: Proceedings of the Genetic and Evolutionary Computation Conference*, pp. 849–856, 2018.

[46] Goldberg, D.E. and Segrest, P. Finite Markov chain analysis of genetic algorithms. In *Proceedings of the 2nd International Conference on Genetic Algorithms*, pp. 1–8, 1987.

[47] Gonzalez-Fernandez, Y., Chen, S. and Bolufé-Röhler, A. and Montgomery, J. Continuous Univariate Marginal Distribution Algorithm on the CEC2013 Real-Parameter Optimization Benchmark Functions. Technical Report, School of Information Technology, York University, 2014.

[48] Goodfellow, I., Pouget-Abadie, J., Mirza, M., Xu, B., Warde-Farley, D., Ozair, S. and Bengio, Y. Generative adversarial nets.' In *Advances in Neural Information Processing Systems*, pp. 2672–2680, 2014.

[49] Goss, S., Aron, S., Deneubourg, J.L. and Pasteels, J.M. Self-organized shortcuts in the argentine ant. *Naturwissenschaften*, 76: 579–581, 1989.

[50] Gould, S.J. Through a lens, darkly: Do species change by random molecular shifts or natural selection? Natural History, September, 1989.

[51] Gould, S.J. *I Have Landed: Ultimate Reflections in Natural History*, Vintage Uk, 2002.

[52] Graves, A., Wayne, G. and Danihelka, I. Neural Turing Machines, http://arxiv.org/abs/1410.5401, 2014.

[53] Greff, K., Srivastava, R.K., Koutník, J., Steunebrink, B. and Schmidhuber, J. LSTM: A search space odyssey. *IEEE Transactions on Neural Networks and Learning Systems*, 28(10): 2222–2232, 2016.

[54] Gulrajani, I., Ahmed, F., Arjovsky, M., Dumoulin, V. and Courville, A. Improved training of wasserstein GANs. In *Proc. of the 31st International Conference on Neural Information Processing Systems (NIPS'17)*, pp. 5769–5779, 2017.

[55] Hansen, N. and Ostermeier, A. Adapting arbitrary normal mutation distributions in evolution strategies: The covariance matrix adaptation. In *Proc. of the 1996 IEEE International Conference on Evolutionary Computation (CEC96)*, pp. 312–317, 1996.

[56] Hansen, N. The CMA evolution strategy: A comparing review. In *Towards a New Evolutionary Computation, Studies in Fuzziness and Soft Computing*, Lozano, J.A., Larranaga, P., Inza, I. and Bengoetxea, E. (eds.), vol. 192, pp. 75–102, 2006.

[57] Harik, G.R., Lobo, F.G. and Sastry, K. Linkage learning via probabilistic modeling in the Extended Compact Genetic Algorithm (ECGA). In *Scalable Optimization via Probabilistic Modeling*, Pelikan, M., Sastry, K. and CantuPaz, E. (eds.). Studies in Computational Intelligence, vol. 33, pp. 39–61, Springer, 2006.

[58] Hausknecht, M., Khandelwal, P., Miikkulainen, R. and Stone, P. HyperNEAT-GGP: A HyperNEAT-based Atari general game player. *Proceedings of the Genetic and Evolutionary Computation Conference (GECCO 2012)*, pp. 217–224, 2012.

[59] Haidt, J. *The Righteous Mind: Why Good People are Divided by Politics and Religion*, Penguin, 2013.

[60] Hepper, F. and Grenader, U. A stochastic nonlinear model for coordinated bird flocks, AAAS publication, Washington ,DC, 1990.

[61] Herbert-Read, J.E., Romenskyy, M. and Sumpter, D.J.T. Turing test for collective motion. *Biology Letters*, 11(12): 20150674, 2015.

[62] Higashi, N. and Iba, H. Particle swarm optimization with Gaussian mutation. *Proceedings of IEEE Swarm Intelligence Symposium (SIS03)*, pp. 72–79, 2003.

[63] Hinton, G.E. and Salakhutdinov, R.R. Reducing the dimensionality of data with neural networks. *Science*, 313: 504–507, 2006.

[64] Hochreiter, S. and Schmidhuber, J. Long short-term memory. *Neural Computation*, 9(8): 1735–1780, 1997.

[65] Holland, J.H. *Adaptation in Natural and Artificial Systems*. University of Michigan Press, 1975.

[66] Iba, H., deGaris, H. and Sato, T. Genetic programming using a minimum description length principle, *Advances in Genetic Programming*, Kinnear, Jr., K.E. (ed.), pp. 265–284, MIT Press, 1994.

[67] Iba, H. and Noman, N. *New Frontiers in Evolutionary Algorithms: Theory and Applications*, ISBN-10:1848166818, World Scientific Publishing Company, 2011.

[68] Iba, H. and Aranha, C.C. *Practical Applications of Evolutionary Computation to Financial Engineering: Robust Techniques for Forecasting, Trading and Hedging*, Springer, 2012.

[69] Iba, H. *AI and SWARM: Evolutionary Approach to Emergent Intelligence*, CRC Press, 2019.

[70] Katayama, S., Pindur, A.K. and Iba, H. Extending deep interactive evolution with graph kernel for 3D design. *Proceedings of the 10th IIAI International Congress on Advanced Applied Informatics*, 2021.

[71] Kauffman, S.A. *Investigations*, Oxford University Press, 2000.

[72] Kennedy, J. and Eberhart, R.C. Particle swarm optimization. *Proceedings of IEEE the International Conference on Neural Networks*, pp. 1942–1948, 1995.

[73] Kennedy, J. and Eberhart, R.C. *Swarm Intelligence*, Morgan Kaufmann Publishers, 2001.

[74] Kimura, M. *The Neutral Theory of Molecular Evolution*, Cambridge University Press, 1983.

[75] Kingma, D.P. and Welling, M. Auto-encoding variational bayes. arXiv:1312.6114, 2013.

[76] Kingma, D.P. and Ba, J. Adam: A method for stochastic optimization. arXiv preprint arXiv:1412.6980, 2014.

[77] Kinoyama, R., Morales Perez, E.A. and Iba, H. Preventing overfitting of LSTMs using Ant Colony Optimization. *Proceedings of the 10th IIAI International Congress on Advanced Applied Informatics*, 2021.

[78] Koh, I., Kim, J.-S. and Kim, S.-B. Identification and phylogenetic analysis of schizophrenia associated retrovirus element in the human genbank database.*Genome Informatics* , 12: 390–391, 2001.

[79] Koza, J. Evolution of subsumption using genetic programming. In *Proc. of the First European Conference on Artificial Life (ECAL91)*, pp. 110–119, MIT Press, 1992.

[80] Koza, J. *Genetic Programming, on the Programming of Computers by means of Natural Selection*, MIT Press, 1992.

[81] Koza, J. *Genetic Programming II: Automatic Discovery of Reusable Subprograms*, MIT Press, 1994.

[82] Koza, J., Andre, D.A., Bennett, III, F.H. and Keane, M.A. *Genetic Programming III, Automatic Programming and Automatic Circuit Synthesis*, Morgan Kaufmann, 1999.

[83] Kurzweil, R. *The Singularity is Near: When Humans Transcend Biology*, The Viking Press, 2005.

[84] Krizhevsky, A., Sutskerver, I. and Hinton, G.E. ImageNet classification with deep convolutional neural networks. *Advances in Neural Information Processing Systems 25 (NIPS)*, pp. 1097–1105, 2012.

[85] Larrañaga, P. and Lozano, J.A. Estimation of distribution algorithms: A new tool for evolutionary computation, Springer, 2001.

[86] Larsen, A.B.L., Sønderby, S.K. and Winther, O. Autoencoding beyond pixels using a learned similarity metric. arXiv preprint arXiv:1512.09300, 2015.

[87] Latty, T. and Beekman, M. Irrational decision-making in an amoeboid organism: transitivity and context-dependent preferences. *Proc. R. Soc. B*, 278: 307–312, 2011.

[88] Le, Q., Ranzato, M., Monga, R., Devin, M., Chen, K., Corrado, G., Dean, J. and Ng, A. Building high-level features using large scale unsupervised learning. In *Proc. of the 29th International Conference on Machine Learning*, 2012.

[89] LeCun, Y., Bottou, L., Bengio, Y. and Haffner, P. Gradient-based learning applied to document recognition. *Proceedings of the IEEE*, 86(11): 2278–2324, 1998.

[90] Levenick, J.R. Inserting introns improves genetic algorithm success rate: Taking a cue from biology. In *Proc. the Fourth International Conference on Genetic Algorithms*, (ICGA91), pp. 123–127, Morgan Kaufmann, 1991.

[91] Lewin, B. *Genes*, John Wiley & Sons Inc.; 3rd Edition, 1987.

[92] Liang, J., Suganthan, P.N. and Hernández-Díaz, A.G. Problem definitions and evaluation criteria for the CEC 2013 special session on real-parameter optimization. In *Computational Intelligence Laboratory, Zhengzhou University, Zhengzhou, China and Nanyang Technological University, Singapore, Technical Report*, pp. 281–295, 2013.

[93] Lim, A. and Zhang, L. WebPHYLIP: A web interface to PHYLIP. *Bioinformatics*, 15(12): 1068–1069, 1999.

[94] Liu, Y.-P., Wu, M.-G. and Qian, J.-X. Evolving neural networks using the hybrid of ant colony optimization and BP algorithms. *International Symposium on Neural Networks*, pp. 714–722, 2006.

[95] Liu, J., Yu, F. and Funkhouser, T. Interactive 3D modeling with a generative adversarial network. In *Proc. of 2017 International Conference on 3D Vision (3DV)*, pp. 126–134, 2017.

[96] Maynard Smith, J. *Evolutionary Genetics*, Oxford University Press, Oxford, 1989.

[97] Merity, S., Keskar, N.S. and Socher, R. Regularizing and optimizing LSTM language models. arXiv preprint arXiv:1708.02182, 2017.

[98] Mesoudi, A. *Cultural Evolution: How Darwinian Theory Can Explain Human Culture and Synthesize the Social Sciences*, University of Chicago Press, 2011.

[99] Miikkulainen, R., Liang, J., Meyerson, E., Rawal, A., Fink, D., Francon, O., Raju, B., Shahrzad, H., Navruzyan, A., Duffy, N. and Hodjat, B. Evolving Deep Neural Networks. arXiv:1703.00548, 2017.

[100] Minsky, M. and Papert, S.A. *Perceptrons: An Introduction to Computational Geometry*, MIT Press, 1969.

[101] Mitchell, M. *An Introduction to Genetic Algorithms*, MIT Press, 1996,

[102] Morgan, C.L. On modification and variation. *Science*, 4: 733–740, 1896.

[103] Mostaghim, S. and Teich, J. Strategies for finding good local guides in multi-objective particle swarm optimization (MOPSO). In *Proc. of the 2003 IEEE Swarm Intelligence Symposium*, pp. 26–33, 2003.

[104] Nei, M. and Saitou, N. The neighbor-joining method: A new method for reconstructing phylogenetic tree. *Molecular Biology and Evolution*, 4: 406–425, 1987.

[105] Nguyen, A., Yosinski, J. and Clune, J. Deep neural networks are easily fooled: High confidence predictions for unrecognizable images. In *Proc. of 2015 IEEE Conference on Computer Vision and Pattern Recognition (CVPR)*, pp. 427–436, 2015.

[106] Niwa, T. and Tanaka, M. Analyses of simple genetic algorithms and island model parallel genetic algorithms. In *Proc. of the 3rd International Conference on Artificial Neural Networks and Genetic Algorithms*, (ICANNGA 97), pp. 224–228, Springer, 1997.

[107] Nordin, P., Francone, F. and Banzhaf, W. Explicitly defined introns and destructive crossover in genetic programming. In *Advances in Genetic Programming 2*, Angeline, P.J. and Kinnear, K.E. (eds.), pp. 111–134, MIT Press, 1996.

[108] Osborn, H.F. Ontogenic and phylogenic variation. *Science*, 4: 786–789, 1896.

[109] Pfeifer, R. and Scheier, C. *Understanding Intelligence*, A Bradford Book, 2001.

[110] Pfeifer, R. and Bongard, J. *How the Body Shapes the Way We Think: A New View of Intelligence*, A Bradford Book, 2006.

[111] Pinker, S. *How the Mind Works*, W.W. Norton & Co., 1998.

[112] Poundstone, W. *Gaming the Vote*, Hill and Wang, 2009.

[113] Prechelt, L. Early stopping-but when? In *Neural Networks: Tricks of the trade* Montavon, G., Orr, G.B. and Muller, K.R. (eds.). Lecture Notes in Computer Science, vol. 7700, pp. 55–69, 2012.

[114] Prusinkiewicz, P. and Coen, E. Passing the El Greco test. *HFSP Journal*, 1(3): 152–155, 2007.

[115] Radford, A., Metz, L. and Chintala, S. Unsupervised representation learning with deep convolutional generative adversarial networks. arXiv preprint arXiv:1511.06434, 2015.

[116] Retief, J.D. Phylogenetic analysis using PHYLIP. *Methods Mol. Biol.*, 132: 243–258, 2000.

[117] Reynolds, C.W. Flocks, herds and schools: A distributed behavioral model. *Computer Graphics*, 21(4): 25–34, 1987.

[118] Ridley, M. *Nature Via Nurture: Genes, Experience, and What Makes us Human*, Harper, 2003.

[119] Ridley, M. *The Evolution of Everything: How New Ideas Emerge*, Harper, 2015.

[120] Rucker, R. *Artificial Life Lab*, Waite Group Press, 1993.

[121] Salama, K.M. and Abdelbar, A.M. Learning neural network structures with ant colony algorithms. *Swarm Intelligence*, 9(4): 229–265, 2015.

[122] Schaffer, J.D. Multiple objective optimization with vector evaluated genetic algorithms. In *Proc. of the International Conference on Genetic Algorithms and Their Applications*, pp. 93–100, 1985.

[123] Schaffer, J.D. Multi-objective learning via genetic algorithms. In *Proc. of the International Joint Conference on Artificial Intelligence*, (IJCAI85), pp. 593–595, 1985.

[124] Schrum, J. and Miikkulainen, R. Evolving multimodal behavior with modular neural networks in Ms. Pac-Man. *Proceedings of the Genetic and Evolutionary Computation Conference (GECCO 2014)*, pp. 325–332, 2014.

[125] Schrum, J., Volz, V. and Risi, S. CPPN2GAN: Combining compositional pattern producing networks and GANs for large-scale pattern generation. *Proceedings of the Genetic and Evolutionary Computation Conference (GECCO 2020)*, pp. 139–147, 2020.

[126] Sebag, M. and Ducoulombier, A. Extending population-based incremental learning to continuous search spaces. In *Parallel Problem Solving from Nature? PPSN V*, Eiben, A.E., Bäck, T., Schoenauer, M. and Schwefel, H.-P. (eds.). Lecture Notes in Computer Science, vol. 1498, pp. 418–427, 1998.

[127] Sehara, K., Toda, T., Iwai, L., Wakimoto, M., Tanno, K., Matsubayashi, Y. and Kawasaki, H. Whisker-related axonal patterns and plasticity of layer 2/3 neurons in the mouse barrel cortex. *Journal of Neuroscience*, 30(8): 3082–3092, 2010.

[128] Simonovsky, M. and Komodakis, N. Dynamic edge-conditioned filters in convolutional neural networks on graphs. In *Proc. of IEEE Conf. Computer Vision and Pattern Recognition (CVPR)*, pp. 29–38, 2017.

[129] Shervashidze, N., Schweitzer, P., van Leeuwen, E.J., Mehlhorn, K. and Borgwardt, K.M. Weisfeiler-Lehman graph kernels. *Journal of Machine Learning Research*, 12: 2539–2561, 2011.

[130] Sober, E. *Philosophy of Biology*, Second Edition, Perseus, 1999.

[131] Srivastava, N., Hinton, G., Krizhevsky, A., Sutskever, I. and Salakhutdinov, R. Dropout: A simple way to prevent neural networks from overfitting. *Journal of Machine Learning Research*, 15(56): 1929–1958, 2014.

[132] Soule, T., Foster, J.A., Dickinson, J. Code growth in genetic programming. In *Proc. of Genetic Programming Conference 1996 (GP96)*, 1996.

[133] Stanley, K.O. and Miikkulainen, R. Evolving neural networks through augmenting topologies. *Evolutionary Computation*, 10(2): 99–127, 2002.

[134] Stanley, K.O. Compositional pattern producing networks: A novel abstraction of development. *Genetic Programming and Evolvable Machines, Special Issue on Developmental Systems*, 8(2): 131–162, 2007.

[135] Stanley, K.O., D'Ambrosio, D.B. and Gauci, J. A hypercube-based encoding for evolving large-scale neural networks. *Artificial Life*, 15(2): 185–212, 2009.

[136] Su, J., Vargas, D.V. and Sakurai, K. One pixel attack for fooling deep neural networks. *IEEE Transactions on Evolutionary Computation*, 2019.

[137] Suzuki, R. and Arita, T. How learning can guide evolution of communication. In *Proc. of Artificial Life XI*, pp. 608–615, 2008.

[138] Szegedy, C., Vanhoucke, V., Ioffe, S., Shlens, J. and Wojna, Z. Rethinking the inception architecture for computer vision. In *Proc. of the IEEE Conference on Computer Vision and Pattern Recognition*, pp. 2818–2826, 2016.

[139] Tero, A., Kobayashi, A. and Nakagaki, T. Mathematical model for adaptive transport network in path finding by true slime mold. *Journal of Theoretical Biology*, 244: 553–564, 2007.

[140] Thompson, J.D., Higgins, D.G. and Gibson, T.J. CLUSTAL W: improving the sensitivity of progressive multiple sequence alignment through sequence weighting, position-specific gap penalties and weight matrix choice. *Nucleic Acids Research*, 22(22): 4673–4680, 1994.

[141] Turney, P. Myths and legends of the baldwin effect mold. In *Proc. of the Workshop on Evolutionary Computing and Machine Learning at the 13th International Conference on Machine Learning*, pp. 135–142, 1996.

[142] Unemi, T. SBART2.4: Breeding 2D CG images and movies, and creating a type of collage. *Proceedings of The Third International Conference on Knowledge-based Intelligent Information Engineering Systems*, pp. 288–291. Adelaide, Australia, Aug. 1999.

[143] Valiant, V. *Probably Approximately Correct: Nature's Algorithms for Learning and Prospering in a Complex World*, Basic Books, 2014.

[144] Waddington, C.H. Canalization of development and the inheritance of acquired characters. *Nature*, 150: 563–565, 1942.

[145] Wan, L., Zeiler, M., Zhang, S., Le Cun, Y. and Fergus, R. Regularization of neural networks using dropconnect. In Proc. of Iinternational Conference on Machine Learning (ICML), pp. 1058–1066, 2013.

[146] Weizenbaum, J. *Computer Power and Human Reason: From Judgement to Calculation*, W.H. Freeman & Co. Ltd., 1976.

[147] Westh, A. *Deep Interactive Evolutionary 3D Modelling*, M.Sc. in Software Development, IT University of Copenhagen, Master Thesis, 2019.

[148] Wilson, E.O. *Sociobiology: The Abridged Edition Abridged Edition*, Belknap Press of Harvard University Press, 1980.

[149] Wu, A.S. and Lindsay, R.K. Empirical studies of the genetic algorithm with noncoding segments. *Evolutionary Computation*, 3(2): 121–147, 1995.

[150] Wu, J., Zhang, C., Xue, T., Freeman, W.T. and Tenenbaum, J.B. Learning a probabilistic latent space of object shapes via 3d generative-adversarial modeling. In *Proc. of the 30th International Conference on Neural Information Processing Systems*, pp. 82–90, 2016.

[151] Yang, X.-S. and Deb, S. Cuckoo search via Levy flights. In *Proc. World Congress on Nature and Biologically Inspired Computing (NaBIC 2009)*, pp. 210–214, IEEE Publications, 2009.

[152] Yang, X. *Nature-Inspired Metaheuristic Algorithms*, 2nd Ed., Luniver Press, 2010.

[153] Yang, X.-S. Multiobjective firefly algorithm for continuous optimization. *Engineering with Computers*, 29(2): 175–184, 2013.

[154] Yang, Y. and Iba, H. Fooling voice based on evolutionary computation. In *Proc. of Evolutionary Computation Symposium*, Dec. 9–10, Hokkaido, Japan, 2017.

[155] Yao, X. A review of evolutionary artificial neural networks. *International Journal of Intelligent Systems*, 8: 539–567, 1993.

[156] Zhang, C., Bengio, S., Hardt, M., Recht, B. and Vinyals, O. Understanding deep learning requires rethinking generalization. *Proc. 5th International Conference on Learning Representations (ICLR2017)*, 2017.

Name Index

Symbol Index

Index